Rail Tales from around Europe: From Å to Zagreb

Rodney Jory

rodney.jory @ gmail. com.

Published by

**MELROSE
BOOKS**

An Imprint of Melrose Press Limited
St Thomas Place, Ely
Cambridgeshire
CB7 4GG, UK
www.melrosebooks.com

FIRST EDITION

Copyright © Rodney Jory 2012

The Author asserts his moral right to
be identified as the author of this work

Cover designed by Catherine McIntyre

ISBN 978 1 907732 60 7

Printed and bound in Great Britain by:
CPI Group (UK) Ltd, Croydon, CR0 4YY

FSC
www.fsc.org
MIX
Paper from
responsible sources
FSC® C013604

INDEX

1.	Prologue	1
2.	Europe	6
3.	Denmark	9
4.	Iceland	18
5.	Norway	24
6.	Sweden	34
7.	Finland	40
8.	St Petersburg, Russia	46
9.	Estonia	51
10.	Latvia	57
11.	Lithuania	61
12.	Poland	64
13.	Russia	71
14.	Czech Republic	78
15.	Slovakia	82
16.	Slovenia	84
17.	Croatia (Hrvatska) and Bosnia	88
18.	Hungary	95
19.	Romania	99
20.	Serbia, Montenegro, Kosova, Macedonia (Fyrom), Albania	105
21.	Bulgaria	113
22.	Turkey	118
23.	Greece	123
24.	The Greek Islands	130
25.	Venice, Venezia	135
26.	Tuscany	141

27.	Roma, Rome	147
28.	Naples, Napoli	152
29.	Sicily and Malta	156
30.	More Italy	161
31.	Spain	166
32.	Portugal	175
33.	France	180
34.	Provincial France	184
35.	Paris	189
36.	Belgium and Luxembourg	193
37.	The Netherlands	198
38.	Germany, the nation	203
39.	Germany, the rail system	205
40.	Germany, the south, the west and the Rhine	211
41.	Germany, Hamburg and the north	215
42.	Helgoland	217
43.	Germany, Leipzig and the east	220
44.	München, Munich and Bayern	224
45.	Berlin	230
46.	Austria	234
47.	Wien, Vienna	240
48.	Switzerland, the nation	249
49.	Switzerland, its railways	253
50.	Switzerland: Parlez-vous Schweitz?	256
51.	Switzerland, North	259
52.	Liechtenstein	261
53.	Graubünden	264
54.	Northern Italy	272
55.	Switzerland, Central	276
56.	Epilogue	290
	About the author	292

1. PROLOGUE

There are two types of train buff. The first is represented by those who collect the numbers off locomotives, or marvel at the engineering of ancient steam engines and modern diesels. The second likes finding out and understanding how railway systems work and riding in them to verify how they do work. These folk also spend time envisaging how long it will be before this or that infrastructure will be upgraded, and what the system might be like 'one day'. I confess to being one of the latter. As a physicist, I also yearn for the day when fuel efficient electric trains can supplant the diesel trains from the system.

The following collection of experiences relates to a six year extended period of retirement spent mostly in Europe with a Eurail pass and the *Thomas Cook European Timetable*.

This timetable is an indispensable reference book for any European train traveller containing timetables for almost every significant railway system in Europe. Its author, Brendan Fox, and his team, whom I have met in Peterborough, do an amazing job keeping the book up-to-date and reliable. The timetable does not contain enough information to find everything needed but, by pairing it with this volume, the Thomas-Cook-carrying traveller should be able to make the most of the European system. The timetable is referred to in many of the following chapters simply as 'Thomas Cook'.

This book is unashamedly railway-biased. How could it not be? You will find yourself dabbling much more into the history, the politics and the *raison d'être* of the locations rather than their appearance. This should both appeal to you and give you an opportunity to learn something which you might not otherwise encounter.

Before you begin, find a map of Europe. If you can't find your school atlas, which is generally good enough, then print a map from the web. An even better companion is the *Thomas Cook Rail Map of Europe*. The descriptions will be much richer if you know where you are. If you are really clever, also find a map of Europe before 1938 so that you can trace the history which you either never knew, or have forgotten.

The travelogue style has been avoided where possible and the descriptions minimised. If you want to see pictures and read a description of the Frauenkirche in München, of the Trummelbach Falls in Switzerland or of Meteora in Greece, then please look these up on the web yourself, beginning with Wikipedia. Wikipedia is a lot less likely to be biased than the travel agents and local directories. Google will find anything you want, but remember that if you enter the German name, the article may be in German. If the web is not your thing, then any encyclopaedia will be even better; at least you know it will be in English.

The spelling of place names in this document is not altogether consistent but the local spelling has been used where the English language has wholly corrupted the German or Italian name, such as in München (Munich), Köln (Cologne), Roma (Rome), Venezia (Venice), Nürnberg (Nuremberg), Firenze (Florence) and Milano (Milan). Using the English version in these cases is either not understood or draws a glance resembling pity from the locals. The paradox here is that the Anglicised name of the country, *Austria*, is widely used by the locals, even though the country is Österreich. Even their email code is '*.at*'. The name *Vienna* is readily understood by the folk of Wien. German uses double dots above the vowel, the umlaut, ü, ä, ö, which modifies the vowel in the same way as putting an e after 'mat' turns it into 'mate' or 'cod' to 'code' in English. Norwegians pronounce Å similar to English "aw" as in straw. The nearest railway stations to Å in Lofoten (accent on the second syllable) are Bodø and Narvik in Norway. For a physicist, Å is the abbreviation for an Ångstrom unit, one metre divided by ten to the power ten.

Travelling long distances by rail, through many countries and regions over several weeks or months, is to me a great joy. If your age is the same as mine, or you are even a tad younger, then you may not relish this form of travel. I have traversed Europe so many times over the years by train, the first being in 1977, that there is a sort of immunity attached. It is not necessary to use overnight trains; you can move from hotel to hotel if you wish. The important thing to note is that this type of travel is very flexible and available to you at a not unreasonable cost, and with an itinerary which is solely yours and can be changed at will. No advance booking, nor even planning, is necessary. You are now, through this book, about to become an armchair traveller!

European railway systems are generally clean and comfortable. Railways most often run extremely frequent services and you can walk-on, walk-off trains in any combination you wish. You can choose to have plenty of space in first class, or sometimes be crowded out in second. Individual train trip costs, in Euro per kilometre, are not inexpensive when compared with coach or air travel, but in terms of Euro per hour, end-to-end, they are better. With a three-month Eurail pass, the value is unequalled by any other form of transport.

Buses I hate. I always have and will continue to do so. The only time you see references here to using a bus is when there is a gap in any logical train journey, probably caused by the failure of someone to build a railway, the need to avoid an obstruction, or occasionally in a city where there is no rail or tram service. Trams are OK with me and with other with rail buffs, sometimes exceptionally so. Air travel is avoided wherever possible but a brief interposition about air travel can be found under Iceland.

Since Great Britain has not chosen to accept the Eurail pass, the Britrail pass being a separate entity, travel around the UK and the Irish Republic has been left for another time. It could make up a book in itself.

This book takes you by train and occasional ferry around Europe, enjoying the pleasures, and sometimes the foibles, of train travel. Join me for a pleasant excursion. You do not need to read the chapters sequentially. Every chapter is self-contained and you can skip or back-track as you wish.

You will find that I tend to equate cleanliness and neatness with comfort and efficiency, both in trains and in a country.

Descriptions of the journeys are enhanced by inclusion of some history, politics and people, both real and fictional. One of my favourite fictional authors is Mary Stewart and I have taken the liberty of including references to her books on occasions. An even greater favourite is C. S. Forester, who takes Horatio Hornblower all over the world, particularly in Europe, in the time of Napoleon. Forgive me if Hornblower is treated as a real character. Countless of his readers see him that way. You will encounter Hornblower from St Petersburg to Gibraltar as you proceed. The one common factor with admirals in those days was that they stayed alive long enough to become one. If you are fictional, it is much easier. J. R. R. Tolkien also rates a mention in a few chapters.

As we go through the various countries and cities, I have taken the liberty of briefly discussing their history and politics. Remember that this is done with a non-educated background as the author is a physicist, not an historian nor an economist so if anything you see interests you, seek further information. Don't go quoting me as an authority.

Finally, you cannot travel around Europe without discussing some overall aspects, which are necessary to understand Europe. Some authors might include these in a preface, which would take many pages, never be read or bore readers to tears. I have included these items in the various chapters as they come to mind, with the hope that the reader will take a little more note and probably enjoy them. I have tried to treat these as fun items, some of which are causing less and less concern to the traveller by the year until some of them will quietly fail to be of any consequence. If you are puzzled in the earlier chapters by some of the terminology, then you might need to run onward a little for the explanation.

Topics to be found in the various chapters, include:

Membership of the European Union (EU)	Belgium
The Schengen Treaty and border crossings	Latvia
The Euro	Estonia
Summary table of the above	Slovenia
Air travel	Iceland
Eurail pass	Europe
Train nomenclature	Europe
Speaking English	Czech
Rail gauges	Finland
Rail voltages	Lithuania
Smoking	Croatia
2009 money problems	Greece
The partition of Europe and the Yalta conference	Romania
Sleeping car trains	Poland
Train speeds	Slovakia
The ICE fleet	Germany
Eurostar and cross channel	Belgium
Future projects	Epilogue

Settle back with a glass of your favourite beside you and enjoy a trip around Europe.

Happy travelling!

2. EUROPE

Europe: our destination for the whole of this book.

The logical place to arrive in Europe by air is Frankfurt. Apart from being a big airport in a big city, Frankfurt can be reached directly from most parts of the world. If your travel agent is able to find you a lower fare from home to another city in Europe then, provided it has or is adjacent to a railway station, grab it. You can pick up the journey at any railway station.

Frankfurt Airport, however, is remarkably efficient and clean. Having cleared customs, all that is needed is for you to follow the signs indicated by a railway icon. The symbol is a modern day train and not the steam train symbol still used in most countries when referring to a rail crossing.

To continue the story requires that we recognise that we are in the European Union, henceforth the EU. We are now in that part of Europe and of the EU which comes under the Schengen Treaty.

The EU will be discussed in more detail in the chapter on Belgium, and the Schengen Treaty in the chapter on Latvia.

As confirmed train travellers we follow the signs down the escalators, easily find signs leading to the ticket office, present the Eurail pass with passport for validation and we are free to travel the railways and byways of Europe. Similar action is required at any arrival point, but none is anywhere as convenient as Frankfurt Airport.

One of the best deals offered by the Eurail organisation is the three month global Eurail pass, a pass which allows one to travel anywhere by train on the national rail network in 22 European countries made up of the 27 EU countries plus Croatia, Norway and Switzerland, but currently (2011) without Britain, Poland, Slovakia, Estonia, Latvia, Lithuania, remembering that Malta and Cyprus don't have railways. This is shown in a table in the chapter on Slovenia. The pass also includes some lake ferries and minor railways, but not all mountain summit trains in Switzerland, such as the *Matterhorn Gotthard Bahn,* and the *Jungfraubahn,* plus ferries between countries where trains would have difficulty, like Sweden to Finland, Italy to Greece. The validity is explained in the Eurail guide which is issued with the ticket and generally increases each year. A three-month pass costs around $US 1,600, €1,400 or $AU 2,200 (2011 prices). The price is within tens of dollars of the return air fare paid from Australia to London. One lasts 92 days, the other around 30 hours each way.

Since I have chosen to make Denmark our next nation of call, we check the destination boards from the airport and pick the next train to Hamburg Hauptbahnhof (Hbf, main station), and we are on our way. A change may be necessary at Frankfurt Hauptbahnhof. Every hour a train will leave. If it is later in the day, then take a local train to Frankfurt Hauptbahnhof, buy some dinner and take IC2020 to Hamburg overnight as described in the chapter under Germany, Rail. From Hamburg Hauptbahnhof take the ICE, Intercity Express, to Copenhagen.

The beauty of this form of travel is that you don't have to do any of these things. Simply decide where you want to go and go there.

Before we go further, the notation of the European railways must be explained.

Several years ago, Britain was the first to divide its railways into local, provincial and Intercity. This was a brave move and one which has generally been followed by most countries. The title *Intercity* was copied almost universally as 'IC' and this classification can be found in most countries. It implies an express train linking major cities with a reasonable degree of comfort, usually including food service. This term was used despite the fact that the word cannot be pronounced from that spelling in most languages. In the race to provide better services, the term *Eurocity,* EC, was coined to indicate an IC service operating across international boundaries with a higher level of service. The DB (*Deutsche Bahn*, German Railways) then adopted the term ICE, *Intercity Express,* to describe their high speed trains. The SNCF (the French Railways, the *Société Nationale des Chemins de Fer Français*), skilled at not copying other languages, adopted the term TGV for their high speed trains which most have forgotten signifies *Train à grande vitesse*. Most other countries with specialised trains have subsequently tacked their own names on to their most modern trains, but most of these do not make international journeys. These must be consulted in their national timetables. Where these trains with local identity cross borders, they are often simply termed EC.

In many countries the local trains are further subdivided into U-Bahn, S-Bahn and regional services. The U-Bahn is generally a purpose built commuter railway, often underground, and very often owned and operated by the city. Eurail pass is generally not valid on these services. The S-Bahn is the suburban section of the national railway, generally confined within the city limits, stopping all stations and running a clockface timetable. Regional trains are those providing a more distant and less regular service.

3. DENMARK

Plus an excursion into southern Sweden

Denmark consists of a single peninsular, Jutland, running north from Germany and an archipelago of islands, the largest of which, Zealand, is nearest the Swedish coast and contains the main city, Copenhagen, *København*.

Denmark is flat – oh, is it flat! – although the locals will point out hills of interest. In the event of the sea rising by more than a few metres, you would find the Danes all heading for Sweden, or living on a lot of much smaller islands and much closer to sea level. North Germany would be no haven for them, as it would suffer the same fate. Since general consensus talks of the sea rising at centimetres per decade, nobody living today is likely to be inconvenienced.

The Danes have an extraordinary system of ferries in operation, connecting both the bigger and smaller islands. The trains once used these ferries as well, with an amazing efficiency. As the train, usually a diesel motor set, approached the waiting ferry, it would hardly stop and trundle straight on to the open gates of the ferry. As the train came to a halt, the ferry doors would be closing and it would seem that the ferry was moving off with the onward momentum of the train. The same thing would happen in reverse on arrival. Where the train was loco-hauled, the through passenger cars would be uncoupled and pushed, using an intermediate set of flat cars, onto the ferry without the locomotive having to cross to the ferry.

Doubtless it was this efficient transport system which made Hitler's occupation of Denmark so speedy. Despite the lack of altitude, the Danes have not borrowed land from King Neptune so there is no significant part of Denmark below sea level. This took away from the Danes the opportunity, taken by the Dutch, to open the sea cocks and flood the land in the face of Hitler's approach.

Since the 1970s the Danes have become fascinated with the idea of building bridges. The first was across the 'Little Belt' linking Zealand with Fünen, the next island, then in 1997 they bridged the 'Great Belt' linking Fünen to Jutland. This has meant that there is now a road and rail link, without ferries, between Copenhagen and Germany. The railway to the German border was electrified and trains can now reach Copenhagen from anywhere in Europe without travelling by ship. This is a much longer route, so through passenger trains by day still take to the water, as we shall see. The Great Belt Bridge is also referred to as the 'West Bridge'.

The overnight sleeper train south to Germany crosses the islands of Denmark and enters Germany through peninsular Denmark, bound for Hamburg and places south. The same journey by day requires at least one change of train to accommodate the change of voltage at the border. Travelling this way, the flatness of Denmark becomes very apparent. The one spectacular part of the southern section of this journey, apart from more windmills, is the bridge over the Kiel Canal, in Germany. A check on the map will show that to reach the North Sea from the Baltic Sea by ship involves sailing around Denmark, and is a very long way. The neck of Denmark is quite narrow. Accordingly, a canal was built through here to accommodate ocean-going vessels. Because of the flatness, the engineering problems for the canal are not great, but not so for the railway. To reach the level of the bridge, the train goes through a complete spiral and returns to ground level on the German side by the same method.

The next move in bridge-building was in 1999, into Sweden, across the Øresund, that dividing piece of water which Hornblower traversed on his way to relieve the siege of Riga by Napoleon's troops. The two-track railway and the highway run through a tunnel, then come to the surface on a small island before crossing the bridge, the longest in Europe at around 8km, into Sweden. Around 20,000 vehicles a day use the bridge, which has virtually incorporated the southern part of Sweden into Denmark, making Malmö a dependent city. This bridge is thus referred to as the 'East Bridge'. As a more modern construction, the bridge/tunnel was compelled to follow all of current environmental practices designed not to disturb the Baltic Sea, which links with the North Sea through this channel. The train fare for ordinary mortals without Eurail is very high, as is the toll on the highway. What else do you do? Swim?

The Danes are not familiar with tunnels, as they once had nothing above sea level which warranted one. They do now, however, have tunnels under the sea associated with both the Øresund crossing and the Great Belt crossing. In the seat pocket on these trains, you will find a safety card, which matches that which you read when travelling for 24 hours at 39,000 feet. The prospect of the train stopping in the tunnel, or of there being a fire, is really emphasised but is so remote as to make it a joke.

The Øresund Bridge has now linked the tracks of Sweden and Norway to the rail network of Europe, and freight can travel without trans-shipment from Istanbul or Bordeaux, or even from London, to Narvik in the north.

The Danes have followed the German pattern and divided their rail services into suburban, regional and inter-city. The suburban, S-Bahn, services in Copenhagen follow the old conventional railway through the city, which is efficient but limited in scope. Regional trains extend to Malmö and beyond in Sweden. Superimposed on this is a modern underground U-Bahn service extending to the airport and with a major set of promised extensions. Regrettably, the electrification of the main line only extends from Copenhagen across the Great Belt to the German border. Lines to Denmark's second city, Århus, and surrounding areas, are not wired and thus require diesel trains operating 'under the wires' from Copenhagen.

The Danes maintain that theirs is the oldest continuous hereditary monarchy in Europe, as well it might be, extending back over 400 years to when Denmark had sovereignty over Norway, Sweden and Iceland. The British monarchy may stretch back further, but it took a holiday from 1649 to 1660 after Charles I unwillingly mislaid his head.

Perhaps it is worth noting here that there are eleven generations from Britain's George I to Prince William, meaning that the genes have been diluted by 50% eleven times since then, reducing the regal genes to less than 1 in 2,000 or 0.05%. Allowing for re-introduction of some of the genes, you can be certain that William only carries about 0.1% of the specific genes of George I. This certainly reduces the apparent value of the hereditary monarchy as seen by some.

The Danes have a special place in the eyes of Australians. When Crown Prince Frederik of Denmark was visiting Australia, he happened to attract the attention of Tasmanian Mary Donaldson, and vice versa. The story does not need any more elaboration except to say that, as Princess, she has produced the second in line to the Danish throne. The Danes love her. Mary and Fred have made trips to Australia, where they ride around on buses and mix with the people. Australians don't mind the idea either.

The largest remaining water crossing of note in Denmark, there are many more smaller ones, is the Fehmarn Strait, which lies between Germany and Denmark. Here the main passenger railway crosses between Germany and Copenhagen, once more on a ferry. This route was developed during the Cold War years, when the older traditional ferry route to Warnemünde or Rostock would have arrived in East Germany (the DDR). The present day route, now followed by passenger trains, is known as the *Vogelfluglinie*, which probably best translates into Australian to 'as the crow flies', and its equivalent in other English idioms. The deserted marshalling yards at the terminals at either end tell that the freight trains no longer come this way.

The Danes, however, have more ideas. They plan to build a fixed road and rail link across this 18km, very shallow gap to allow passenger and freight trains from Germany into Denmark and on to Sweden, and to do it without help from the government of Germany. Current thinking is for an immersed tunnel and a 2020 completion.

Denmark joined the EU in 1973 at the same time as Britain and Ireland, and was granted four 'opt-out' clauses. The present government has as its policy to remove these clauses. One of these was exemption, as was given to Britain, from joining the Euro. The Danes have had two national referenda seeking the approval of the electorate to join the Euro. Both have been rejected on the basis that 'we don't need to give up the Danish kroner' which is similar to the original British attitude to the pound. Consequently the Danes, for all the wrong reasons, still use the kroner, which trades at around 7.5 to the Euro. In Copenhagen, however, the Euro is much more readily accepted by the local traders than elsewhere in Scandinavia.

***

So, after that brief introduction to Denmark, let us set out from Hamburg Hauptbahnhof to see the Danes.

The trains on the *Vogelfluglinie* route are four-car German diesel ICE-TDs, of which very few were built specifically for lines elsewhere and then abandoned in favour of electrifying the lines, albeit a much more long-term programme. A ferry crossing does not fit easily with electrification, so here they found a good home. The ICE-TD (tilting diesel) is also used on the occasional IC trains which venture from Hamburg north into peninsula Denmark.

This little train whips out of Hamburg Hauptbahnhof and travels for about two hours across the flat plains of northern Germany. The most notable features are windmills; hundreds of them. This part of Germany is quite flat and the wind never stops. Germany generates more than a token of its power from the wind. At Puttgarten the ship is waiting and the train drives straight on, sometimes without a stop. Passengers adjourn to the top deck, where there is the inevitable bar and cafeteria where they serve delightful seafood, Scandinavian-style. This provides quite a change from German fare. After about 45 minutes, arrival in Rødby is handled in the same way. The ship stops and the train rolls off and keeps going on for another two hours to Copenhagen. The total journey takes less than five hours and brings you to Copenhagen Central Station.

Wonderful, Wonderful Copenhagen. Indeed it is.

As can be expected, Copenhagen is flat and surrounded by lots of water. In the days before trains and bridges, Copenhagen was the principal trading port of the area, as its name implies. Today it is the centre of one of the largest agglomerations of population in northern Europe, spreading across both Denmark and Sweden, thanks to the Øresund Bridge.

Copenhagen International Airport at Kastrup, under which the train across the bridge to Sweden stops, is the main hub for Scandinavian Airlines.

The city is not too large to walk about and certainly never boring. In short, it is a delightful city. It is sufficiently large (perhaps 1.7 million) that it is not distorted by the arrival of a cruise ship or two.

The first on the tourist list must be the *Tivoli*, right across the road from the station. There is no other place in the world quite like 'The Tiv' in Copenhagen. It is a vast park in the middle of the city, filled with every type of family-style entertainment you could want. The pantomime theatre performs four times a day, there is a small orchestra playing for those who wish to relax and there are major performances in the theatre. The Tivoli Boys' Band marches through twice a day. The whole area is landscaped like a village and is easy to navigate. The major attractions are, of course, the sideshow events, everything from a roller coaster to a placid children's merry-go-round. There is every type of food imaginable on sale, from the best restaurants to the very worst in junk food. Then there are the junk stalls and the souvenir stalls. International visitors go mad and buy hats and things which they would not be seen dead buying at home. Granny would hate one of those. The locals simply smile and enjoy themselves in their own way. The Danes know how to live.

If you compare this with the dust, flies and bedlam of the Sydney Royal Easter Show or the Adelaide Royal Show, you would never go to another place like those in Australia. The same applies to those of North America, Britain and anywhere else you would like to name.

It is tempting to say that 'The Tiv' was the model for Disneyland and all of the innumerable theme parks around the world. 'The Tiv' is not a theme park; it is a good family recreation area, where you can walk around and partake of nothing and yet still enjoy yourself.

Above all, Copenhagen is clean. According to the brochures, you can happily swim in the inner harbour and you feel everything is 'neat and tidy' wherever you go. Possibly only the tourists make a mess.

Proceeding inland across the Great Belt Bridge on to the island of Fünen, one comes to the city of Odense. This is a pleasant city by anyone's standards, but to an outsider is best known as the birthplace of Hans Christian Andersen. Even today the 1952 movie of his life, starring Danny Kaye, is still shown. It is the voice of Danny Kaye which brings us the song *Wonderful, Wonderful Copenhagen*. Most memorably he told us the story of the *Little Mermaid*. Children of today remember the Walt Disney version of 1989.

The *Little Mermaid*, slightly less than life-sized, sits on a rock at Langelinie in the harbour of Copenhagen, slightly north of the city, and she must be the most photographed mermaid in the world. Is there any competition? An athletic person can reach her dry-shod and so she is subjected to all forms of abuse, even to having been stolen completely. She has even had her head cut off several times. In 2010 she went on her first holiday and visited Shanghai for Expo 2010. The figure in the harbour is, of course, not the original, which is kept well out of reach. There is an extension to the mermaid story attached to the chapter on Warsaw, which will be visited later.

The city abounds with carvings and artworks of all types. Near the *Little*

Mermaid is a full-sized replica of Michelangelo's *David* from Firenze (Florence). Maybe she would not have been so unhappy in love had she met him earlier.

North of Copenhagen is the old ferry crossing from Helsingør on the Danish side to Helsingborg in Sweden. Kronborg Castle located there is not madly spectacular but when the name of the location is translated into English as *Elsinore* you can see why people want to see it. *To be, or not to be.*

For accommodation in the area I have often used the youth hostel in Lund, in Sweden, which is easily accessible with a train pass now that the bridge is open. The town centre of Lund is about a half hour from Malmö, thus an hour from Copenhagen, and in the station yard is the Youth Hostel, made up of five carriages of an old Swedish sleeper train, still on the tracks. A night here in a regular sleeping compartment is very little different from other nights, except it does not rock and is quiet. There is neither 'clicketty clack', nor 'ka thump'. The cost is about the same as the surcharge for a couchette attached to a moving train. It is rumoured that the hostel is to close in a year or two, so consult the web before you go that way.

From the station in Copenhagen, one can head by foot towards the City Hall and the main square. The absence of hustle and bustle is quite evident and the centre of the city has an appearance which is uniquely Copenhagen. Cross the square and head up the Strøget for the main tourist shopping precinct of Copenhagen, apparently the longest pedestrian street in Europe. Beyond, one can find the Royal Palace, with its daily changing of the guard, and eventually the *Little Mermaid*. If you expect to see a changing of the guard at the palace comparable with London, you will be most disappointed. The guard is of around 16 soldiers and does not sport horses or a band.

A different view of Copenhagen can be seen by taking a boat cruise around the harbour. There you will see the commercial aspect of Copenhagen and also the cultural area. The Opera House, donated by Mr Maersk, whose name can be seen on the sides of container traffic all over the world, sits on the shore of the harbour, opposite the palace, and is quite a spectacular building. The Opera House does not quite match that of Sydney, as it has a dominating rectangular roof,.

On the western side of the harbour, across the bridge from the city, contiguous with the city street pattern, is the Church of the Our Saviour. It is the tower, visible across most of the harbour, which makes this church unique, as it is in the form of a corkscrew. A narrow catwalk winds its way around the outside of the steeple, becoming narrower as it goes up. The church makes money out of unwary travellers who are prepared to try the climb, but few manage to go very far. It is quite likely that health and safety regulations have closed the tower, in the same way that they have closed individual entry into the Leaning Tower of Pisa. The apocryphal history, all worthwhile buildings have such a story, recounts that the architect was told after the building was completed that the screw had a left-hand thread, which is a work of the devil. He promptly climbed the tower and threw himself off. Good story, but completely false!

The city of Malmö, in Sweden, fits into the story at this point. Malmö is the largest city in southern Sweden and a major port. A very new and extensive tunnel network allows trains from Copenhagen to pass through Malmö station en route to Göteborg and Stockholm.

One notable outpost of Denmark is the island of Bornholm in the Baltic Sea, south of the Swedish mainland. A Danish train takes you from Copenhagen, via the Øresund Bridge, to the port of Ystaad in Sweden, where you board a Danish ferry for Bornholm and the port of Rønne, after another 45 minutes. The residents of Bornholm are very insular, very proud and very Danish. There is no special reason for going there except to see Bornholm as she is.

The last sleeper train travelling by ferry in Northern Europe runs from Malmö to Berlin, via Trelleborg and Sassnitz. It is operated by a private company and runs nightly in summer and three times weekly in winter. The only other ferry in Europe carrying trains is across the Straits of Messina to Sicily in Italy.

***

From Copenhagen we wish to travel north to Norway but, to anyone's surprise, there are no direct day trains to Oslo and no night train, even though the distance is such that either trip is quite within reason. Whether this is due to the Danes' dislike of Norway, the Danes' love of ferries, the presence of cheap flights, or the need for such a train to be organised by the Swedes, is not apparent; but there it is. Only one journey is possible by day but not encouraging, with a change in Göteborg.

Several ferry journeys are possible, including a very short ferry trip from Hirshals at the top of peninsular Denmark to Kristiansand, the long trip from Copenhagen to Oslo, or another from Frederikshavn to Oslo. The suitability of any ferry is thus selected by the desired times and departure ports. Two of these treat you to a cruise up the Oslo Fjord which is worth waking up early to see.

The other alternative is to take the train to Stockholm and then to Oslo. By taking the early morning fast Swedish train from Copenhagen, one can be in Stockholm for lunch. This train really is of the highest standard in first class, with 'at seat' service of about everything. The seat reservation fee is correspondingly high. This can then be followed by a fairly ordinary afternoon train from Stockholm to Oslo, An ordinary fare-paying passenger would not take kindly to this extended trip, but with a Eurail pass the extra distance is of no financial consequence.

***

One of the disadvantages of travelling in Scandinavia is the multiplicity of currencies. Each of Norway, Sweden and Denmark uses its own kroner and each is slightly different from the other. It is thus necessary to carry three more wallets to keep up with border crossings. Best advice would be to withdraw whatever cash you need from an ATM rather than keep changing cash, as the *Forex* exchange offices charge per transaction. Then you wait until your travels are all over and present all of your no-longer-required notes to an exchange office at home, one which tells you it charges no commission. Coin cannot be changed back, so one must minimise the coins in the pocket and buy a few Mars bars to offload the remainder as you cross a border. Notes from these countries are readily recognised without penalty by exchange offices in other European countries, but the same cannot be promised of the currency of other countries we shall encounter.

This is a reminder of the pre-Euro days of German marks and French francs, of guilders and lira and of pesos and schillings. How did we manage?

4. ICELAND

Although separated by many hundreds of kilometres of the Atlantic Ocean, Iceland is definitely part of Europe.

Thomas Cook tells us that there is a ferry from Denmark to Iceland once a week between April and September, which perhaps qualifies Iceland to be in this discussion. It takes, however, several days.

This brings me to the comparison with aircraft.

The first commercial air services were spacious, clean, courteous and punctual. This was at a time when rail services were slow, dirty, non-caring and otherwise rather unattractive. Regrettably, some still are, but the number is decreasing. Train was cheaper than air; the latter being horrendously expensive in those early days. If it cost a lot, it must be good.

The pendulum has now swung the other way, but Mr and Ms General Public are reluctant to admit it.

Air travel is arduous, crowded, time-consuming, environmentally unfriendly and often intimidating. You must allow at least five hours for an air journey which takes merely an hour from take-off to landing, when you take into account travel to the airport, finding a parking space, checking in, security, the inverse on arrival and then finding a way to your destination, which may be ultimately by rail. You may nowadays be dumped in a secondary airport, which may carry the same name as the city to which you want to go, but will take you as long as the flight to reach. Consider a Ryanair flight from London to Frankfurt (Hahn) or to Vienna (Bratislava). You will have a bus ride of two hours on arrival at either of these, and incidentally, how long did it take you to go from London to Stansted *by train*?

Flights originating in London going to Birmingham, Liverpool, Manchester, Paris and Brussels have all but disappeared, as the rail journey gives a much better service. The same better service is true from London to Glasgow, Edinburgh and Amsterdam, but the public has yet to be persuaded. Flights within Germany are a thing of the past.

What of the 'additional extras'? On many of the 'cheap' flights, you either have to buy a lunch box or go without. You pay for each bag you load on. Mr O'Leary from Ryanair points out that you can probably buy what you want at the other end more cheaply. You are about to be charged for a pee in the air. 'Go before you leave.' Mr O'Leary again. In most international train journeys of this length, you can sit down to a three-course meal.

Then there is the environment. No-one will argue when you state that, anything for anything, aircraft are the most polluting form of travel we have today. Modern diesel trains have very efficient engines whose energy use and pollution per passenger mile is extremely low. Electric traction fares even better, depending on the source of power.

Finally, safety. At the top end of the safety regime always come trains, with aircraft one order of magnitude lower, then going down through buses, cars, pedestrians, bicycles to motorbikes as the least safe. The least safe part of any journey by train or aircraft is travelling from home to the station or to the airport; that by a very long way. Since railway stations are generally closer to the population, they involve less travel than when you have to travel by taxi, car, bus or even train to the airport, so rail becomes much safer than air. You should think this through. The advertisers never give you time to check this one.

To reach most major airports in Europe today, it is possible to take a direct train from the central railway station and from many other locations in the network, without change. The Swiss, of course, have it all sewn up as the international airports of Geneva and Zürich are an integral part of the rail network. Frankfurt Airport in Germany is destined to become a major rail interchange in its own right. At what airport in the world, outside Europe, could you meet convenience like that? US airports are not rail-friendly and, although airports like London and Sydney have railway stations, they can only take you to the centre of the city, which is one place you generally don't need to go.

So here I sit and say, 'Do the logical thing; travel by train and enjoy it.'

If you are travelling to Iceland, however, you have little choice than to travel by air.

***

Geologically, Iceland is part of both America and Europe, because in Iceland, as anywhere down the middle of the Atlantic, the continental plates of Europe and America meet and are gradually moving apart; did someone say centimetres per century? This accounts for Iceland's high geothermal and volcanic activity.

Iceland has no railways and hence, like Malta, does not qualify for this book. Thomas Cook, however, gives both countries an entry and so will I.

Iceland's history goes back into the early Viking days when the country was an intermediate stop-over en route to Greenland and North America. There are claims that it has the oldest parliament in the world, but if you set the parameters tightly enough you could correctly claim anything.

Iceland functioned as an independent nation until about the 1400s when the Icelanders chopped down their last tree. With nothing to build boats, they were doomed. They threw themselves on the mercy of Norway, which accepted them under its wing and they remained under their care, and then that of Denmark, until 1940. Hitler occupied Denmark, which then left them without a king. For Herr Hitler, a base in Iceland would have been ideal for his Atlantic U-boat operations, so Britain occupied Iceland.

In 1944, when the crisis was approaching the end, the King of Denmark was still in London and Hitler was still in Copenhagen, Britain gave Iceland its independence, after a short period of US occupation. History does not specify what the King had to say. By this interesting quirk of fate, Iceland qualified for Marshall Aid assistance from the US.

Iceland did not apply for membership of the EU when the opportunity first arose, as this would have meant sharing control of the large fishery resources which it commands. Iceland had already been at odds with Britain over the distribution of these resources; a war which was sensibly solved amicably.

History now repeats itself six centuries later, as the piggy bank of Iceland has once more run dry and the country is standing outside the doors in Brussels, cap-in-hand,. Iceland actually fell off the financial shelf in 2009. The Icelanders are now hell-bent on securing membership of the EU before the tide goes out completely. Their application is not well advanced (2011), but one would imagine that Brussels would fast-track an application for a rather large number of not unselfish reasons. Perhaps 2013 or 2014 are possible dates of entry. Iceland, with about 320,000 people, would become the smallest, by population, of any EU nation,

Iceland is a geographically small nation, rendered smaller by the fact that a large proportion is icecap, one of the relics of the last ice age. Habitation is limited to the coastal strip and the single circumnavigating road. A bus service follows this road around and takes three days to make the circuit, remaining overnight at appropriate towns. The middle day's journey is listed as, 'No winter service', and an indication is given that the service runs from 1 June to 15 September, only three-and-a-half months in each year.

During the period which is not winter, however, there is a lot to be seen and enjoyed.

For the geologist, the Icelanders will show you the chasm which separates those two plates, how it is moving and how the geothermal heat arises. Then there are the volcanoes, which are as inaccessible as they are unpredictable. The most recent threw the European airports into confusion. The previous large one occurred under the icecap and gave the vulcanologists plenty of time to speculate on how the ice would behave and how long before the water would emerge. Apparently the photographers waited for as long as their editors would let them, but one by one were called home. When the water broke out, there was one photographer left and he had the scoop of a lifetime. Even today you can see the miles of ravaged plains where the water emerged and found its way to the ocean. Everything was wiped out, power-lines, roads, bridges, etc., and communication was broken for days. The Icelanders anticipated all this, but the questions of where and when could not be answered until the event.

The Icelanders also allege that they caused the French Revolution. Their volcano, *Laki*, went up in 1785 and, as with its successor in 2010, spread ash through the atmosphere around the globe, only to a much greater extent. The words now used are 'nuclear winter' or 'volcanic winter'. For the next few years there was no summer, hence no crops and hence no food. The best way to trigger a revolution is to starve the antagonists and this is what happened in France. Marie Antoinette said, 'let them eat cake', but there was a good chance that she had the only food, not just the only cake.

Apart from many of the natural features like geysers and waterfalls, all of which are spectacular, four items are of special interest, most not available anywhere else in the world. New Zealand may claim a couple and so also may Greenland.

The geothermal power station is a huge affair. Water is forced down into the hot rock and emerges as superheated steam under pressure. This generates electricity, runs industry, heats the houses and buildings and ultimately runs under the footpaths to keep them from freezing, before finally reaching the sea. In terms of energy, this is completely 'green'. There is no carbon dioxide as there is no fuel input. Everything seems great. The only snag was the capital cost.

One of the by-products is *Blue Lagoon*. This is a lake which receives some of the waste hot water from the power station and remains permanently at the temperature of a good hot bath. As might be imagined, this attracts lots of tourists and is easy to recognize in the brochures.

A tour can be made onto the icecap, but it is not possible to go independently. A bus takes you to the nearest accessible point, where you are kitted out in a heavy jumpsuit arrangement, loaded into tracked vehicles and off you go onto the ice. You may only move 100 metres from base and drive in circles for all you know, as the landscape loses all natural features. It is foggy and you have absolutely no idea of direction. After half an hour of this, you are back at base. The icecap melts from the bottom, the only place where the temperature may be above zero, and theoretically has no water on the top surface. If you are a good observer, however, you can see some trickles of water on the surface and they will run downhill.

The fourth item of real interest is *Glacier Lagoon* on the southern coast, at least a day's journey from Reykjavik. This lagoon is the end point for one or more glaciers which are melting and continuously producing icebergs. As well as this, the lake has access to the ocean so it is slightly salty, bringing down the freezing point of the water to quite a few degrees below zero Celsius. Thus you have a lake of the order of a few kilometres across, with water well below zero C and icebergs the size of houses floating about in it. Throughout, there are major banks of fog, as might be expected. An operator has taken advantage of this and you can go around the lake on a small boat, see the foot of a glacier, wind amongst the icebergs and do all those things that are not available anywhere else in the world. A pilot boat precedes the boat to ensure that the adventure of the *Titanic* is not repeated. Our skipper maintained that they did not provide lifejackets, because if you fell in you would be frozen before they could pull you out. This is not far from the truth. Some years ago a James Bond movie was filmed on this lake. First they closed the lake off from the sea so that the salt content dropped and the lake froze. There was then an enormous, flat, frozen surface, with icebergs frozen in place like small mountains. Today such an escapade would be frowned on.

While Iceland is not on the Eurail itinerary, it is certainly worth a deviation.

5. NORWAY

As distinct from not only Denmark but from most of northern Europe, Norway is relatively mountainous.

The distance north to south of Norway is quite staggering; unappreciated by most because of the inability to show Scandinavia on a regular Mercator map of Europe. Norway indeed stretches from latitude 58 degrees north to over 71 degrees north, an extent of 13 degrees of latitude. Latitude 71 is almost meaningless to anyone in the Southern Hemisphere, where Tasmania stops at 45 degrees south and even South America stops at 56 degrees south. Pt Barrow in Alaska, though, is also 71 degrees north.

The Arctic Circle is at 67 degrees north.

The extent of Norway is the same as that in Europe from Rome to Copenhagen, in North America from New York to Orlando Fla., or in Australia from Melbourne to north of Rockhampton. The Norwegian coastline is a staggering 2,500km which, when the fjords are taken into account, reaches 8,500km. When you consider that the coastline of the whole EU is estimated at 6,600km, the importance of the seas to Norway becomes obvious.

Oslo is well in the south of Norway at a mere 60 degrees north, and corresponds in latitude to the Shetland Islands, Stockholm, Helsinki and St Petersburg. To most Europeans this is very far north, but acceptable; what they don't appreciate is that the top of Norway is as far distant from Oslo as Frankfurt is to the south. In North America, however, the 60 degree line stretches across Canada from the top of Labrador, the middle of Hudson Bay, the northern boundary of British Columbia, the extreme north of the Alaskan panhandle, and slightly south of Anchorage. Most North Americans would consider that to be beyond comfortable habitation.

Norway is one of the richest countries on Earth, per capita. It has huge oil resources and huge fishing resources. It is not surprising that it is not a member of the EU, although it did apply in 1973 at the same time as Britain and Denmark, but the populace rejected the final accession by referendum.

Norway split from Sweden amicably in 1907 and created its own monarchy. Norway was, of course, occupied by the Nazis in WWII. Theirs is a constitutional monarchy, established 1905, with the sovereign playing mainly a titular, but irreplaceable, role as head of state.

Since its refusal to join the EU, the economy of Norway has expanded through discovery of enormous oil and gas reserves. With its long coastline, Norway has sovereignty over huge amounts of ocean, to the North Pole and across to the boundaries with Greenland. Norway includes Jan Mayen Island, right out in the Atlantic, and Spitsbergen (Svaalbad), which stretches out toward the North Pole.

Norway is a member of the Schengen Treaty, although an exceptional member, as the country is not in the EU. Nonetheless, entry into Norway is entry into the EU and vice versa.

Norway's kroner requires yet another wallet for you to carry and it has a different value from those of Iceland, Sweden and Denmark. The Norwegians generally do NOT accept Euros and there are signs in many shops to tell you so. Expect to receive about seven or eight kroner for one Euro.

***

The first arrivals on the Norwegian coast, after the retreat of the glaciers, were typical coastal dwellers and they saw no reason to check behind them. As the mountains became less forbidding, they pondered over the mountains and saw that they must be inhabited by trolls.

Trolls were non-aggressive beings who liked to play practical jokes. They were rarely seen, but the results of their handiwork were often noted. How else do you explain such things? Trolls had numerous personal attributes, one of which was to be able to change into any form they wished; with one exception. They always wore a tail. It is not hard to think up a sequence of events involving a troll appearing as a beautiful maiden and the later discovery of a tail.

Norwegian trolls are not really aligned with the trolls of the *Three Billy Goats Gruff,* nor of the trolls of J.R.R. Tolkien.

So the trolls became part of the everyday folklore of the Norwegians. Everywhere you go in Norway, you will be told of the trolls and exhorted to buy images of trolls in every form. Generally, they are atrociously ugly and make good talking points. Granny might not appreciate one of those as a souvenir, but everyone would have a good laugh.

***

One normally arrives in Norway in Oslo.

Oslo lives up to its reputation as being one of the ten most liveable cities in the world. With a population of about half a million, it nestles in the head of the Oslo fjord and accepts warmth from the Gulf Stream. This is enough to keep the fjord from freezing and gives a passable climate in mid-winter. This does not mean that it is not cold, but it fares better than many other places.

One can't help feeling on arrival that this is a nice place to be.

On the western side of the fjord an enormous shopping complex, the Aker Brygge precinct, with restaurants and boutiques, has been developed, making use of the existing buildings. Above the head of the fjord is the city hall and related buildings, while on the eastern side the old port image still remains. At the head of the fjord are the small craft which abound in any such area, including those wanting to take you out for a cruise for any purpose. The fishing boats assemble each morning and sell their wares, including hot, freshly-cooked prawns (shrimps, *reker*) by the kilogram.

On one trip to Oslo, I eagerly bought a kilogram of prawns only to find that my meteorologist travelling companion, Andrew, did not like prawns. So I had a whole kilogram to myself. I was not upset. On another occasion my engineering colleague, Wayne, and I misjudged the time taken to reach the station and headed north, standing in the vestibule of the first class compartment spreading the odour of prawns to anyone who came by.

Away from the fjord, the city is much more traditional, being clean, neat and suffering from very few of the drawbacks of a European capital. Nazi occupation did little to harm the structure or the culture of Oslo. One would imagine that Oslo is today small enough, however, to be disturbed by the presence of a cruise ship, but, since these bring money, who will complain?

Oslo has an efficient, but limited, Tunnel-bahn network and a network of buses. A new through railway has been superimposed on the old, giving a strange mixture of ancient and modern, but the mixture works well.

From Oslo we begin by taking a rail trip around the south of the country to Stavanger. This is not fjord country and, while attractive, does not match the north. From Stavanger a ferry can take us to Bergen, the second city of Norway.

Bergen is, of course, where Norway shows itself. This is troll country and from where the Vikings populated the east of the British Isles. If you are of British origin, then the chances are that about twenty generations ago one of your forebears came from here. Haakon's Hall, on the rise above the city, demonstrates the Viking background of the city. Bergen is the home of Edvard Grieg, of *Peer Gynt* fame, and his house can be seen here.

Starting from Bergen is the *Hurtigrute*. This is a daily shipping service which operates from Bergen through to Kirkenes, on the Norwegian side of the Arctic Russian border. The trip takes seven days and is still one of the wonders of European travel. The service was once very exclusive, with references required before booking, and in those days the ships were considered large. Today with the same sized ships overshadowed by the big cruise liners, the *Hurtigrute* has become much more of a service ship and in that category it serves the purpose well. We will run into the *Hurtigrute* again.

It is possible to return to Oslo from Bergen by a day or by a night train. If travelling in the summer, the joys of the journey can be seen for most of the night, and to sit up overnight in a Norwegian train is not a punishment. On the other hand the price of a sleeping compartment is quite high. Norwegian railways will not sell one berth; a single traveller must take the whole double compartment for a double price. Norwegian Railways does not provide couchettes.

Starting again from Oslo, there is also the journey the brochures describe as 'Norway in a Nutshell'.

Norway is carved by countless fjords; some short, some huge. The Sogne Fjord stretches inland for around 150km and baffles anyone wanting to cross it, or even reach it for that matter. At a very convenient point on the innermost reaches of the Sogne Fjord is the little port of Flam, and 863 metres above it is the town of Myrdal on the railway from Oslo to Bergen. This is on the boundary of the *UNESCO World Heritage Area, Western Norwegian Fjords,* so there is something to see.

The morning train from Oslo towards Bergen takes the line to the higher part of the ranges over the highest point at Finse, at 1,222 metres above sea level. For much of the journey snow is evident on the ground all year and a very large proportion of the higher sections is in snow-shed formation to keep the line open during the winter. After about three hours the train comes to Myrdal, from where you take the *Flamsbana*. The *Flamsbana* was the rail connection (electrified) from this main line down to the sea, thereby allowing passage from Oslo to the fjords of the west of Norway. The line is 20km long and drops those 863 metres with a maximum gradient of 1:18 which applies over 80% of the track. The maximum speed is 30 kph down and 40 kph up and the trip takes about 55 minutes. The line was started in 1923 and opened in 1940. Railway enthusiasts come from all over the world to travel on this train. Once it was free to Eurail pass users, and my memory tells me that three trips in one day was my limit on one occasion. Fancy finding me here again!

After allowing time for a two-hour walk about the head of the fjord at Flam, now of the order of 100km inland, a ferry takes passengers on a cruise of around four hours, arriving at Bergen in time for dinner. In this part of Norway the word 'sunset' is not a sensible way of giving the time, as it can vary over more than eight hours. This cruise gives a really good picture of the manner in which fjords cut the country and how they made coastal travel simple, but cross country travel a nightmare. The Norwegians have now built tunnels linking the heads of the fjords, so driving across Norway is now a reality. This boat traverses most of the length of the Sogne Fjord and shows some of the most beautiful scenery imaginable. It arrives conveniently in Bergen in time for the night train back to Oslo. The *Flamsbana* and the cruise to Bergen is a MUST for any traveller.

Thomas Cook places both the Bergen Line and the Flam line on the list of Scenic Rail Routes of Europe and awards the star for the editor's personal choice to both. This star is restricted to 23 locations, most of which will be referred to in this book.

With a Eurail pass, there is an inexpensive way of seeing more and costing less. It is possible to take a seated night journey Oslo-Gol-Oslo on the Bergen line, have a reasonable sleep, and be ready for another day in Oslo (or Bergen-Ål-Bergen). The Norwegian Railways might not like this idea very much, but it said nothing to me when it knew nothing. Since it is light during the summer for most of the trip, here is another chance to see their mountains.

Norwegians all speak English and, with only a small margin of error, I would postulate that they speak English better than you do. A physicist colleague did his sabbatical in Trondheim, so his primary school-aged children went to the local school and were required to learn Norwegian. The school discovered that their knowledge of English was so poor that they had to put them into English classes first, so that they could learn language structure, etc. before they could begin teaching them Norwegian. English is compulsory for all Norwegian kids.

'Why can't the English teach their children how to speak?
Norwegians learn Norwegian,
The Greeks are taught their Greek.
But use proper English, you're regarded as a freak.
Why can't the English,
Learn to speak?'

Alan Jay Lerner, – '*My Fair Lady*'

On another occasion I had promised my meteorologist travelling companion that he would not find anyone in Norway who could not speak English. He laughed at this and suggested that we might find some old sea captain who did not. On the following morning we went to the dock to buy prawns for breakfast. Sure enough, the old fisherman did not speak English. The nearest person, of course, translated.

Travelling north from Oslo by train is generally through pretty countryside, with plenty of lakes, rivers and mountains, but none is overwhelming… at least not yet.

Take the very chic morning express train from Oslo Central and head north for Trondheim.

Ultimately you arrive at the village of Dombås, 660 metres, where you leave the train and wait for, then join, a two-car diesel rail motor for Åndelsnes on the Rauma line. The train heads off on its 90-minute journey down the Rauma valley and almost at once you feel that this is not an ordinary journey. The train slowly loses altitude but the clifftops do not, so that as the train reaches Åndelsnes, you are at sea level but the mountains about stretch up for ever. The *Trolltindine*,Troll Peaks, tower up to 1,700 metres above sea level.

Ancient legend has it that the mountains are actually trolls who were turned to stone by the light of day. Trollwegen is Europe's highest perpendicular mountain wall, as 1,000 metres is sheer precipice. This then is the haven for walkers, rock-climbers, hang-gliders and all those sportsmen and women in between. Here you certainly have no difficulty in believing the tourist brochures.

Having seen Åndelsnes, which is the base for these numerous activities, your next opportunity is to take the bus to Ålesund. This 130-minute journey follows the fjords at sea level and gives plenty of opportunity to see Norwegian coastal scenery, Ålesund faces out into the North Sea, was once a fishing centre and has reasonable accommodation available. Ålesund is also a stopping point for the *Hurtigrute*, last seen in Bergen. Not only is it a stopping point, but during the summer it takes its passengers on an excursion up the Gerainger fjord, taking from early morning to late afternoon. Further, it will take day-trippers. For a modest sum, therefore, you can take a trip on the high quality Norwegian *Hurtigrute*, see an outstanding fjord and return. This is the other sub-area of the *World Heritage Area, Western Norwegian Fjords*. After a second, or subsequent night in Ålesund, you are ready to make the return trip to Dombås and then on to Trondheim.

Trondheim is one of Norway's larger cities and once again relies on the ocean for its existence.

From here, the line continues north to Bodø. The overnight train carries second-class seats and a sleeper car but, as mentioned earlier, seats are comfortable in Norwegian trains and sleepers are expensive. Besides, for several months of the year the trip is mostly in daylight.

The terrain covered by this trip is not over-exciting; in fact, once the line runs above the tree-line it becomes very repetitive. At around 0500 the train crosses the Arctic Circle at 66° 33' 44" North. Nothing very special happens here, except that the inevitable tourist shop is visible on the adjacent highway and a small beacon has been erected on each side of the line. The crossing is near the highest point on the line, so the countryside is fairly barren. At Fauske, about an hour before the end of the journey, those wishing to take the bus to Narvik, more than seven hours further on and through a lot more inland country, are invited to leave the train. The train continues to Bodø.

Bodø is the northernmost extremity of the Norwegian rail network, but, even though it is well north of the Arctic Circle there is a lot of Norway yet to cover.

Back in 1982 I was able to identify and take the family on the weekly steamer plying between Bodø and Narvik. We called at everywhere en route, off-loading goats and chickens, and took around 24 hours. It was huge fun and a great experience for the kids, but, alas, such things are no more.

Once I made an excursion to see Norway in the winter, but only the part as far as Bodø. The trains were, of course, properly heated and, although snow was on the ground everywhere, there were no hold-ups in the train service. Crossing the Arctic Circle carried no special interest to the passengers and we arrived in Bodø on a cold, dark morning. Overcoat, scarf and beanie were the order of the day. The train schedule allowed me four hours in Bodø, where I wandered around the city and the docks. The ground was icy and in many cases difficult for a stranger to walk on, but nothing locally was stopped by this. It was business as usual, as it must be. Away from the coast there was frozen snow to be contended with, but well trampled. At about 0800 the prawns came on sale on the dock and I could be seen munching my half kilogram bucket of prawns, trying desperately to keep the prawn smell off myself and off my limited selection of warm clothes.

Back to summer. For those who are not happy with long, uneventful bus rides such as the one from Fauske to Narvik, there is yet another alternative. In the distance over the ocean from Bodø, you can see a range of mountains which are the Lofoten Islands. This string of islands sticks out (not a very geographically correct expression, but it says what is wanted) into the ocean and into the Gulf Stream, and thus enjoys a more temperate climate, in the same way as the Scilly Isles do in Britain. From Bodø a ferry, not large, but large enough for a restaurant and comfortable facilities, runs usually twice daily to a small village by the name of Moskenes out on the seaward end of the Lofoten Islands. Thomas Cook has it listed in the ferry section and I am pleased to say that I was instrumental in having it included. From Moskenes there is a journey of around 5km to the town of Å in Lofoten. You can choose bus, taxi or even foot; someone will pick you up.

Å is the most amazing village. Each year the cod come to the area around these islands and the fishermen of Å are waiting for them, as they have been for a thousand years. The catch is dried on outdoor racks and sent to places in southern Europe, where it is a delicacy.

The fishermen have moved from their traditional village accommodation, on piles over the water, back into the trees, and the traditional buildings have become hostel accommodation for the arriving tourists. The restaurant is second-to-none. As you can gather from my enthusiasm, it is a location not to be missed.

> *The sun was shining on the sea, shining with all his might:*
> *He did his very best to make the billows smooth and bright—*
> *And this was odd, because it was the middle of the night.*
> *The Walrus and the Carpenter*, – Lewis Carroll

Midsummer's Day is a long one, from 25 May to 11 July or thereabouts. It is an uncanny sensation to be able to walk around at midnight, in an amenable climate, in daylight. One must pause a minute to think of Midwinter's Night. Apparently golfers come here, and further north, to play 18 holes at midnight.

The bus back to Narvik via Svolvaer, along the island chain, is a long one but balanced by some of the most magnificent coastal, mountain and island scenery available. By leaving Å early in the morning, it is even possible to take a two hour round-trip cruise into the fjord from Svolvaer, have a kilogram of prawns on the dock for lunch, and still arrive in Narvik in time for dinner. On the most recent occasion I was there, 6 June 2011, the temperature in Svolvaer was 23C at noon, warmer in the afternoon and still 23C in Narvik early next morning. The sun shone on the town all night.

A shorter journey can be made from Bodø to Svolvaer by ferry, but you miss Å. It is even possible to take the *Hurtigrute* from Bodø to Svolvaer.

Narvik is near the head of a long fjord and, under German occupation, featured greatly in the battle between Mr. Churchill and Herr Hitler in WWII.

Narvik is the northern extent of the European rail network, albeit Swedish, and is at 68 degrees north of the equator, north of the Arctic Circle. The climate, at least in summer, is still agreeable. There is so much more of Norway yet to go, three more degrees of latitude to Nordkapp.

Back in 2006, my meteorologist colleague and I took the train to Bodø, as far north as the Norwegian train can take you, hired a car and then drove consistently for two days to reach Nordkapp. The experience was justified, the country on the way is not exciting, the tree-line is not very far above sea level, but there are towns, even substantial cities. Tromsø, Hammerfest, Alta. Alta is the northernmost city in the world at 69 degrees north. Like you find in crossing Australia, words fail; it has to be seen to be believed. Everywhere, except at the very top, the climate was mild and the roads were good. All this is due to the Gulf Stream, which is generated by a large flow of very cold water from the melting ice of the Arctic flowing south under the Atlantic Ocean, complementing a very warm flow, the part we normally refer to as the Gulf Stream, coming north from the tropics on the surface to take its place. In a half-century or so the polar icecap may have completely melted, possibly as a result of natural climate change. Then there will be no Gulf Stream, and at what price to Norway and Britain?

Nordkapp faces out over the Arctic Ocean and, in marked contrast to the drive up, was exceptionally cold and windy. It was bitterly cold at 71 degrees N facing out toward the North Pole and well above the tree-line, which reaches the coast much further south. The concessionaire has made the best of his asset and the cost of entering the area comes well over the €100 level.

We arrived after the evening meal on 20 June. There were 39 buses lined up and an equivalent number of car passengers, all coming to see something fail to happen. All were lined up to see the sun 'not set'. Most of those buses and cars carried Europeans; Germans, Italians and those from smaller countries. It was pleasing to see no Australians, no British and no Americans. How many of the last would even consider *driving* to Pt Barrow in Alaska, a location at the same latitude?

As the clock rolled around, the sun headed down, but always behind cloud. Then, at very close to the witching hour, the clouds broke and there was the sun, about 20 degrees above the horizon; the lowest it would go today. Hundreds of cameras clicked, most with flash, to take a photo of the sun above the open ocean, a shot you can find anywhere there is ocean, twice a day every day. Strange! Then they all headed for their cars or buses to return to one of those towns or cities to find their night's sleep. We headed back to Narvik. From Nordkapp it is as easy to go back by car or bus to the railhead at Rouvaneimi in Finland, to Kirkenes or even to Murmansk in Russia if you have a visa.

To avoid retracing steps home from Narvik, Swedish Railways provides an alternative way south to Stockholm. That is the subject of the next chapter.

6. SWEDEN

Sweden is probably the nation in the EU closest to the 'ideal' welfare state and, as a consequence, the standard of living is high, age expectancy is high, taxes are high and costs to an outsider are very high. Their life expectancy is in the top bracket of nations of the world, approaching 84 for women and 80 for men; it all depends on your definition.

A visitor immediately notices the costs. Their MOMS (VAT, GST) can be as high as 25% and the basic price component is high as well.

Sweden has always had a policy of neutrality. Its constitution is one of the eight oldest in the world, again depending on definition, and it has not been subjected to the over-lordship of any other nation since it parted from Denmark. Mind you, it has had both Norway and Finland under its wing for some of that time.

The old royal line in Sweden came to an end during the time of Napoleon, and Bonaparte, no doubt seeking an easy alliance, gave them Marshall Bernadotte as king. Bernadotte became King Carl XIV John and immediately continued Sweden's policy of neutrality, snubbing Bonaparte in doing so. The Swedes managed to remain neutral, doubtless because of Bonaparte's preoc-cupation with Russia and Britain, and has done so ever since. Hitler did not touch Sweden, although on both sides were occupied countries. All this has doubtless helped the ultimate Swedish economy, and a landscape with virtu-ally no destruction for 200 years is a joy to see.

Currently the heirs of Bernadotte still hold the Swedish throne, although an almost nominal position. Sweden passes the throne to the eldest child, not necessarily the eldest son, by act of parliament in 1980, being the first European monarchy to do so.

Sweden joined the EU in 1995 at the same time as Austria and Finland

and, like Austria, needed to change its constitution to do so. By then a requirement of entry to the EU was to join the Eurozone. The other two countries have, but Sweden has somehow managed to fail to meet the entry requirements and still merrily trades in Swedish kroner, and will probably continue to do so, standing along with Britain, which has an exemption, as the big, permanent abstainers.

As in Denmark and Norway, the traveller is obliged to buy the local kroner to move about. The Swedes will not take Euros! The fistful is not, however, very large as the Swede pays for everything with his credit card. He walks into a hamburger shop, orders a hamburger, swipes his card, collects his goods and walks out. He does not need to sign or enter a number. It takes some doing if you come from a country where signs keep urging you, 'Minimum transaction on credit card is $50', or similar, but you can learn. Then, every so often, you come across a merchant whose goods are indispensable to you and find that he will not take a card or that his machine is out of order. The most notable exception like this is to buy a ticket on the local buses or Tunnel-bahn. A Euro will buy you nine Swedish kroner.

As a surprise to most, Sweden ranks as the third largest country by area in Europe, not including Russia. Its northerly extent does not show on European maps, because of the inability to depict the northern regions on a standard map projection. Sweden has a northern border with Norway and thus does not have access to the Arctic Ocean.

All Swedish ports are in the Baltic,and are frozen in during winter, certainly to big ships, so Sweden has developed a rail link across the mountain range into Norway and to the port of Narvik which is ice-free. From here Sweden exports its iron ore from Kiruna and such other products as use the oceans.

***

Having covered all that preamble about Sweden, we can now resume our eastern journey. Southern Sweden and access to Stockholm were discussed in the chapter on Denmark, so we pick up the journey in the Norwegian city of Narvik.

Narvik, you will remember, is on the Gulf Stream coast of Norway, 68 degrees north of the equator and has a relatively mild climate, but don't go there in winter from choice. The Swedish train leaves Narvik twice daily, although the rails and crew to the border are Norwegian.

The train trip from Narvik to the border is nothing short of spectacular. In 43km the track must rise to 513 metres to the top of the watershed near the border, and, in doing so, winds about the sides of the fjord. Then it reaches the ski resorts which, while not being very high, have lots of snow in the winter. Every so often you pass a huge iron ore train using gravity to take it down to Narvik. Once in Sweden the track changes mode, for here the Kiruna ore trains are going uphill toward Narvik and the gradients are kept as low as possible.

Kiruna is a mining town and, while it is not exceptionally grubby, its format is easy to detect.

When I came here with my family back in 1982, we enquired in the store about the youth hostel. No, it would not be open until the next day which was the beginning of the summer, all three weeks of it, but she would call the proprietor. The proprietor came to us and told us we could have a room but, since the facilities were not ready, would we first buy our provisions. This we did, only to be followed out by her presenting us with a basket of fruit and a smile saying, 'for the children'. We enjoyed our stay in Sweden.

At Kiruna the train is fully assembled with sleeping cars, etc. for the journey to Stockholm. In contrast to Norway, the surcharge for a sleeping berth in trains in Sweden is not so high and there are no exclusion rules. The reasons for this are obvious when you join this train, as it takes 24 hours to reach Stockholm and there are very few major towns between to break up the journey.

From Kiruna you are in Lappland, as you would be this far north in Finland. In Norway there be trolls; Norway is mountainous. The Lapps are nomadic people. They herd the reindeer (in North America, the caribou) and they move where the reindeer take them. They are a fascinating people and worthy of time spent observing their culture.

There are some amazing national parks in the Kiruna area, which allow for walking trails in the summer and winter recreation in the remainder of the year. Their remoteness ensures that they are unspoiled and only used by the genuine. There are very few other places in the Arctic regions of the world (this is well above the Arctic Circle, remember) where climate and accessibility make such places viable. At such latitudes in Alaska, Canada and Russia, the land is effectively uninhabitable and life-threatening, except to the very fine sprinkling of locals who have come to terms with the climate.

So the train continues seemingly endlessly over plains, through forests, past mountains and often through them. Wildlife in the form of reindeer and the occasional moose can be seen, perhaps even a bear, but not a white one. The crossing of the Arctic Circle is shown twice, the current location and that of a few years ago. The Arctic Circle is currently drifting northwards at a speed of about 15 metres per year, something of which I was unaware until I saw the signs.

On one occasion when I was in this train, we emerged from a tunnel with a great jolt and screeching of brakes. The conductor went stomping to the rear of the train and returned with a rifle. 'Bang! Bang!' The conductor returned the rifle and we continued on our way. We had hit a moose as we emerged from the tunnel. It was neatly put out of its misery; no doubt hauled out of the way and left for the next opportunist to dispose of the carcass. Protein would be at a premium in that area and should not be removed. Insect, bird, animal or man may make good use of it.

After a long journey, but by no means tiresome, the town of Boden is reached. Boden is adjacent to the city of Lulea and the head of the Gulf of Bothnia which is icebound in winter. Here the train is once more rearranged and continues on its way over much more conventional terrain to Stockholm.

At Lulea one can take the bus into Finland, which we will discuss later.

***

The city of Stockholm is built on a huge number of small islands where Lake Mälaren drains into the Baltic Sea. The drop in level is only a metre or so, but enough to maintain a flow and to distinguish fresh from brackish; the Baltic is not terribly salty.

Logically, Stockholm is best appreciated from the water.

A round-the-harbour cruise for a couple of hours gives a good understanding of the city, why it is where it is and its history. Most things worthy of note can be seen from the water. On any such cruise the Swedes will point out their own unique architecture and history. Not one bit of it has come under enemy influence in more than two centuries.

It is rumoured that the mediaeval residents of Stockholm felt themselves reasonably safe against enemy invasion, except for one navigable channel which was undefended. They resolved to fill this and set about throwing rocks into the channel so as eventually to fill it. This practice is said to have continued for something like 400 years and their aim was achieved, only to be completed at a time when one big piece of earth-moving equipment could have filled it in a day, or cleared it in the same time. Discovering the truth can spoil some very good legends.

Stockholm is not Venice or Amsterdam, but a hop-on-hop-off ferry is probably the best way to see the main sights, a few of which can be recounted here. For about €10 (he takes Euro) you can go anywhere, all day, on his route.

The main shopping centre seems not unlike most of a city this size and the 'seen one seen all' mentality could prevail. This is not warranted and many hours could be spent poking about the main streets and back streets, with or without credit card.

The old city, Gamla Stan, has an island of its own and is not all that spoiled by having the railway skirt its shore. Here are the oldest buildings and institutions of the city.

The headquarters and museum of the Nobel organisation is in an unassuming building on the island and worthy of a visit. The palace, of course, dominates the route of the tourist. As in Denmark, the changing of the guard is small by London standards but a preserved tradition.

The *piece de resistance* of Stockholm is the annual presentation of the Nobel Prizes. This takes place each December in the great Concert Hall of the city. My connection with this is that, over 20 years ago, I was able to negotiate for my organisation the privilege of annually sending two Australian students to join the very small contingent of around twenty students, Swedes included, who were to join the festivities. They were given the opportunity to attend the lectures by the laureates, to meet the laureates informally, to attend the ceremony, and finally to attend the great dinner and ball at the conclusion; perhaps even to meet the King and Queen, or at least the Crown Princess. What 18-year-old student could fail to be impressed by that collection of events?

The Swedes have a living piece of history in their midst, in the form of the warship *Vasa* in its preservation museum on Djurgarden Island. The *Vasa* was the pride of the Swedish Navy and turned turtle on its voyage in Stockholm harbour on 10 August, 1628. There was a large loss of life and much egg on face. The cause is alleged to have been design meddling by an absentee king who believed he was an expert in naval architecture. The parallel with Henry VIII and the *Mary Rose* in 1545 is too close not to notice.

The *Vasa* was brought to the surface on 24 April, 1961 and immediately put in the hands of the conservators. The waters around Stockholm are too cold for the usual worms and beasties to consume the timbers, so the ship was close to intact. After 300 years under water the timbers had metamorphosed, and a huge amount of treatment was required to make the ship capable of facing the open air in which it was created.

Swedish heritage has been preserved in an open air museum at Skansen. This island, once reserved as a royal hunting ground, is the final resting place of houses, villages, activities and the like from all parts of Sweden, somewhat akin to Ballenberg, near Brienz in Switzerland. The area doubles as a recreation resort, so Swedes adjourn to the Skansen for a day out in the sun with the kids.

On the same island is the resort area of Grona Land, a sort of mini-Luna Park, Blackpool or Coney Island. It is hardly an attraction for the legitimate visitor but it is a notable landmark.

The backbone of the excellent Swedish railways, the hourly service from Stockholm to Malmö, was mentioned in the Danish chapter. Stockholm central station is the core of the city from where mainline trains can take one to Copenhagen, Malmö, Göteborg, Oslo, Lulea and Narvik, as well as to the airport and to the adjacent university city of Uppsala, which enjoys a very high international reputation.

In the city the traditional rail lines have been used to form a substantial suburban S-Bahn system, although somewhat complex. On top of this is superimposed the tunnel-bahn network, mainly underground. To reach the departure point of the Silja line ferries to Finland, take the tunnel-bahn to Gärten on T13, the orange line, and follow the signs for a ten minute walk to Vartahamnen.

7. FINLAND

Finland is a difficult country to classify. It is not Scandinavia and the Finns have no wish to be equated with Russia. It has lived either inside Russia, or under the shadow of Russia, for much of its existence.

Finland existed under Swedish rule for some 700 years and Helsinki was established as a city in 1550. Helsinki had built its own fortification on many of the islands in the harbour. They were adequate to cope with any invasion but, alas, in 1808 Alexander came from behind by land. The cannons of the Finns were facing the wrong way. You are probably reminded of the Japanese invasion of Singapore in WWII. The world was too involved with Napoleon to worry about a tiny country like Finland, and Bernadotte, next across in neighbouring Sweden, was certainly not out to annoy anyone. In the following year Finland became part of Russia.

So the Finns lived under Russian rule until 1917 when Finland declared its independence. I once very unthinkingly asked a lady in Helsinki if the Finns had ever had a king. There was a long pause until she finally answered, 'Well, we had the Tsar!'

The Russians did, however, exchange a large slice of territory nearer to St Petersburg for a similar sized slice of useless territory in the north after the winter war in 1939-40. The argument was that the border was too close to their capital. This has never endeared the Russians to the Finns, but like the diminution of Germany, they have learned to accept it.

For 40 or so years the Finns lived on a knife-edge. They dare not antagonise the Soviets and they could not, therefore, join the EU or NATO, despite their (unspoken) wish to do so.

Then came the memorable day around 1988 when Soviet General Secretary Mr. Gorbachev said that he saw no reason why Finland could not join NATO if it wished. This caused a scurry. Finland, Sweden and Austria each applied to join the EU, the last two having first to amend their constitutions, and, after being hoisted to the top of the list, were admitted. Finland adopted the Euro at the first opportunity and is now an exceedingly Western European member of the EU with a very large land border to Russia, even though there are very few crossing points because of the geography.

***

There are two ways in which the non-air traveller can reach Finland from the west: by ferry from Stockholm and by the rail route across the top of the Gulf of Bothnia, the mid-portion of which is now operated by buses.

The ferries are huge, the regular floating casinos once more. One can take a Silja line or Viking line ferry from Stockholm, have a feast at the very moderately priced buffet, spend the night at the casino without using your cabin, and arrive next morning in Helsinki. The Silja line also operates a ferry to Turku and does a round trip every 24 hours. One waits at Vartahamnen, the day ferry comes into sight, speedily manoeuvres itself into place and begins disgorging passengers and cars. While the last passengers are still coming into the terminal the new passengers are moved forward and, within an hour of arrival all the passengers and cars are on board and the ferry is Turku-bound.

Turku is on the Swedish side of Finland and a train waits to collect Helsinki passengers from the Silja ferry as the same turnaround is repeated. A couple of hours on a comfortable, but not luxurious, IC train will see you in the capital.

The land route involves taking the Swedish train north along the western side of the Gulf of Bothnia to Lulea, and then taking the replacement bus to Haparanda on the border. I was lucky enough to take this service around 20 years ago when it was still a train. The small railcar from Boden stopped at all stations to load or unload passengers and goods. It would not have been surprising to see goats and chickens. On arrival at Haparanda it was 'all off' and if you wanted to go on to Finland, you walked across the bridge to Tornio and the Finnish train which would take you to Kemi. The latter provided the same type of service.

Today the bus takes you from Lulea (rail tickets accepted) and runs to Haparanda where, if you are quick, you can find the Finnish bus going to

Tornio and on to Kemi. Hesitate and you have to wait some time for the next bus. This is all complicated by the one hour time difference between Haparanda and Tornio.

At Kemi the train can take you, by now overnight, to Helsinki.

There was once another surface method. In winter the Gulf of Bothnia freezes, very solidly (water freezes from the top down), and road traffic would drive across the Gulf, some 200km, into Finland. This is no longer allowed, seemingly by stuffy safety regulations, because of bigger trucks which might fall through or, more likely, because of the big ice breakers which might keep the sea lanes open. Whatever, the ferries are now bigger and the road around the top is much better so the trucks find other routes.

***

The railway gauge, the distance between the rails, across most of Europe, all of North America, most of Australia and numerous other parts of the world, is set at 1435mm (4'8½"). It is alleged that this became standard because Roman chariots in Britain had their wheels set so that they would follow the tracks of the horses' hooves which led them. The wheel gauge was thus the distance between the centre lines of the horses or, more bluntly, the distance across a horse's backside.

Little did George Stephenson know that by setting his trains at this gauge, he would set the size of equipment built in the 20th century, by Boeing and NASA for instance. The rail gauge determines the radius of curvature of the track, hence the length of the trucks. It also determines size and curvature of the tunnels which determines the loading gauge. All of this determines the size of any single item carried. Since both NASA and Boeing have components transported by rail, this determines the maximum size of any component. Thus, many of the products of NASA and of Boeing have been limited by this gauge. It is alleged that the space shuttle had to be redesigned to fit through the rail tunnels of North America.

Most of Europe from Britain to the far Polish border, to the north of Sweden and Norway, to Istanbul and Athens and to the Pyrenees, operates on the standard 1435mm gauge. Hercule Poirot was to travel from Istanbul to Calais in the same coach. Where there was need to choose a smaller gauge, as in the mountains of Switzerland, a 1000mm gauge was usually chosen; the metre preceding the railways by about half a century.

Finnish rail gauge is 1524mm, very close to Russian gauge of 1520mm. Hence the train from Helsinki can take you onward to Russia, but there is no real advantage in lamenting the loss of the passenger rail connection at Haparanda/Tornio, as nothing could run through from the Swedish gauge at 1435mm. The Russians have the facility to change the wheel gauge at the Polish border on selected through trains to the west, to 1435mm.

Ireland uses 1600mm, which became transposed to Victoria and South Australia, while Spain and Portugal run at 1668mm. The Spaniards are very busy building fast trains on new 1435mm tracks to connect into France.

The great Isambard Kingdom Brunel, when he built the Great Western Railway in England, chose 7'6" as his gauge. This is the reason why the track is less winding and the bridges more substantial on this route today.

***

Don't tell the Finns, but Helsinki is not a large city. It makes up for size, however, in its unique charm and appeal.

As in many cities the centre of Helsinki is about the railway station, sloping away toward the port. The port, and almost the city, is dominated by the presence of the huge ferries from Sweden which stand in the port, reaching a dozen decks high, until they ceremonially leave together at 1700 daily, as if in a race.

One item to notice is the church in the rock, a small but beautiful church which is built in a hollowed-out basin of natural rock. This you will not see anywhere else.

Helsinki has its mermaid too, standing larger-than-life on a pedestal in the park heading to the docks. Actually, she is not a mermaid, but don't let that spoil the story. Every year, during their short summer, she is given her annual scrub. The town band and My Lord Mayor come marching down in company with the fire engine. The fire crew hoists the ladder out immediately above her, douses her with soapy water and proceeds to scrub, with an ordinary household scrubbing brush. Of course, the watching populace is free in its suggestion as to where they might scrub. There is a great need for this to be done because she has a year's accumulation, minus the rain's cleaning, of pigeon and seagull dung all over her. Our kids loved the spectacle back in 1982.

The International Physics Olympiad was held in Finland around 1990 and we were located at Espoo, slightly out of Helsinki. Our facilities were not of as high standard as the Finns had, since IPhO planning had commenced, taken on the task of hosting G7 as it was then. To handle security, Finnish police were drafted in from all over the country and fed where we were supposed to be eating; we were downgraded. One wonders whether there was a policeman to be found in non-metropolitan Finland.

On our first free day at Espoo, I declined to take the bus into Helsinki and was soundly berated by one of the locals for not going to see her beautiful city. 'You have come all the way from Australia and do not see Helsinki!' She simply would not believe me when I told her I had been to Helsinki five times before.

One night I had taken the Russian delegate out to dinner, they still had no Western currency. On returning, asked the Belgian delegate what they had for dinner. His response was not very complimentary. This was very unfair but does indicate that Finnish food may not be exciting. This reaction was followed by M. Chirac, the French Premier at the time, who, on the eve of the selection of London for the 2012 Olympics, was noted to comment that one would never want to go to London as the food was as bad as that of the Finns. That would have lost him support from at least the Finns and, remember, London only defeated Paris by four votes. One of the London papers carried the headline, 'M. Chirac, you have *oeuf* on your face.'

On another occasion I had the fortune to stay with the leader of the Finnish team in Helsinki. She took me to their country cottage out of town, on a lake, as it must be, and treated me to one of the more delightful weekends I can remember. The cooking by her brother-in-law put flight to any ideas that Finnish food may be below standard.

History has given Finland two official languages, Finnish and Swedish. 95% of the population speaks Finnish and, of the remainder, there is a substantial population who speak Lapp. There is no language problem in Finland. Written Finnish appears complex as it has double letters and a pairing of letters unseen in any other language of Latin script. Strangely enough, the nearest related language is Hungarian, so the origins of these peoples may be common. Since 1989 we must acknowledge that the Estonians, up until then subsumed in the USSR, have a language closely allied to Finnish.

The Finns claim to have the largest per capita usage of telephones in the world. It might be so, but again this will depend on your definition. They are irked because, when dialling codes were given out, the more dominant Western European countries were given two digit codes (Britain 44, France 31, Switzerland 41, etc.) but the Finns were given 353. *C'est la vie*!

Apart from the line to Turku, the principal rail lines from Helsinki run north to Rouvaneimi and east to Joensuu. Both are attractive journeys, but hardly to someone who might have no affinity for lakes. See what I mean about spelling!

North of Rouvaneimi you will find the headquarters of Santa Claus. Some entrepreneur found a niche from which to make money and here you will see the factory, the elves and, above all, the gift shop where you can buy almost anything that you could not conceivably want when it comes out of your suit-case at home. You are exhorted to send postcards from here to your loved ones at home, written and dated today and mailed on 1 December. Granny would like one of those. Of the old boy, there is no sign.

From Helsinki one can take the ferry to Tallinn across the water in Estonia. 'Tallink' ferries ply between Helsinki and Tallinn in two hours, today at six daylight services a day, supplemented by a frequent hydrofoil service of 90 minutes 'during the ice-free period' and a second shipping line. The memories of the very sparse service before 1989 tell how things have changed.

Another choice for those with a visa is to take the Russian train to St Petersburg.

Whichever way you go, east or south, make sure you take with you a large number of €5 and €10 notes to make your way easier and the inevitable roll of perforated blank, that is, toilet paper. The latter should not be necessary but, if you need it and you don't have it, trouble can ensue. You can leave what is left over in the WC on the train out of Warsaw.

8. ST PETERSBURG, RUSSIA

St Petersburg is not correctly in the province of the Eurail pass traveller, as one needs a visa to enter Russia, which the Russians do not regularly give to itinerant travellers. Nonetheless, St Petersburg logically fits here as it is at the end of a train journey which can be started on Eurail, and the timetable is given by Thomas Cook.

St Petersburg is the second largest city in Russia after Moscow and, after London and Paris, thus the fourth largest in Europe. Different definitions of 'largest' will produce different lists. It was a created a city in the same sense as Washington, Brasilia and Canberra, but considerably earlier. It is still 'young' by European standards, being founded in 1703.

One takes a train from Helsinki main station on Russian gauge. There are five trains a day, all taking about three-and-a-half hours. The trains are new and well appointed by anyone's standards. When I took the train in the 1980s there was but one train per day and it took much longer. It was necessary then to have a pre-purchased visa and the trip endured all of the searches by both immigration and customs, which were the policy of the Soviets. They checked the ceilings and under the seats, in the lockers, in the WC, etc., although why anyone would want to smuggle INTO the USSR is beyond me.

There are, of course, about a dozen services a day between Moscow and St Petersburg, which will be alluded to in a later chapter. There is also a daily service, on a traditional Russian night train, from Riga and Vilnius, which will be discussed later, and another from Kaliningrad via Vilnius.

Another important access to St Petersburg is the three-times-a-week ferry from Helsinki. This again requires a pre-paid visa.

St Petersburg was created by Tsar Peter the Great in 1703 as a monument to his patron saint, St Peter. He wanted the city to be built on Western European lines and to be the showpiece capital of all Russia. We are talking of Tsarist Russia at this time, not the USSR of Cold War days. After listening to the various guides, one might be forgiven for having generated a mental picture of Peter rolling up the royal shirtsleeves and wielding a shovel. This undoubtedly was not the case, as the general Russian population was made up of serfs until 1851. Bearing this in mind, we hear that Peter first of all built the fortress of Peter and Paul on the banks of the River Neva to secure the site and began the construction of a city. Peter also built the original church of St Isaac's, named because this saint had his day on Peter's birthday.

Subsequent generations after Peter added to the city, but it was not until Catherine II, a German lady who was married to Peter's grandson, referred to as Catherine the Great, that the greatest changes became evident. Catherine reigned as Empress from 1762 to 1796, during which time the city grew greatly. Catherine built the Winter Palace as the home of the Tsars, in which is now housed the Hermitage Museum and art collection. Catherine did this purely for herself and friends, and the general populace had no access to it until long after her death.

During WWI the name of the city was changed to Petrograd, as it was considered that 'burg' was too German and to be avoided. Britain changed Battenburg to Mountbatten and Saxe-Coburg Gotha to Windsor at about the same time. Nobody changed the name of Adelaide, who was the German-born wife of William IV.

Lenin died in 1924 and the city was renamed 'Leningrad' in his memory.

The power of the city dwindled and Moscow once more became the capital.

Only after the collapse of the USSR and the restoration of the Russian government did the people vote to return the name to St Petersburg.

In the days before the end of the USSR, I was fortunate enough to be able to stay in a private home for a few days without fetters. There was little of material wealth for the populace and consumer goods were very rare. The house in which I stayed would not accommodate one person by today's Western standards, but it housed an extended family and would still welcome a visitor. The streets were wide, the trams and trains ran and the people were seemingly happy. They knew no better. The city was run by the aged mommas of the population. Everywhere the controller was an elderly lady. They sold in the tiny kiosks, they drove the buses and monitored the gates. Undoubtedly they were the widows of WWII, and there were very many of those, and those of latter times. There was no pension scheme and their only alternative to starving was to go out to work. Many of them surely did both.

As distinct from in the 1980s, it is now possible for the tourist to see as much of St Petersburg as desired.

The transport system is excellent, although undoubtedly the locals will describe it otherwise. The trams run frequently, although they may not be too modern, and buses are everywhere. The pearl of the system is the subway, begun in 1955. Since the city was built on marshland, the subway is very deep and any escalator down makes Holborn or Angel in London seem shallow. They claim it is the deepest in the world, probably correctly, and the cleanest, and this may also be true. Most of the stations are works of art, perhaps not comparable with Moscow subways but certainly eye-catchingly so. Trains operate on five lines, criss-crossing one another in an apparently random style as happens in nearly all cities. My school principal colleague, Tony, was impressed to see the doors on the platform open in concert with the doors on the train, similar to the Jubilee line in London, but not eclipsing Moscow where the track and the platform are in separate tunnels. A single token will take you anywhere for around one Euro. The traffic, particularly at peak periods, is reported as chaotic but then these folk have never seen a congested Western city.

The first thing noticed by the casual tourist, after the transport system, is the amazingly wide streets, Parisian-style, interlaced with the canals; not quite Venice or Amsterdam but certainly with a resemblance. This encourages cyclists and, as the city is dead flat, these are flitting about everywhere. This does not compare, of course, with Amsterdam or Oxford.

The city is large enough not to be distorted by the cruise liners which call. It is not unusual to see up to seven of these monsters in the harbour, and consequently the tour groups moving from place to place, with their numbered ping pong bats held high. These ships can issue one or two day visas to those whose passports are recognised by the Russians, and this would be the best way of reaching St Petersburg. The visas are only valid for those going on group tours and do not allow individual touring. The consequences of being mislaid by the tour or, worse still, being left behind by the ship, are unthinkable.

One then must recognise the splendour of the buildings of St Petersburg.

The church of St Isaac's is the most spectacular of many which you would need days to see. The church was rebuilt many times, each time bigger and more glorious. The Admiralty steeple, with the ship on top, is visible from anywhere while the fortress of Peter and Paul dominates the other side of the Neva.

The Jewel in the Crown, perhaps a bad expression in Russia, is undoubtedly the Hermitage Museum. This was begun and mainly stocked by Catherine the Great and can rightfully be compared with the Louvre in Paris for the art collection, or the British Museum in London for artefacts. Combine the latter with the Royal Collection in London (Buckingham Palace, Windsor Castle, Hampton Court) and you may surpass the Hermitage, but not by much. A three-hour, whirlwind tour of the Hermitage can take you past, with no time to stop, most of the Great Masters of any era: Rembrandt, Renoir, Rubens, da Vinci, Michelangelo, Matisse, through to Picasso and his contemporaries. Contrary to some beliefs, the works are said to have been correctly acquired, although when you negotiate with someone as powerful as Catherine your bargaining powers are limited. There are small disputes over ownership, mainly with the Germans, but these have arguments on both sides. Britain does not have a clean nose in this area when one introduces the subject of the Elgin Marbles. It is estimated that there are over three million pieces of work in the Hermitage, of which about 1.7 million are on show. Catherine certainly did a good job.

Then there is the ballet. St Petersburg is the traditional home of classical ballet, having been the home of the aforementioned Peter Ilyich Tchaikovsky and thus of *Swan Lake*. Visiting tourists are taken to the Grand Palace Theatre where *Swan Lake* is performed every night during the tourist season. This may not be *the* top company of St Petersburg, but would surpass any other classical performance worldwide. The ballet is presented in exact traditional style with all of the Western 'additions' omitted and finally true love wins the day. Sixteen remarkable swans provide the support backdrop and the principals leave nothing to be desired.

The visitor is now left with several days more of sights to see in St Petersburg, and still there will be more remaining to be seen.

It is not easy to visit St Petersburg, because 'drop-ins' are not catered for. Anyone given the opportunity should grab it.

9. ESTONIA

If you liked Helsinki you will like Tallinn even more, although it is so different.

During the Middle Ages Tallinn was Danish, but it was conquered by Russia in 1710. In 1918 the Estonians somehow managed to gain their independence, but the country was absorbed into the Soviet Union in 1940. It was invaded and occupied by German forces and bombed by the Soviets. Finally it was absorbed into the USSR, with the approval of Churchill and Roosevelt, after 1945.

The Soviets did all they could to 'integrate' Estonia into the USSR but they did not break the back of the Estonian will. Large numbers of Russians were drafted into Estonia, making a large change to the demography, but still the Estonians saw themselves as Estonians. Approximately half of the population of Estonia is Russian, but they have come to accept that they are Estonian and are indistinguishable.

Finally, as the USSR collapsed and the Berlin Wall came down, Tallinn declared its independence on 20 August, 1991 and it was all over. Western countries were quick to recognize Estonia, and Russia was powerless to do anything. From here has grown a very prosperous and well organized nation. Estonia pegged its new currency to the German mark and has had no need to shift, even when the mark was replaced by the Euro.

Estonia joined the EU in 2004 along with the other nine former Eastern nations, joined the Schengen Treaty in 2007, and on 1 January, 2011 was given entry to the Eurozone and the right to use the Euro. It has been said that Estonia would have made a more credible entrant to the Eurozone on its admission than France or Germany.

It was interesting to note how the Estonians handled the transfer to the Euro. Late in 2010 tickets on items in stores carried three prices: the cost in local currency, the cost per 100g in local currency and the cost in Euro.

They left no doubt on the conversion. Probably the Germans carried out their transfer in the same way as the Estonians. The French still have cash register receipts giving the price in francs. Italians still complain that the Euro gave them 10% inflation, because everything which previously sold at 1,000 lira, and the Italians sold in round figures despite the clumsy currency, suddenly became €1; 10% more.

***

The Euro was established in 12 participating EU countries on 1 January, 1999 and the coins and notes began circulating on 1 January, 2001.

There are now 19 substantive countries using the Euro (as of 2011):

EU members (17): Netherlands, Belgium, Luxembourg, France, Germany, Spain, Portugal, Estonia, Austria, Slovenia, Slovakia, Greece, Finland, Irish Republic, Cyprus, Malta, Italy.

De facto participants (2): Kosovo, Montenegro.

Microstates: Andorra, Vatican, San Marino, Monaco, Liechtenstein.

Over 328 million people live in these countries.

There are then 18 countries, the balance of the 37 which we encounter west of Belarus, which do not use the Euro.

The values quoted in the table below for €1 are from Thomas Cook, August 2011, but have been further rounded (except where the rate is fixed as indicated by *) to take account of the fact that rates change continuously.

EU members which choose to remain outside the Eurozone (3):

Britain	0.9 pound		
Sweden	9 krona		
Denmark	7 krone		

EU members which will join the Eurozone possibly as early as 2014 or 2015 (7):

Poland	4 zloty	Hungary	280 forint
Latvia *	0.71 lat	Romania	4 leu nou
Lithuania *	3.45 lita	Bulgaria *	1.96 lev
Czech	25 koruna		

Others (8):

Norway	8 krone	Bosnia	2 markka
Switzerland	1.1 franc	Serbia	100 dinar
Iceland	160 krona	Macedonia	60 denar
Croatia	7 kuna	Albania	140 lek

The immediate number of potential Euro nations by 2015 is thus 26, while 11 will still be using their own currency.

It is interesting that two of the 19 countries listed, Kosovo and Montenegro, use the Euro by default, but are years away from becoming members of the EU. Sweden is required under treaty to join the Euro, but is able to avoid this requirement through a technical detail and is likely to continue to do so. The government of Denmark has expressed its intention of joining the Eurozone provided it can gain the consent of its electorate.

Thus life for the traveller becomes a little easier each year. Britain, Norway, Sweden and Switzerland will, however, for the foreseeable future, use their own currency.

Rule Britannia, Britannia opts out again; Britons never, never, never shall be slaves!

The day when it would be possible to travel without visas and border checks and using a common currency, from the Atlantic to the Russian-Ukraine-Belarus-Moldova border, has obviously come closer but it is a painfully long way off.

Don't expect to buy currency at this rate from the moneychangers. They ask for no commission but their profit comes from the wide gap between the 'buying' and 'selling' rates. At minimum this is usually 10 to 20%. If you are selling a currency which the vendor will have difficulty in selling, like Turkish lira, you will be given a very poor rate. Except for small amounts, buy currency at an ATM which always has the best rate. Mr. Forex has a commission on top of his exchange rate. To cash a travellers cheque anywhere today will involve a huge commission. Don't even consider travellers cheques.

Take a pause here to survey the money exchange offices throughout Europe, and probably most of the world. At the head of almost every exchange list are the 10 currencies:

US dollar	Euro
British pound	Swiss franc
Norwegian kroner	Swedish kroner
Danish kroner	Japanese yen
Canadian dollar	Australian dollar

Of course, the omission of the local currency often reduces the list to nine.

The list gives rise to some pondering. Why Australia is never omitted must be a measure of some confidence in the Australian dollar, or maybe Australians always want to change money. Perhaps it is a function of the liberal long service leave provisions in Australia.

This list does not, however, apply in Latvia, Lithuania and Estonia, where Canada and Australia have been sacrificed to include the Latvian lat, the Lithuanian lita, the Polish zloty and the Russian rouble. Australians and Canadians apparently don't come this way often.

***

Coming by ferry from Helsinki over only 85km, you will arrive at the port of Tallinn and can clearly see the location of the old town on the high ground to the right. To avoid additional climbing, follow the old rail track slightly further to the right. This picks up the tram track, which stops conveniently near the railway station and not far from the city gates. You can take the tram for two stops if need be.

The old city of Tallinn is an unspoiled walled city with a clear and unconfused history. Hours can be spent walking about the city seeking out at its history and art treasures. Only when you walk out of the gates do you see in the distance the commercial centre of the city with its modern buildings, but with its ancient Soviet-style trams.

There are buses which continue from Tallinn to Riga and Vilnius and then connect on to Kaliningrad, in Russia, so have your visa if you go that way, or on to Warsaw. All of this, and what follows here, is set out clearly by Thomas Cook, but there is no real idea given of the tribulation, and fun, necessary to make all the rail connections.

The adventurous rail traveller can be satisfied, although at a price.

None of Estonia, Latvia and Lithuania is included in the Eurail pass (2011), but the fares are very low. Tickets can usually be bought on the train, but if you do purchase them there you will only be sold a ticket to the next border and have to repeat the process once you cross. You may be able to buy tickets for Euros at the initial station, but if the operator is not willing to sell them to you then you are on your own. The best advice, repeated often here, is always to carry a load of €5 and €10 notes so that you are in a better bargaining position and do not finish up with large amounts of lats or litas in your change. Chances are that your opposite number can dispose of small Euro notes better than he can large ones.

Make sure that you are not offloaded at the Russian frontier. You may find that the returning train either does not stop or is not allowed to take passengers. Don't test it!

The trains of Estonia, Latvia and Lithuania are logically Russian gauge (1520mm) and most of the mainline services come and go from Russia. Unlike the buses, the rail does not link the three capitals directly.

The only train from Tallinn to Valga, on the Latvian border, which arrives before the last train to Riga, is the first for the day, departing very early from Tallinn, giving only a 10 minute connection in Valga. Otherwise, an overnight stay in Valga is necessary.

It was in Valga that I was caused to abandon my thesis that everyone will understand English; at least, everyone forward from the USSR days.

After arriving in Valga, still inside Estonia, near sunset, I asked someone about accommodation. 'This way' was the signal I received from everyone, with more different signals than people. It began to rain, so I headed toward what I thought was the centre of the city and never found one. In doing so I crossed the border into Valka in Latvia and still found nothing. Eventually I came across some teenagers, who recognized my plight and at first declined to try any conversation. Only once they realized that my Estonian (or Russian or German) was non-existent were they prepared to attempt a few English words and we were on our way. Ultimately one of the lads offered to escort me to a hotel and we retraced my long path back to the other end of Valga, carrying out a hilarious conversation in one-word sentences. By the time we reached the hotel, his English had improved by many hundreds of per cent and he bade me goodbye, soaking wet by now, at the head of the driveway.

'Good evening, Sir. I'm afraid we are fully booked tonight.' They were the only hotel in town. After some arm-waving, we established that there was indeed a B&B with rooms free, but guess where? About 500 metres from the station! The hotel clerk made a booking by phone for me and I was very glad to arrive, dry out, shower and find a bed at the hostel. The fact that I had no dinner was partly made up by the magnificent breakfast that the proprietor served. Then there was a quick hike to the station and onto the local early morning train bound for the next capital, Riga.

On my next visit to Valga, I had no trouble in finding someone at the station who could speak English well. After consulting the accommodation board outside the station, we decided that there was an amenable lodging house a little closer, which made sense. The name was 'Aaia', or similar. On arrival there I found no sign of habitation, but a lad sweeping leaves nearby, who spoke excellent English, was kind enough to phone the proprietor for me; the number being on the door. The proprietor arrived by car in a matter of minutes and he took me into the building which was his place of work, apparently a clothing wholesaler, with a granny flat attached. Here he established me in a private room for the grand sum of about €15. Never have I had such luxury for so little. I was able to find dinner nearby. In the morning his wife arrived in her Mercedes at 0500, as she had volunteered, and drove me to the station. The tip I left for her exceeded the cost of the room.

On my most recent visit, I walked directly to the B&B of my first acquaint-ance. They were full but the manager and his wife gave up their own bed to accommodate me. They charged €30 for dinner, bed and breakfast; the meals being large and very satisfactory.

10. LATVIA

The first train for Riga leaves Valga at something past five in the morning. As you leave you will see the train for Tallinn, which you would take if you were headed northbound. The conductor will sell you a ticket at something less than €10, but since you are in Estonia when you leave Valga, the conductor will accept Euros so you can put off changing currency.

This route from Valga to Riga takes you well to the east of Latvia, much closer to Russia. The country is forested and marshy, sometimes passing by water for hundreds of metres on end. It gives some idea of what Russia might be like.

Not so many years ago the central block countries of the EU met in the city of Schengen and, in the middle of the river where Luxembourg, Belgium and Germany meet, drew up a treaty which eliminated immigration checks at borders. It effectively abolished borders completely. The question of a border for goods and tariffs had been removed in the original Treaty of Rome in the days of de Gaulle, but until then the immigration barrier for people still remained. The Schengen Treaty is much more widespread than at first sight, as it deals with drugs, people smuggling, sharing of data and things that ordinary mortals don't consider. Slowly but steadily other EU countries have joined the Schengen Treaty, with the notable exception of Britain and Ireland. Mrs Thatcher was not having an open border for all those Polish plumbers to come in. When the effects of the Schengen Treaty reached the Danish border, they met the four countries of the Scandinavian bloc, which have never had borders between them. This was fine for Denmark and Sweden, but Iceland and Norway are not members of the EU. So the Schengen Treaty took on external members and allowed Norway and Iceland to join, and thus admitted these two countries which are not members of the EU. So, if you arrive in Oslo, immigration will admit you, or otherwise, to the EU.

Since the end of 2008, 25 of the 27 nations in the EU have become part of the Schengen Treaty (not including Britain and Ireland), bringing the total to 28 including Norway, Iceland and latterly Switzerland. The EU members Bulgaria, Romania and Cyprus have not yet necessarily met all of the Schengen obligations. It is possible to travel between 25 of the 28 countries of the Schengen nations without showing a passport, although some countries may choose to do spot checks as they see fit. Once in a Schengen country, you may travel throughout all of them unfettered. Some borders do not physically exist, such as those between Germany and the Benelux countries, between Germany and Austria and between the Scandinavian countries.

Landlocked countries like Austria, Czech Republic, Slovakia and Switzerland have no borders to guard except at their own airports. The borders of the Schengen bloc to the east are administered by Finland, Estonia, Latvia, Lithuania, Poland, Hungary, Romania and Bulgaria, which has a touch of irony when remembering that all of these but Finland were once satellites of the USSR and three of them, Estonia, Latvia and Lithuania, actually part of the USSR.

It is currently possible to travel from the English Channel to the Russia-Belarus-Ukraine-Moldova border through 25 countries without showing your passport. This includes journeys such as Narvik to Sicily and Lisbon to Tallinn. The area of the Schengen bloc is nearly as big as Australia, but of course Australia abolished all land borders in 1901!

Remember, however, that Britain and Ireland are in the EU but not in the Schengen Treaty. I need my passport stamped to cross the Channel into Britain.

On arrival once in Oslo by air from London, I watched the lady in front of me being interrogated and finally led away by a policeman. The immigration officer pointed out to me that Oslo was an entry point to the whole of Europe and they had to be very careful. No doubt this lady was only being taken for private questioning so as not to hold up the line, but it appeared very daunting.

Before 1989 there was no border marked between Russia and Latvia/ Lithuania/Estonia and the map shows much of the border as a straight line.

After independence all three countries set about fencing the border; the border which was to become that between the EU and Russia. This is quite a change from only a couple of years back when all three countries were part of the USSR.

***

Riga is a much more modern city with its architectural treasures spread about in a more diffuse manner.

The history of Latvia, post-USSR, matches that of Estonia, but the Latvians were unable to recover quite as quickly after the recession of 2009 and they have not yet been invited to the Eurozone. Apparently there was a problem with inflation. We still must deal in Latvian lats, which have been fixed against the Euro for many years. Like Greece and Ireland, these three countries made good use of their entry into the EU and spent a little beyond their means. When the plug was pulled, there was some discomfort. Brussels is in a strange position as it has more control over the finances of applicant members than it has over members and clearly it is about to make no mistakes. Access to the Euro for Latvia and Lithuania is expected in 2014 or 2015.

While in Riga I attempted to trace some of the history of Commodore Hornblower, as recounted by C. S. Forester. Hornblower arrived at the mouth of the river and did all he could to defend the village at the mouth from the oncoming troops of Napoleon. By various means he halted them until Alexander defeated Napoleon and routed him from Moscow. Hornblower was able to sail away before the ice trapped him. This is all very well but I visited that village by local bus and found that it is so far downstream as to be removed from Riga.

Once in Riga, you can very simply buy lats in any quantity you wish at the station. There is a self-serve restaurant in one of the tunnels which serves a great assortment of local food at a modest price. The whole restaurant is under the branches of an enormous tree.

Proceeding southward from Riga by train is the best part of the journey. The first step is on the afternoon Latvian express train to Daugavpils, still in Latvia, where an overnight stay is necessary. Daugavpils is a large city with plenty of accommodation, so this poses no problem. Several hotels can be found after about 15 minutes walk directly in front of the station and have quite satisfactory accommodation at a modest price. The comparison with Valka/Valga can bring a smile to your face.

11. LITHUANIA

Although you are still in Latvia, the next part of the story belongs in Lithuania. Before joining the train from Daugavpils in the morning, you will be required to pay for a ticket in lats. They will not sell you a ticket on the previous evening but will tell you the price. So make sure that you have enough lats to cover the cost. On the express train the price is about €30 (in lats), a little more than you paid in total to come from Tallinn.

Very early on the following morning in Daugavpils, you join the overnight express from St Petersburg on its way to Vilnius. The train is a traditional Russian express. In only a very few places inside the reach of your EU entry can you find such a train which is available to you. If you are in second class you will find sleeping bunks attached to all walls of a carriage, with bodies rolled in blankets everywhere. As the day dawns the bodies awaken, the beds are converted to seats and, by breakfast time, a semi-respectable sitting car arrives in Vilnius. If you elect first class, then you are given a two berth sleeping compartment with bed made up and a complimentary breakfast. This will cost you perhaps three times as much as the second class seat.

The connecting train to Warsaw from Vilnius departs less than three hours after the train from Daugavpils arrives. You spend either three hours or twenty seven hours in Vilnius. Going north, the connection time is even less.

Lithuania's latter-day history matches that of Estonia and Latvia, but its mediaeval history is far more remarkable. Lithuania once controlled vast areas of what is now Poland and its kings were a force to be reckoned with. Not so today.

As in Latvia, the merchants of Lithuania will accept your Euros and its litas are convertible at a fixed rate. You are advised to convert your lats and litas to Euros or spend them before you leave Lithuania, as you may find it difficult to change them further west.

***

Rail electrification across Europe is made up of a large number of varying voltages depending on the nation's history. The following table gives an outline of the voltages of the various countries, but cannot include all of the variations inside any country. From the table it can be seen that travel can be seamless between many pairs of nations, now that taking locomotives across boundaries is a regular event. Some boundaries, however, will always require a change of locomotive, or the use of one which can adapt to more than one voltage.

List of current systems for electric rail traction

750V DC	England (3rd rail)
1.5kV, DC	France (southern)*, Netherlands*, Spain*
3kV DC	Belgium*(part), Czech (northern), Italy*, Poland, Russia, Moldova, Slovakia (northern), Slovenia, Ukraine (part)
15kV, 16.7Hz, AC	Germany, Switzerland, Austria, Luxembourg, Sweden, Norway
25kV, 50Hz AC	Bosnia, Bulgaria, Croatia, Czech (southern), Denmark, England, Finland, France (part), Greece, Hungary, Latvia (eastern), Lithuania, Macedonia, Montenegro, Portugal, Romania, Russia, Scotland (southern), Serbia, Slovakia (south west) Britain, Ukraine. * High speed lines in France, Spain, Italy, the Netherlands and Belgium
Non-electrified	Ireland, Northern Scotland, Albania, Wales
No railways	Iceland, Malta, Cyprus

Source:
en.wikipedia.org/wiki/list_of_current_systems_for_electric_rail_traction

The reason for raising this matter here is that Lithuania is electrifying its system, at a voltage (25kV, 50Hz) which is inconsistent with all of its neighbours, all of which have a common voltage (3kV DC), but very little has yet been done.

Travelling south from Vilnius you are still on Russian gauge heading for Warsaw. If you check the map you will see that Belarus extends westward south of Lithuania toward Poland, but that there is also an enclave of Russia further west, including Kaliningrad on the Baltic Sea. This was another of Stalin's acquisitions after WWII, when the old East Prussia was divided between Russia and Poland to give Russia a port on the Baltic Sea, accessible through Lithuania. The 'defection' of Poland and Lithuania to the West has left Russia with no direct access to Kaliningrad, and a treaty had to be hastily put together to permit this once Poland and Lithuania were to join the EU.

The direct consequence of this is that there is only a very short stretch of common border between Poland and Lithuania, and it is across this border that all the EU traffic must travel. There was once a minor railway crossing within this range and this has become upgraded to the main trunk route for freight and passengers. Undoubtedly the highway goes this way, but I have not checked.

As our train going south in Lithuania is taking us beyond the reach of the wires, a reasonably modern diesel rail motor takes us on our journey. Initially the speed is good and the ride smooth but, as the distance from base increases, the speed goes down and the quality of the ride decreases. Ultimately our Lithuanian rail motor arrives at the very simple island platform, with no facilities, at Sestokai, concurrently with the standard gauge train from Warsaw. The two trains exchange passengers, run the Polish locomotive around its train and proceed back the way they came, in even less time than the loading of the Baltic Sea ferries.

You move your watches back an hour, note the new rail gauge (1435mm) and recognize that you are soon to be in Poland and on the way to Warsaw.

12. POLAND

Poland has been pushed back and forth across Europe for centuries, and only with entry to the EU can it be promised any stability. In the years before the twentieth century, it had fought wars with Germany, Lithuania, Russia and many of its other neighbours, with varying degrees of success. Still the Poles soldiered on as a proud nation.

Germany occupied Poland in World War I and, after its release, a fairly large Poland was given some sense of independence.

On 1 September, 1939 Hitler threw down the barriers, marched on Warsaw and WWII had begun. There were many terrible atrocities carried out over that time but none overshadows that of the Jewish Ghetto of Warsaw. Firstly, Hitler forced the Jews to wear identifying armbands and they were not allowed on public transport, and ultimately not on the street at all. He built a wall around the Jewish quarter and rounded up all the Jewish people into that ghetto. Figures vary but the numbers range from 300,000 to 450,000 people; about one-third of the population of the city at the time. Over the next year or so these people, about 1,000 per day, were systematically taken by train to Treblinka and marched into the gas chamber. At least 300,000 people disappeared from Warsaw and the same picture, on a lesser scale, was repeated elsewhere in Poland. As the war ended there were only a few thousand Jews left in Warsaw. Time ran out on Hitler. Then, of course, the ghetto was razed. Today this is an almost holy place in Warsaw.

The next aspect that we don't remember is the insurrection in July 1945. Hitler was weakening. Stalin had reached the other side of the Vistula and was waiting. Urged by the Russians, the home army rose up against the Germans. The Russians did not move. The slaughter was atrocious and it has been estimated that over 40,000 Poles and 25,000 Germans died over that six week period. It was probably more. Every day for six weeks more people were killed than died on 11 September in New York. Finally the Poles gave in. The leaders were summoned to Moscow, supposedly as heroes, but then tried and imprisoned. All were to die in prison. News was minimal. Churchill had no idea what was going on. In the end Stalin had put out that these men had collaborated with the Germans and were put down by the Soviets. That was the cruellest part. Of the Polish resistance, there was nothing remaining. Hitler ordered that the city be razed. What was left of Warsaw was burned to the ground and flattened. Warsaw did not exist. Stalin simply walked in and took over.

At the Yalta Conference, Stalin was the victor, as discussed in the chapter on Romania. Of the people of Eastern Europe, millions were passed into Stalin's hands without a murmur. A huge slice of Poland on the Russian side was absorbed into the USSR and the Poles were forced to leave. A sizable piece of eastern Germany and half of East Prussia were given to Poland, but not before the German people had been almost all evacuated. Poland lost about one-third of its territory. The balance of East Prussia, including the Baltic port of Kaliningrad (formerly Königsberg), became part of Russia. The German version of the Readers' Digest atlas of those days shows all of the new post-war boundaries, except that it only shows the partitioned parts of Germany being 'under occupation'.

When I questioned whether the German nation might have wanted those bits of Germany back in 1989, the answer came back very quickly. There are very few German people left there and the areas are incredibly poor as no-one has cared for them. For Germany to absorb the areas into the German Republic would have been at immense cost and out of proportion to any benefit. Absorbing East Germany (the DDR) caused sufficient strain, from which the Republic still smarts. Hence these bits were left, as might be imagined, to the Poles as they had become part of the Polish nation.

Then comes the amazing part. After 1945 the people returned to Warsaw. It has all been rebuilt. The whole of the old city has been restored to as it was before WWII. It was done by the Poles without outside money, without Russian help, without Marshall Plan money. The old post-mediaeval city has been completely restored; all the palaces and public buildings have been rebuilt. There are two buildings remaining which are pre-WWI. Only two.

They are run-down and deserted. Now this amazing rebuilding took place *before* 1988, during the Soviet days and under Gomulka. In 1987 when I was there for the International Mathematics Olympiad, Warsaw was all there, but looked run-down and grubby, worse than Romania and Bosnia look in 2011. There were Soviet-style small stores and long queues for goods which had run out, no lights, no advertising signs, vodka as easy to buy as Coca Cola today and Coca Cola almost unobtainable. Grubby, messy, horrible, but it was Warsaw and it was Poland, even though the Soviets were in command.

Between 1988 and 2004 that all changed. The Soviets moved out, global business moved in. In 2004 Poland joined the EU and on 31 December, 2007 became part of the Schengen Treaty. Today, you could be mistaken for thinking you were in Germany. Warsaw is a big, alive, city with lights, trams, subway, well-lit monumental public buildings and an old city, which looks as if it was there in 1683. You can come and go as you please and all those nasty days of passports and visas have gone. There remain a few anomalies. One is the gigantic tower block which the Soviets gave to Poland for their government. It stands above the city as a reminder that all was once not so good.

Legend has it that there were two mermaids who swam together into the Baltic Sea. The first found a comfortable rock to sit on, and there she is today in Copenhagen for Hans Christian Andersen to write stories about and Danny Kaye to sing about. The other was more adventurous; she swam further up the Baltic and into the River Vistula until she came upon this city, whose residents were always being be set upon by their neighbours. She took up sword and shield (a veritable valkyrie indeed) and has been helping them ever since. Her statue occurs all over Warsaw. There is a small replica in my lounge room.

Also in Warsaw is a statue of Nicolai Copernicus, who lived before Galileo in the 16th century. It was Nicolai who first concluded that the Earth and the planets revolved around the sun and was prepared to say so. Herr Copernicus had the sense to live well away from Rome so that the Pope could not reach him, and had even more sense to have his book published away from Rome, and have it released on his deathbed. It was partly from his work that Galileo and later Newton were able to formulate the beginning of Physics as we know it now.

So this is the Warsaw of today; a fascinating city with an unbelievable recent history.

From the west one can arrive in Warsaw by train from Berlin or from the direction of the Czech Republic, as well as by numerous other smaller border crossings. Those trains were very mournful in the Soviet days, mainly taking refugees out to the west. Today there is a frequent train service from Berlin, requiring dedicated trains since the voltage changes at the German border. The *Jan Keipura*, the overnight train between Berlin and Warsaw, is one of the more palatial overnight trains in Europe with two berth sleepers at quite a reasonable cost, being equipped with showers and an acceptable dining car.

***

Overnight trains in Europe generally carry three types of accommodation. The top level is the sleeping car, *Schlafwagen*, which is shown in the timetables with the icon of a bed with a pillow. These are normally two beds to a compartment, one above the other, and have the beds made up with sheets, etc. They often come with a complimentary breakfast. Usually there is a washstand and a bottle of water, with the communal WC at the end of the car. One can expect a surcharge of the order of €100 for such a berth, comparable with the cost of a night at a motel. Such a berth generally requires a first class ticket, but in some countries this is not necessarily so. Most railways will sell a single berth which may be a cabin containing one bed, or simply give the exclusive use of a cabin with the upper berth folded away. The *Jan Keipura* carries some of the best sleeping cars in Europe.

Less exclusive is the couchette, *Liegewagen*, which is simply a padded bench, perhaps the extent of three seats, or even the back of three seats, folded out. A couchette car is shown in the timetables with the icon of a bed without a pillow. A compartment may include four or six such berths. A couchette might come with a pillow and a blanket and, since you are not usually aware of whom your fellow travellers will be, you are expected to remain in your street clothes. Top berths are usually a little warm and very difficult for an old guy like me to clamber in and out, especially for middle-of-the-night visits down the corridor. The person in the bottom berth risks being stepped on intermittently. One can expect a surcharge of the order of €30 for such a berth, comparable with the cost of a night in a hostel with similar accommodation. Such a berth may require a first class ticket, but in most countries a second class ticket is adequate and Thomas Cook makes this clear in the timetables.

Finally, night trains carry second class seating compartments. Where trains are full, these are a tolerable, but not exciting, form of travel. Where trains are lightly occupied, you stand a chance of being able to commandeer a compartment to yourself, especially with two people. Often the seats pull out to give an enlarged flat sleeping space. It is usually only necessary to draw curtains, spread out luggage and laundry and generally make yourself appear uninviting. Most people will not seek to use a compartment which might be already occupied by a dirty old man. Certainly a woman by herself or with children will not go into a compartment where there are no other women. Universally there is no first class sitting car on night trains. The additional cost to buy a first class ticket would be better spent on a couchette or sleeper. Nobody pays heed to the passenger with the first class pass. Occasionally night trains will include second class aircraft-style seats, 'recliners', available at a small surcharge.

These standards tend to decline as you proceed into Southern and Eastern Europe, but so does the surcharge. Scandinavian sleeper trains follow a different logic, as do those in Russia-Belarus-Ukraine. The latter are generally not available in the area of the Eurail pass unless you are travelling into those countries, when you will require a visa.

It is said that the standard gauge once stopped at the Vistula, and from Warsaw eastward toward Moscow the tracks were Russian gauge. Apparently the Poles were very quick to eliminate that anomaly and the gauge change is now at Brest, across the border in Belarus.

***

Coming from Lithuania, the standard gauge train begins at Sestokai and carries a once daily service to Warsaw. The first major town in Poland is Bialystok, a name which may jog the memory of fans of the musical, *The Producers*. The train mainly serves Poland and has passengers joining and leaving throughout the six-hour journey. As it proceeds, the train moves faster, the ride improves and ultimately is taken over by an electric locomotive.

There are many outstanding places to visit in Warsaw, beginning with the old city and extending through the various concentration camps and ghettoes. You will leave very chastened.

My memories of Poland are overshadowed by a rather nasty train crash on 19/10/11. Our train was headed from Vienna to Warsaw and, just inside Poland, without any warning I found myself thrown from side to side in the compartment, empty as it happened, and after a few seconds of juddering we came to rest tilted about 15 degrees from upright. The train had been crossing from one set of tracks to another and while the loco and first 3 cars continued on their way, car 4 and those behind it were derailed and thrown about. All 4 cars remained standing, fortunately, although the angles were somewhat odd and the relationship of the cars one to another, was anything but in a line. All wires were down and one car had its roof sliced open. My car, the last, was probably the least damaged. In all this, no-one was hurt which very much upset the inevitable TV cameras when they arrived and had no grizzly human interest story to promote.

The Polish emergency services and railways were great. In a very short time we were ushered off the train and to a close-by small village where we were installed in the local hall and given coffee. Railway authorities appeared and re-arranged onward bookings, a bus collected us and took us to the next available train and nothing was lost except a few hours.

Had this been a bus in a smash of this nature the personnel damage, and death, would have been enormous. It was the train itself which saved us.

I can only conclude by saying that, with the amount of travelling I do it was bound to happen eventually and had my travels been by road I might not have escaped unscathed.

Throughout Poland there are many more cities worthy of a visit. Krakow and Katowice for their ancient buildings, Gdansk and Gdynia for their modern-day history and from where you can continue by train to Hell, out at the end of a long spit into the Baltic. It bears no relation to the place down below and is a little more prominent than its namesake in Norway. The end of communism began with the actions of Lech Walesa in the shipyards of Gdansk. All of these cities are readily accessible by train.

Poland has not yet been admitted to the Eurozone. One must use the zloty, of which there are about four to the Euro. Poland's economy is large compared with the other EU-but-not-yet-Euro nations, but sits alongside Latvia, Lithuania, Hungary and the Czech Republic in not expecting to join the Eurozone until perhaps 2014 or 2015. Change your zlotys back to Euros before you leave Poland, or don't expect a great return if you bring them home. This is in contrast to the advice for Scandinavian countries, from where notes are better brought home to be changed.

Regrettably the global Eurail pass holder must pay fares in Poland, as Poland is not included in the global pass (2011) although Poland does recognise lesser passes. Fares are quite reasonable by German standards.

One of the less complicated ways of leaving Warsaw is to take the night train to Szczecin in the NW of Poland and almost on the German border. This city was once Stettin in Germany. It is an easy trip from here to Berlin or Hamburg. The overnight train on this route is the only one leaving Warsaw after the train from Sestokai has arrived.

This part of Europe probably suffered as much as any during the Soviet years, as the German side of the line was in the DDR (East Germany) while the present day Polish side was originally part of Germany and unwillingly carved off into Poland. The countryside seems pleasant but not prosperous, and reminders of the Soviet days are still in evidence.

13. RUSSIA

Back around 1949 when I was in primary school, we were taught that the longest straight railway track in the world was across the Nullarbor Plain on the Transcontinental Railway in Australia (478km), and the third longest stretch was between Nyngan and Bourke (187km) in Western NSW.

The latter was built to take produce from the Central West of NSW to the head of navigation on the River Darling, whence it could be shipped by paddle-steamer to the Murray Mouth and then onward to Mother England. This use has long since been discontinued and the track was cut late last century. What is not remembered is that the new line from Alice Springs to Darwin, in the Northern Territory of Australia, was built partly to link these same areas to the port at Darwin, enabling days to be cut from the time required to trans-ship goods to Asian markets and thus allowing meat to be chilled rather than frozen for the journey. Rail is still an important factor in world transportation.

What our Grade Six teacher could not tell us was the location of the second longest straight stretch but he, whose experience overseas was limited to wearing a uniform for His Majesty, believed that it must be on the Trans-Siberian railway. In the event it was not so, as we shall discuss shortly.

Moscow is well out of the reach of the Eurail pass user, both from the ticket point of view and for visa reasons, although Thomas Cook does give the trans-Siberian times. To complete the rail picture, it will be included here.

Russia has a vast railway network, all on broad gauge, 1520mm, and, if Belarus is included, extending from the Polish border at Brest to the Pacific at Vladivostok.

My first experience was to meet a Russian business colleague in Moscow on a very eventful weekend.

My entry to the USSR, as it was then, was from Helsinki on the train to Leningrad, as described in the chapter on St Petersburg. My host showed no surprise at being asked to meet me there and to show me around that city, then we embarked on the train journey to Moscow. This is on a heavy train on Russian gauge with very well-appointed sleeping compartments, each extolling you to lock the doors by night; the only difference between here and Western Europe being that it was in Russian.

The story has it that when the mandarins of the Tsarist days wanted to build the rail line to Moscow, Alexander took out an atlas and a ruler and drew a straight line between Moscow and St Petersburg. That, he is alleged to have said, is where the line shall go! And it did. It follows the straight line through marshes and forests most of the way, with tunnels, cuttings and embankments where required. So it is very likely that this contains the second longest straight stretch in the world.

The USSR was in torment at the time of my visit, since Mr First Secretary Mikhail Gorbachev had been sent on holiday by a bunch of old guard communist leaders who clearly did not understand the situation. My hosts duly took care of me, showed me the sights of Red Square, etc., and then gave me a little time to myself. As you might have guessed, I used this to familiarise myself with the Moscow subway system.

Like London, Moscow is plagued by a number of rail terminals placed around the city and with no direct links to the centre or to one another. The basis of the subway system is thus the ring of about 5km diameter, linking most of these stations to one another and linking all of the radial subway lines as they cross. It is truly a spectacular system. All of the stations, at least in the centre, are built in separate tunnels and are linked to the travelling tunnels by smaller tunnels adjacent to the doors of each coach, with doors at each end. This adds to the quietness of the operation and the lack of any forced draft effects. The newer parts of the Jubilee line in London use a similar system.

The dominating aspect of the subway stations is that they are all works of art. In the West they would each qualify as an art gallery. The guidebooks tell you which stations to visit and what you will see. A day would not be enough to see the technical workings plus the major works of art of the Moscow subway.

Then came the blow. My hosts came to see me in my hotel to tell me that the government had been overthrown, there were tanks in the streets and I was not to leave my hotel under any circumstances. Public services had come to a halt, but not the subway, and they would have difficulty finding their way home. I took their advice, but not before I had beetled around to the Australian Embassy to register my presence. Barriers were going up in the streets.

'Tanks, in the streets!' said my host. Well, I asked, what about Prague, and Budapest? 'That was different. This is Moscow!' I failed to accept his argument. Mr Yeltsin had emerged on the steps of the Russian White House took control. It is interesting to recall that he was accompanied there by the French Ambassador, this both indicating EU sympathies and adding to the safety of the event. To bop off the French Ambassador would arouse international ire. You are perfectly safe in Moscow with a foreign passport, but in a crowd no-one asks if you have a passport. This advice made a lot of sense.

My rail ticket out of Moscow was for several days hence. Try as I might, I was unable to advance that booking, nor find an air booking.

As it happened there was no need for alarm. The tanks were probably not armed and children were playing on them. Any casualties were caused by misadventure. Mr Yeltsin carried the day.

On the day of departure, I prepared for a short subway ride to the terminus and allowed plenty of time for my train. 'But no,' said my hosts. 'we have a car and if we have a car you will use it.' For the next hour or so we travelled about in ever-increasing circles, searching for a path without roadblocks. In the end I was returned to my hotel and permitted to use the underground. I had allowed enough time.

The next surprise was an eventful one. My hosts had provided me with a ticket to Brest and I had a ticket from Brest to Warsaw and on to Berlin. What I had not realised, and why should I, was that, although the timetable showed a through train, the tickets that I held were not for that through train but for those components of the train which were subtracted or added in Brest, and the components were isolated from one another. I was about to be offloaded in Brest, in sight of my Polish train, but unable to make the transit. It took a lot of arguing and a lot of US dollars to be allowed to move from the Russian cars to the through cars. Nonetheless, I am here to write about it and I am not still sitting on the platform at Brest.

Don't expect a similar event today, but then I did not at the time either.

This reminds me of another event, completely out of context, of the same era. My friend, Wes, had been to Prague with his wife on a semi-official visit for an agency of the Australian Government. As he was boarding the plane to leave, he was apprehended. 'Would you come with us, Sir?' His wife tried to follow but he persuaded her to continue, the logic being that at least she could report on his whereabouts when she arrived at her next destination. Apparently some Czech official had been apprehended in Australia and this was the reprisal; Wes was the best opposite number they could find at the time. After some time and a fair amount of verbal harassment, he was allowed to rejoin his wife on the much-delayed flight. My circumstances were easy compared with that.

***

My most recent visit to Russia was through a travel agent who arranged tickets, accommodation and visas in advance. This somewhat spoils the whole trip, but is unavoidable. Tim and I flew to Moscow and, as you guessed, my bags remained in London. Dressed in shorts and shirt, as I was, is no way to begin a journey in Moscow, so we followed the advice of the hotelier and went to the local market. Here we found how the locals afford their goods and how they dress well. For instance, I was able to buy a pair of tracksuit pants for 10 roubles, less than €10, and these I still carry with me wherever I travel, ready to wear over the shorts. They have lasted around ten years and show no sign of reaching the end of their life.

To cut a much longer story short, the bags were retrieved, we did a day tour of Moscow with a personal guide, spent some time on our own, mainly on the subway, and finally set forth on train #2, the *Rossiya*. This train is erroneously called the *Trans-Siberian Express* by most Western travel agents, but this is not so. It is simply the once-every-second-day service train across Siberia. There are also once weekly trains of slightly lower quality to Beijing via Mongolia, and to Beijing omitting Mongolia, both with international borders. Luxury, the term may be relative, private trains are also available, provided through the travel agents, but that would not be Russian train travel. The notable thing about the *Rossiya* is that it takes seven days to reach Vladivostok, crosses seven time zones and there are no international borders to cross.

Fortunately Tim and I had elected first class, which meant that we had exclusive use of a four-berth cabin, with the top bunks folded away. To have been cramped into that little compartment with two other strangers for seven days, would have been more than one could take. Neither of us is small. The compartment is your world. There is nowhere else to go. The dining car is inhabited by train staff, smoking, and there is no other alternative. Memo for any reader contemplating this train: 'Go first class!' Even if you travel as a foursome, four people in an oversized bathroom for seven days is not a great idea.

This begs the question on sending people to Mars. Space on such a vehicle would be much more at a premium than that in a train, and there are no intermediate stations on which to alight and stretch your legs. The journey must last 259 days. The psychological and sociological problems are so enormous as to be probably insurmountable. If they are to come back, which they might not, those people have to do so in the same manner.

Meals we could take in the dining car, and these were cheap but not appetizing. Anything which looked as if it might be worthwhile was not available. The train stopped quite frequently for the exact number of minutes shown in the timetable and on every station were locals out on their daily (alternate days, alternate directions) sales drive. The food appeared appetizing but we were very wary of trying it. Packaged food, for instance by Mr Nestlé, would have posed no problem, as would drinks by Messrs Pepsi or Coca Cola, readily available in most places. We carried our own 20-litre bottle of fresh water, without which we could have managed but it provided a useful fall-back.

The journey goes on and on. The scenery is ever-changing and provides adequate reward for the traveller. I cannot give an adequate description so all I can do is to recommend that you take the journey yourself. There are no outstanding features such as the Rocky Mountains of Canada, or the Nullarbor Plain of Australia. The track is never straight. It follows contours and rivers; it avoids mountains and lakes. There is plenty to see.

Some of the cities are startling. There are BIG cities in Siberia. Yekaterinburg is where the Tsar and family were murdered. Novosibirsk is a huge city with a very productive hinterland. It is alleged that the line between these two cities is the busiest freight route in the world. For the whole of the journey across Siberia the line is double track and electrified. This is a far cry from the long distance routes to which we are accustomed, such as in North America or Australia, which are invariably single track and have not heard of electricity.

Lake Baikal, one of the largest freshwater lakes on Earth, provides the major diversion. Originally, as we were taught by that same teacher in primary school, the tracks ended on opposite sides of the lake and the trains were either ferried across or the tracks were laid on the ice. At that time I had never seen naturally occurring ice or even a large lake. Today they skirt the lake and operate a through service all year. Our travel agent booked us off for two days at Irkutsk, and we spent the first day in a village on the shore of the lake by courtesy of a sweet old widow who provided accommodation for a living. She spoke excellent English, all learned from her passing trade. Among her treasures was a real Russian sauna, which we used at her encouragement.

One of the important aspects of history is that James Baker, then US Secretary of State, went on a fishing holiday on Lake Baikal with Edouard Schevardnadze, his Soviet opposite number, immediately before the break-up of the Soviet Union. Their personal friendship must have contributed much to the peaceful dismantling of the USSR.

Lake Baikal had started to thaw. The ice sheet, of the order of a metre thick, had recently broken up and was floating about on the lake at the behest of the wind. On some occasions the lake would be a wall of ice, a few hours later it was clear. Even to observe the behaviour of the lake was an experience. Today we wish we had taken a dip in the lake, purely to say we had done it. At the time it was not inviting.

In Ulan-Ude is a huge bronze statue of the head of Lenin weighing 42 tonnes and standing seven metres high, erected to celebrate the centenary of Lenin's birth.

> *'He stood on his neck,*
> *With a smile well bred,*
> *And bowed three times to me!'*
>
> W.S Gilbert – *The Mikado*

One guidebook comments that he now knows how Dorothy felt when confronted by the Wizard.

Exactly 48 hours from our arrival in Irkutsk our journey was resumed and we arrived at Vladivostok at 2333 on the ninth day by Moscow time, but seven hours later, by Pacific Time. We did dip a toe in the Pacific Ocean, but no more.

Airlines work on local time and it was early morning, so a trip by local public transport was in order and we joined Aeroflot for the journey back to Moscow, switched the clocks back seven hours, and arrived at the time we departed. Even by air that is a long way.

Another really long way is the distance between the airports in Moscow. Of course, Aeroflot and British Airways are at different locations, so a long taxi ride diametrically across town was in order. I know that there is a train service, but no-one can tell me enough about it to be certain of a connection.

The concern for haste was not necessary because the BA aircraft had picked up a bolt in one of the tyres. After some hours they allowed us to board, only to be told that they had found another and they were sure that we would prefer that they changed the wheel now rather than wait until we reached Heathrow. On a separate occasion our party was delayed in Moscow because BA judged that the tar on the Moscow strip was too molten for a safe take-off. The temperature range in Moscow is alleged to be from -40 Celsius to +40.

So we made it back to Tim's residence in London, too late for the train or the tube from Heathrow; yet another argument for favouring train over plane.

In summary then, although Russia is not a Eurail adventure, it can provide rail adventures second to none.

14. CZECH REPUBLIC

Before World War I, the area occupied by the Czech Republic was part of the Austro-Hungarian Empire under Kaiser Franz Josef I. After WWI it was packaged with Slovakia and became an autonomous republic of Czechoslovakia. Hitler made his first territorial advances against the Czechs in 1938 and he promised Chamberlain these would be the last. 'Peace in our time!' This was not to be, and the land of the Czechs was soon absorbed into the German Reich.

At the end of WWII the Czechoslovakia package was returned to its owners and immediately it became one of the Soviet satellites, behind the Iron Curtain, under communist rule. After the USSR broke up, the 'Velvet Revolution' in December 1989 removed the communist power and Czechoslovakia became a democratic republic, with no turmoil and no fighting. On 1 January 1993 came the 'Velvet Divorce' when, by mutual consent, the country split into the Czech Republic and the Slovak Republic, Slovakia.

The Czechs joined the EU in 2004 and acceded to the Schengen Treaty in 2007, but it may well be 2014 or 2015 before the Czechs can join the Eurozone. There are currently about 25 Czech korunas to one Euro.

Before 1990 there were a few sad trains which entered Czechoslovakia from Germany and Austria, but most were refugee trains. Since then the Czechs have smartened up their railways with new rolling stock, but little visible upgrading of infrastructure. The most direct trains from Vienna/Budapest to Berlin pass through Prague, but the German ICEs through Nürnberg are often faster.

One visits the Czech Republic to go to Prague, among the more beautiful cities of Central Europe. Prague received a bashing through all the changes of management over the years, but very little of the destruction is now visible.

The city is renowned for its beautiful old buildings, its music, the river and the views across the city.

Trains come into the central station, *Hlavni*, in the centre of the city. At the Metro station you can buy a 24-hour ticket which covers all trams, buses and the underground. Korunas can best be bought in small amounts from an ATM and their value decreases once you leave the country.

Take the Metro to Staromestska, changing first at Museum, and follow the signs for a short walk back. This is the centre of the Prague that you came to see! Standing in the cobbled square, you can see the city hall, the clock, and the old church. It is all right here! In the main square are the local stalls. Try an 'Old Prague Pork', cooked on the spit in front of your eyes. Or try one of those things with the baked bread wound around a spindle.

A pleasant walk through narrow streets can take you to the Charles Bridge, completed in 1402. This magnificent structure links the two sides of the town and is the talking point of the city. As with most tourist locations, this has been taken over by the hawkers, here trying to persuade you to have your caricatures drawn, amongst all the usual activities.

Several years ago when the river flooded, the bridge was in danger of being destroyed. A large laden barge was moored upstream and, if it had broken loose, it would surely have crashed into the bridge and taken it away. Plans were in hand to blow up the barge if it broke loose. You will now see a baffle around each pier to divert any possible future catastrophe.

My meteorologist friend, Andrew, waited until he was on the Charles Bridge before he proposed to Rachel, who is now his wife. It is a spectacular bridge.

One interesting intercession you may see is the marionette production of Mozart's '*Don Giovanni*'. This opera was first presented in Prague and the locals show some pretence at owning it. There are two such theatres and a visit to one of them to see the production is worthwhile.

Prague did not escape Hitler's persecution of the Jews, and the city prides itself on an historic Jewish quarter with more amazing history and reports of these terrible events.

As in many cities, the best view can best be seen from outside. Take the tram across the river and to the top of the hill, then walk along the hillside path, without going down, to see the best views of Prague. At the funicular railway, the midway station, turn and go up . Here once again you will see a great view of the city. You can also go up the local 'Eiffel Tower', or visit their hall of mirrors. There is a splendid restaurant at the halfway point of the funicular. This will show you Czech food at its best.

You cannot cover all of that in one day, but if you have no more than one, this will show you a lot of Prague.

There are quite a few larger cities around the Republic, but none match Prague. From the communication perspective, Breclav has become an important European transport hub, with trains connecting on the hour to Vienna, to Bratislava and Budapest, to Prague, Dresden and Hamburg, and to Warsaw. Regrettably, my experience does not extend beyond the railway station.

Olomouc is an interesting city with crazy trams and cobbled streets. One gains an idea from these how such cities grew.

The International Chemistry Olympiad was in Olumouc in about 1988. I arrived in the town by hire car and found no-one who could communicate with me, until finally someone directed me to a scientific establishment out of town. Here, after using the word 'chemistry', I was directed to a laboratory only to find a young lady whose English was as good as I could ask. On the desk beside her was a chemistry journal opened at an article by my colleague in Canberra.

The use of English as a medium of communication in Europe grows every year. Most train announcements on international trains are spoken in English, following the local presentation, and in many cases the use of French as a secondary language has disappeared. Even the domestic trains in many countries, certainly in Germany, Austria and Switzerland, now often give recorded announcements in English after the local tongue. One can be confident that anywhere, provided you are both civil and polite, you will be answered in English. If the officer concerned is not fluent, you will be passed to one who is. It is tempting to say that this might not apply to citizens from the Land of the Free as they do not always meet the 'civil and polite' requirement, according to European definition.

Both bank tellers, for instance, that I spoke to in suburban Belgrade were quite fluent in English and could be accepted in any English-speaking city in the world, except perhaps London, which is no longer solely an English-speaking city. Some announcements in Warsaw Station were given in English.

The most notable use of English is in graffiti where often vulgar English words, of which I had forgotten the existence, are among those most frequently used.

The primary reason for the advance is, of course, television, which talks in a form of English which enables one to learn and provides, in most countries, subtitles in the *lingua franca*. This must be coupled with the fact that English has been compulsory in all schools in many European countries for many years, and the proportion of the population who missed English at school diminishes as you watch. The secondary and short-term reason, certainly in Germany, is undoubtedly the World Cup in 2006, during which the most prevalent common language would have been English. This would have meant that those who spoke good English would have improved greatly, and those lacking in confidence would have gained it. Railway and other authorities would have instructed their staff to give announcements, where needed, in English and such an effect is not reversible. The French language may fade away almost as fast as memories of M. Chirac will. Nearly all of the German train announcements now finish up by thanking you, in English, 'We hope you enjoyed your journey with *Deutsche Bahn*! Have a pleasant day.' It becomes very tedious.

Once out from under the Soviet yoke, many countries did their utmost to forget Russian and to learn English.

15. SLOVAKIA

After WWII Slovakia, minus the bottom end, (Zakarpattia Oblast, now part of the Ukraine) remained as part of the Republic of Czechoslovakia but in 1993, in the 'Velvet Divorce' the two nations parted and the Slovak Republic, or Slovakia, became an independent nation.

Slovakia joined the EU in 2004 and acceded to the Schengen Treaty in 2007. It joined the Eurozone in 2009. Slovakia thus has everything going for it, but one. It does not take a Eurail pass (2011).

***

Bratislava is a dream for those who like to see a town dripping with history. Bratislava shows no damage from all of its arguments with its neighbours over the last century, and is surely there to be enjoyed.

One tends to forget that Bratislava is on the Danube, only 60km downstream from Vienna. As an alternative to the train from Vienna, the boat can provide an interesting, and not lengthy, journey to Bratislava.

The old city of Bratislava (in German, Pressburg) is extremely compact and a joy to wander about. The central city square includes the city hall with the inevitable clock and a very accommodating tourist office.

One of the idiosyncrasies of the city is the art works in the street. Don't be surprised to see a bronze model of a worker coming up from a manhole in the midst of your path.

The local market in the city square, which becomes the Christmas market in December, should not be missed.

The Danube, now much broader and in less haste than in Vienna, is adjacent to the city centre and is crossed by a very obvious and large, modern bridge. At the far side of this is an alternate return rail journey back to Vienna.

***

Calculating speeds of trains is easy, anywhere in Europe. One only has to notice the kilometre posts going past, attached to the stanchions. They read in kilometres and tenths, so 13 above 8 is 13.8km from somewhere. To obtain the speed it is only necessary to count, in seconds, the time taken to cover one kilometre and divide that into 3600 to obtain the speed in kilometres per hour, or divide it in 2250 to obtain it in miles per hour. A stopwatch is not needed; all that is necessary is to count the seconds as best you can. To be a little more accurate then, count the time for three kilometres and divide by three.

In case you don't want to do the arithmetic, here is a table which may be helpful:

Seconds per kilometre	Kilometres per hour	Miles per hour (rounded)
12	300	185
15	240	150
18	200	125
20	180	112
24	150	92
30	120	75
36	100	60
40	90	56
48	75	46

Since Slovakia has not been included on the Eurail pass, I have not spent a lot of time elsewhere in the nation. I did manage a train trip to Poprad in the mountains to the east where I saw a good selection of the very pleasant mid-European countryside.

16. SLOVENIA

In its time the Austro-Hungarian Empire, based in Vienna, incorporated most of the neighbouring countries which were generally Roman Catholic. To the south these included the nations of Slovenia and Croatia, bordering onto the Ottoman Empire ruled from Istanbul.

The old Kaiser, Franz Josef I, presided over all of this until 1914, when his heir, the Archduke Ferdinand, was shot in Sarajevo, now the capital of Bosnia. This led to a declaration of war, signed by Franz Josef, and World War I began. Once this was all over, Austria was stripped of most of its 'possessions' and became a republic, while all the countries to the south, now called the 'West Balkans', were lumped into a potpourri known as Yugoslavia, including Slovenia, Croatia, Serbia, Montenegro, Bosnia and Macedonia; six countries which were as different as chalk and cheese in terms of economy, culture and, most of all, religion. The only country not included was Albania.

Slovenia had a long border with Austria and had more affinity with Austria than with Belgrade, from where it was governed.

On 25 June, 1991, Slovenia declared its independence from Yugoslavia at a time when Belgrade could do little about it. Non-Slovenian officials were told that they could either stay and continue in their jobs, or return home. A border was set up with Croatia and a new nation was formed.

Returning from the International Physics Olympiad in Cuba in 1991, we were in Mexico City waiting for a flight out and with us was the Yugoslav team, the last ever of this name. They had been staying overnight with the Yugoslav Ambassador, a gentleman from Ljubljana, as they had no Western currency. We met the ambassador at the airport and he told us that Slovenia had declared its independence overnight and that he had aligned himself with Slovenia. This meant that he had no fallback position if the coup failed, but he was adamant that he was doing the right thing. He was both a Slovenian hero and a Yugoslav rebel. What happened to the man, I have no idea.

One statement he made came over as good sense. The European Union will never allow a war within 200km of Salzburg. He was right, of course, and Slovenian independence was never fought over except in the first ten days. Since there was no fighting and no destruction, Slovenia was subsequently able to concentrate on its own development.

Slovenia turned its face to Europe and was admitted to the European Union in 2004 along with nine other applicant nations, none of which were in the Balkans. Entry to the Schengen Treaty followed shortly afterwards and the Slovenian-Croatia border became the southern boundary of the EU, and was managed in the same way as the remaining EU boundaries, with Slovenia receiving financial assistance to monitor this.

The Slovenia-Croatia border had hitherto been in name only and persons, goods and families walked across at will. Now there was an immigration barrier which was unwelcome to most. Slovenia has a very small access to the Adriatic Sea and this has been a source of friction with Croatia. The port of Koper on this small piece of coast has been developed and this has become an important seaport for EU countries not using Italian ports.

Slovenia was one of the first from the new entrants to the EU to meet the monetary criteria and join the Eurozone.

Before the break-up, access from the EU to Yugoslavia was difficult and it was not easy to travel by road toward Greece. Trains going south from Vienna were very restricted.

Today this is very different. Austrian trains continue beyond Maribor into Slovenia and there are several services per day to the capital, Ljubljana, Of more importance appears to be the link between München and Ljubljana via Salzburg, which boasts several direct trains a day plus an overnight service, the *Lisinski,* which appears to carry through carriages from everywhere to everywhere else. This includes from Belgrade to Switzerland and Germany, although the main route north from Belgrade appears to be via Budapest.

Ljubljana is a modern city and has well-appointed roads, buildings and transport. There is neither grot nor grime visible, as one is prepared to find in these countries, and it can be seen as a responsible part of the EU.

Most of these factors have now been discussed under the various countries, so it is a good time to summarise them. The following table compares the 31 European countries which are members of the EU, the Schengen Treaty, the Eurozone or the global Eurail pass (2011).

Selected European countries by membership (31):

	EU Membership	Schengen Treaty	Currency	Eurail Pass
Germany				
France				
Belgium				
Netherlands				
Luxembourg				
Italy				
Great Britain			Pound	
Iceland	2012, 2013		Kroner	
Denmark			Kroner	
Sweden			Kroner	
Norway			Kroner	
Irish Republic				
Finland				
Estonia				
Lithuania			Lita *	
Latvia			Lat *	
Poland			Zloty *	
Czech			Koruna *	
Slovakia				
Hungary			Forint *	
Romania			Leu nou *	
Bulgaria			Lev *	
Austria				
Switzerland			Franc (CH)	
Greece				
Spain				
Portugal				
Slovenia				
Malta				
Cyprus				
Croatia	2013		Kuna	

EU membership: Blank = member (27); dark horizontal bars = non-member (4) with potential date of accession.

Schengen Treaty: Blank = full participant (25); dark horizontal bars = non participant (2); light horizontal bars = not yet implemented (3); vertical bars = not specified (1).

Currency   Blank = Eurozone (17); no shading = local currency (14). * indicates that the nation has undertaken to join the Eurozone (7 from 14).

Eurail   Blank = Global Eurail pass accepted in 2011 (22); light horizontal bars = Global Eurail not accepted (6); Vertical bars = no train service (3).

Kosovo and Montenegro use the Euro, *de facto.*

A summary of the microstates of Europe is given in the chapter on Liechtenstein.

No other nations of Europe fall into any of the categories above (2011).

Six other nations lie within the periphery of the EU and are not on this chart: Albania, Macedonia, Serbia, Montenegro, Kosovo and Bosnia.

17. CROATIA (HRVATSKA) AND BOSNIA

Hrvatska. Once the naughty boy of Yugoslavia, Croatia is now enjoying a very definite trend to modernisation and toward the EU.

Thrust into the rag-bag of Yugoslavia after World War I, Croatia was never happy with its lot. Its pronounced enmity with its historic rival and neighbour Serbia was celebrated across the world with battles, mainly on the soccer field but in other more clandestine ways. Australia, which had many post WWII migrants from Croatia and Serbia, saw many of these fights and it is alleged that there were Croatian fighting units set up in hidden places in Australia. Fortunately that has all but disappeared. Croatia is predominantly Roman Catholic, but of the Croatian variety which contains a frightening amount of nationalism.

Following the collapse of Yugoslavia in 1990, Croatia had at least two wars. In the south the anti-secessionist forces from Belgrade (Serbians) lay siege to Dubrovnik and in the north there were battles between Bosnian and Croatian forces. It is not for me to say who was responsible for these but the fact that there were substantial numbers of Croats in a primarily Muslim country, or sub-country, since Bosnia is a 'federation', was certainly a contributing factor.

Peace came at last and Croatia is concentrating on its entry into the EU, something which they hope will happen as early as 1 July 2013. Most barriers have been overcome and it is alleged that Croatia meets entry requirements to the EU better than many of the existing members do.

Following this would come entry to the Schengen Treaty, which would move the EU boundary further south and extend it along the very long border

Croatia holds with Bosnia. It would also give the EU a huge expanse of sea-coast border; one littered with countless islands which are, and will continue to be, a haven for pirates of all varieties. Slovenia would lose its external EU border except for its very small seacoast and Hungary's external EU border would decrease. Croatia's accession will be a major change in EU border regime.

Croatia's entry to the Eurozone is not mentioned in the discussion, but that would be an event very much in the future.

Currently my passport must be stamped on entering Croatia. EU passports may be exempt. Their currency is the kuna, which sells at around seven to the Euro. Some merchants accept Euros, but that is their choice.

From Austria, Zagreb is most easily reached from Vienna by a train via Maribor and through Slovenia, along what was a little-used line south from Graz before the borders opened up. This involves crossing the Semmering Pass in Austria. An alternate route has been established from Vienna via Wiener Neustadt, through Hungary, without much rise in terrain. This follows some single track and much is not powered, so it is an interesting exercise for the track-watchers. A third option, usable only by Eurail pass holders as it involves a circuitous route, takes the evening service from Vienna to München then the overnight service into Zagreb, something not available when travelling direct.

Zagreb reflects much of what I have said above about the economy of Croatia. The city is clean and open, ready to do business with you. Outside the front of the station is an underground shopping mall, which is so clean you feel you could eat your meal off the floor. Even at night there is a cleaner with a broom and dustpan ensuring that it is. No-one would dare smoke in here. Such an area reflects on the changing mentality of the Croatian people.

One evening I sat outside the station waiting for my train. There were plenty of seats and I felt I could sit there in comfort without having some disagreeable person sit next to me; in other cities you may collect anything from a persistent beggar to simply a smoker. Lots of people were moving about. Trams came and went. A chap was playing a French horn on the other side of the tram tracks; nothing special, anything that came into his head, but no doubt he collected a few kuna. He was replaced on the next night by a lady with a keyboard. It was a splendid summer evening, even though it was

November. Then the rain began. The milling about stopped. Suddenly there were only those standing under the tram shelters with me under the front of the station. The situation returned as the rain passed.

The long coast of Croatia is a well promoted holiday region, despite what else it may offer, and it is well worth a visit. The three major coastal cities of Split, Rijeka and Dubrovnik may all be reached by train from Zagreb although there are limitations in reaching Dubrovnik. As well as this an irregular ferry service taking about 20 hours, with possible overnight accommodation, operates between the three. Even more irregular ferry services cross into Italy. Split is an interesting old city turned into a major port and commercial area. The age of the buildings confirms the former, and the pace of the people the latter. Once more, the place is relatively clean, for a port. The standard of travel between Zagreb and both Split and Rijeka will go up when Croatia adopts and enforces a no smoking policy on trains, as it must under EU regulations and might already have done by now (2011).

To reach Dubrovnik is another story, as it involves travel through Bosnia (correctly *Bosnia and Herzegovina*). The trains are of a much earlier vintage and of much lower standard than those to which one is accustomed. Included in your kit should be the inevitable roll of toilet paper, lots of €5 and €10 notes, water to last the journey and food likewise.

The train journey to Ploče (for Dubrovnik) takes all day after departing from Zagreb, so morning arrival in Zagreb is necessary if an overnight stop is to be avoided. The train from the north, the *Lisinski*, arrives in Zagreb at 0840 (2011 timetable) after which it is first necessary to buy a ticket from the Bosnian border to Metkovic. Bosnian tickets cannot be bought in Vienna or Budapest. Then one has to find the departure platform, all in time to make the 0853 departure. I have done this twice so it is not impossible. The Bosnian conductor will sell tickets on the train for Euros, at his rate of exchange, so all is not lost if a ticket cannot be bought at the station. He will only sell a ticket to Sarajevo, after which another ticket must be bought to the next border.

The train is tired and grubby with smokers abounding. With luck a first class compartment will be empty and you may be spared the smokers. This train knows nothing of speed but it does keep moving. There is hardly time for passengers to get on and off before the train is on its way again. Despite the fact that it is the only through train of the day, it does not stop at the smaller stations, but at each one the Bosnian equivalent of the 'Fat Controller' (from *Thomas the Tank Engine*) emerges from his office and waves the train on. The same happens in all countries, of course, but here the trains move slower and the situation is much more laughable.

After a couple of hours the train arrives at the border of Bosnia and one must go through the farce of having a passport stamped out of Croatia into Bosnia.

After slightly over nine hours the train has covered the 496km to Sarajevo, the capital of Bosnia with the notorious history. This city is where the Grand Duke Ferdinand, the nephew of the Emperor Franz Josef I, was shot in 1914, triggering the beginning of World War I.

The city of Sarajevo matches the train, with poverty visible. Bosnia is a pathetically poor country and a long way from membership of the EU.

Another four hours is needed to reach Metkovic, 194km further on. This involves yet another border crossing, for Metkovic is in Croatia again, as is the destination of the train, Ploče. Fear not, there is more to come.

***

Smoking is banned on all public transport throughout the EU but the laws still vary on railway stations. There are designated smoking areas at many big German and Austrian stations but, since they are badly defined, they are not terribly effective. One suspects that the next move from the EU will be to ban smoking in all railway stations, bus stations, bus stops, etc., and this is keenly awaited by the non-smokers. The smokers, many of whom need a smoke only because it is allowed, are probably equally as enthusiastic. Most were as much in favour of banning smoking on aircraft as were the non-smokers. The banning of smoking on trains had the effect, of course, of transferring the problem to the platforms where the addicted grab their last chance before boarding and first after leaving. Throughout Europe, as in other places in the world of course, one sees passengers swinging out of doorways in stationary trains, most anxious to have that puff but unwilling to leave the train. The braver use the platform. Were they not allowed to do this, the craving would not exist. Heathrow tells you that smoking is only allowed in designated areas and then leads you to the designated areas outside near the taxi rank.

The ban on smoking in trains, however, has not (2011) yet reached countries outside the EU and smoking on trains in such countries as Croatia, Bosnia and Serbia is still allowed. Smoking is never permitted in sleeping cars but when one is constrained to travel in a sitting car in one of these countries, the effect is devastating for the non-smoker. Surely this will change shortly.

***

Metkovic has two hotels in the town, owned by the same person, and one a few kilometres out on the road. On my first visit the former were full and the management arranged for me to be collected by the proprietor of the latter. On my second visit, a bystander in one of the cafés (drinking holes) discovered my difficulty and fished out the aforementioned manager from one of the tables. He treated me like the prodigal son and soon established me in one of his hostelries.

The bus station in Metkovic is a busy one, through which all the buses travelling along the coast must pass. Establishing which bus goes where is not easy as, apart from the language, they set out their timetable in a very different form from ours. This problem was eventually solved and the bus had me en route to Dubrovnik, Croatia.

The part of Croatia on which Dubrovnik sits is an enclave, divided from the main body of Croatia by Bosnia's only access to the sea, a very narrow one at that. At one point, islands of Croatia are close enough to be joined potentially by a bridge over the narrow entrance, which would require Bosnians to go under a Croatian bridge to reach the sea. There is a long way to go to bring full stability to the area. Recognise now that to reach the final destination, Dubrovnik, one must again cross into Bosnia and out again. By now I hope you are curious enough to check in a post-1995 atlas to see which one of us is crazy.

The Siege of Dubrovnik in 1990 was a truly terrible affair with mass killings from all manner of sources. Monuments and memorials abound, as the folk who died have close relatives still living. Since all is in Croatian, one can understand little without a guide or guidebook. The conditions were as one would expect of Europe in the seventeenth century or of Africa in the twentieth, but certainly not Europe in the twentieth. We are only a few hundred kilometres from Salzburg. Fortunately the damage to the irreplaceable parts of the city was minimal.

The walled city of Dubrovnik is a sight to behold and well deserving of its UNESCO listing. One can spend hours or even days walking the walls, inspecting the churches, going to the various places of antiquity or visiting the port. Of course the cruise ships visit here and the town, being so small, is soon over-run by groups following a guide, but all subsides when dinner is called on the ship.

So the sun set on Dubrovnik and I returned, with four crossing checks, to Metkovic for the night. On the next day I chose to take a cruise around the islands from Dubrovnik. It involved the same two very cheap bus rides and another eight border checks. Then it was back to Metkovic, Croatia, to the hotel for the third night.

On my first stay in Metkovic I was at the out-of-town hotel and needed to take the 0700 train back to Zagreb, the only one for the 24-hour day. The proprietor agreed to drive me at 0630 and I was duly ready in good time. After nearly an hour the proprietor had not arrived, so I started on the walk to the bus station only to be flagged down by the proprietor driving up behind me after about ten minutes. I had been early and she was on time as the clock had moved for daylight saving. Call me Phileas Fogg. So I made the train. The journey from there back to Zagreb was as tedious as the forward one, if not more so.

This sounds a horrible journey and doubtless it is, but if all railways were sleek ICE trains the fun would disappear. One only has to go anywhere internationally by air to experience a more horrible journey involving more passports, baggage checks, security checks and interminable waits. Even Bosnia is better than that.

Bosnia is made up of several sectors which are of Croatian origin, Serbian origin or of Muslim origin respectively. It fought a war over who owned what, which involved charges of genocide that will never be proven or otherwise. A solution was said to have been found by locking the leaders in a room, Sistine Chapel-style, and not releasing them until a solution was found. Thus Bosnia appears as unstable as the old Yugoslavia was, with very covetous neighbours on all sides. The EU keeps close watch. Bosnia today still looks very little different from pre-1990 Bosnia or Yugoslavia and its economy must match. Of all the old Yugoslavian or 'West Balkan' states, Bosnia would have the least chance of entering the EU and may one day be a country surrounded on all sides by the EU and with only a tiny access to the sea.

18. HUNGARY

Hungary has had a rough time over the centuries. The Magyars settled there while the British were fighting the Wars of the Roses and minded their own business until they, like their neighbours, were taken over by the Ottoman Empire; in simple terms, by the Turks. Finally they were freed from this bondage by the Habsburgs in the early 1800s, only to find that the Habsburgs did not choose to go home and Hungary became part of what was later the Austro-Hungarian Empire under the Kaiser in Vienna.

This state of affairs was changed by World War I, and the consequent passing of the Habsburgs, after which Hungary had a few years under its own flag. Hitler was the next to arrive and the Magyars did not fare as badly as they might have. They were rescued from this by the Soviets in 1945. Stalin's fire was a few steps worse than Der Führer's frying pan, particularly when you remember the brutal fighting involving Russian tanks in Budapest in 1956.

Hungary was one of the first countries openly to encourage leaks in the Iron Curtain, and they finally achieved their independence around 1989.

Now they have chosen to hand the power over to Brussels by joining the EU in 2004 and becoming part of the Schengen Treaty in 2007. Thus no passports are required to enter or leave Hungary, unless you wanted to go to the Ukraine, which would be a whole new story. Hungary is obliged to join the Eurozone but this seems unlikely until 2014 or 2015. In the meantime one uses forints which come at about 280 to the Euro, a very cumbersome amount.

Budapest, the capital city, is alive. It no longer shows the years under Soviet domination and has a commercial image comparable to that of any Western city. Even so, none of the old grandeur of the city is lost. You could well be in Vienna. The city of Buda, on the bluff overlooking the Danube, and the city of Pest on the plains of the other side, became one by natural course of events. The 'chain bridge' across the Danube is a latter-day construction which allowed the union of the cities.

One arrives by train at the south station, *Keleti Pu*. If ever there was a din, it is here. The loud speaker operates almost continuously and such a small amount is in English, international trains perhaps, that it is not worth trying to follow. Once your mind becomes convinced that it is not going to stop, it all becomes easier. The station is fairly primitive and passenger services come almost completely from takeaway-style stands.

Fear not if you cannot read the language. It is more closely related to Finnish than anything else. Sufficient signs are in English to find your way around and a fair proportion of the locals can speak English.

There are a couple of reputable moneychangers, and a couple of less reputable ones, where you might invest perhaps €20 (4,000+ forints!) in local currency at the first instance. This will cover you for local train tickets, something to eat and a trip to the loo. In general, nobody takes Euros. You may collect a map from the tourist office, free of charge, forward from the platforms and to the right.

This reminds me of another rule for rail travel. *Always go immediately before you leave the train.* If you have been sitting still for some time, the need will come upon you almost certainly and with urgency. As soon as you are off the train you will then have to find the loo in a hurry, after which you find that it costs 50c and in a currency which you do not have. The one in Budapest is a long way from the platforms and requires forints.

A tour of Budapest starts by going outside from the front of the station and going left about 50 metres and down into the subway. The surrounding area is being dug up for a new underground line, M4, so this will keep changing. You can buy an all-day ticket, either at the machine or at the ticket office, which will take you on all trams, underground and buses, for the balance of the day.

The murals in the tunnels give pictures of James Watt, George Stephenson and Isembard Kingdom Brunel, telling you that the British engineers were once here.

For the first view of Budapest, take the subway to Szell Kalman ter (formerly Mosckva Ter), across the river in Buda. Here you will find a large circus full of trams and buses. At the head of the staircase leading up to the top road there is a number 16 or 16A; a very small bus. This bus will take you up the hill to the fortress area. Stay on board for ten minutes or so until you see the battlements and the church on the left. From the battlements, Fisherman's Bastion, you can see the city of Pest, the island, the Danube, the parliament, the chain bridge, St Stephen's church, the city and the citadel. Hungary's parliament building is clearly based on the Palace of Westminster and commands the river frontage of Pest.

The church of St Matthias, next to you, is certainly as beautiful as it is made out to be and has tremendous significance for the Hungarians. The roof is tiled like St Stefan's in Vienna, and is possibly even more beautiful. The entry fee in forints is well worth the experience.

Midst the hawkers outside the church is a real one. Two gentlemen in period costume are offering to let you have your photograph taken with their eagle; a large live one.

On the other side of the road from the church and slightly forward, is a very agreeable restaurant, *Arany Hordo*. It has a suit of armour standing outside. Try it for lunch or at least for a cup of coffee. Buy Hungarian and buy big. They speak good English and take credit cards. The cost of dinner in this restaurant, with tables outside, is a little more than usual but the atmosphere, including the string trio playing Strauss and gypsy melodies in the evening, makes it well worthwhile. If you can be there on a warm evening, looking down over the lights of Budapest with a violin playing behind you, you are in Hungary. While the sun is setting, the view from Buda across the Danube to Pest from the surrounding walls of the bastion is as good as it can ever be.

After your visit to the restaurant keep walking forward, past the Presidential Palace until you come opposite the chain bridge where you have an excellent view down the hill over the wall. There you see another eagle, a huge bronze one, clutching a sword and staring down over the city for which it is a symbol. The funicular, from the strange-looking building near the wall, will take you to the bottom, forints only, where you can walk across the chain bridge and into the city and see what Pest is like.

One very creepy display, a short distance out of Budapest, on the local train or bus service, is 'Statue Park', a park filled with Soviet statues. These have obviously been rescued from the hearth before being melted down, and provide a strange supplement to Hungarian recent history. A bronze replica of Stalin's boots is one of which they are very proud. It is likely, but not specified, that these are the boots from the eight metre high statue of Stalin in the city park which was toppled in October 1956.

Your departure will bring you back to *Keleti Pu* once more, where you lose the wonderful feeling of Budapest. There are, however, some very nice Hungarian restaurants nearby but not visible from the front of the station. The information office recommended the *Huszar* restaurant, for which you walk forward from the station, under the overpass and turn left opposite the Grand Hungaria Hotel, then forward about 100 metres. This provided excellent food with a real Hungarian atmosphere.

There are other cities in Hungary, but none to match the presence found in Budapest.

Hungarians will direct you to Lake Balaton, further back toward Austria, but this you will find is quite over-rated in a country which has no access to the ocean.

19. ROMANIA

It has been said that Brussels has a greater control over applicant countries to the EU than over its members. Romania certainly proves this. Romania was admitted to the EU in 2007 and it really did set minds turning as to whether this was a dilution of standards, as even today much of the required upgrading of the nation's financial system, its governance and its resources do not meet EU standards. While Romania, again with Bulgaria, was required to join the Schengen Treaty shortly after becoming part of the EU, its implementation still has not (2011) come to pass.

***

'My object all sublime,
I shall achieve in time…'

W. S. Gilbert, - *The Mikado*

I did achieve my object, both to reach the Black Sea coast at Constanta and to visit Transylvania. This was November 2007, in the period before Romania joined the EU but after it had given up its restrictive border practices.

Constanta is a long way from anywhere, 2590km from London according to their sign and 22 hours by train from Vienna. It is the most easterly major city of the EU, being further east than St Petersburg. If you are to continue reading this chapter, please find a modern day map of Romania to enable you to see where you are.

Romania is a poor country, almost on a par with Bosnia. All those years under Ceausescu and the Soviet domination took their toll. It is not hard to see why Romania was given accelerated entry to the EU as:

1. It completes the EU border with Russia/Belarus/Ukraine/Moldova between Hungary and Greece, which forms a sort of inverted iron curtain for the EU (their choice).
2. It gives the EU access to the Black Sea.
3. It completely encloses the remaining, non-EU, former Yugoslavia republics in an enclave inside the EU.
4. It denies Russia access to Serbia and the Mediterranean, except by crossing EU territory.

The fact that the accession of Bulgaria and Romania added another 20 million people to the Common Market is perhaps of lesser significance. The EU is spending billions of Euros upgrading the road and rail from the Hungarian border to the port at Constanta. This money will all go into the Romanian economy.

Like Croatia and Bosnia, the Romanians still seem dedicated to full public service employment, hence there are more Fat Controllers and more security guards at the borders than you find elsewhere. The Romanians have not learned that setting a few of these people on cleaning up the country would help. There is rubbish everywhere. The Romanians have at least given up the habit of confiscating your passport if you stay overnight in a hotel. The small stores have not opened out and may still consist of the 30cm by 30cm window with the momma on the other side and all her goods around her behind glass. It is slowly changing but taking a long while.

The most notable thing in Romania is the number of beggars. These are probably the *Roma* who, under the Schengen Treaty, are now gracing the streets of other cities of the EU and causing problems for the French government. There are over 200,000 of these people in Romania, their country of origin. Their method is usually to use small kids to stop you in the street and there are packs of grubby eight-year-olds screaming around all railway stations. Don't let your bag out of your hand here, mate.

Taking the overnight train from Vienna to Bucharest (17 hours continuous journey) I then travelled five more hours to Constanta. Although we changed time by one hour, Constanta is so far east that it was pitch dark by 1700. There I was able to figuratively dip the toe in the Black Sea and have a wander around the city after dark and again in the morning. It was not so cold that I could not wear shorts; I was too hot in my Moscow tracksuit. But that is me, and perhaps only me!

Next I headed for Brasov, the other city which claims to be Romania's second city. Crossing the Carpathian Mountains by train was like *Jingle Bells* and *The Nutcracker* rolled into one. There had been a good fall of snow over-night and the trees, some still with leaves, were all covered in snow. There had been no wind so nothing had moved. Absolutely delightful.

Brasov is the big city of Transylvania, which is why I was there.

There are two Draculas. Vlad was a prince of Wallachia in the 14th century and, because his badge was a dragon (dracul), he signed his name as Dracula. His castle, now without trace, was on the Brogo Pass where he monitored the traffic between Wallachia and Transylvania. It did not pay to be out of favour with Vlad as he had the habit of impaling his enemies on a spike, hence 'Vlad the Impaler'. It is suspected that Vlad had a medical condition which can now be understood (a little like George III who had Porphyria and Abraham Lincoln who had something like Parkinson's), which caused his eyes and gums to be red and his gums to withdraw making his teeth seem like fangs. He was 'long in the tooth'. His domestic habits left a little to be desired. From this real man, the legend evolved and persists today.

About 100 years ago Bram Stoker created the novel *Dracula,* based very loosely on these legends. Englishman Jonathon Harker visited Dracula in his castle after having been collected by Dracula at the Brogo Pass. Stoker chose Bran Castle near Brasov as his model. The literary Dracula has far more fascinating qualities than his progenitor, but that simply adds to the interest. Dracula has absolutely nothing to do with Frankenstein, who was created by Mary Shelley in the mid-1800s, not far from Brienz in Switzerland.

After hiring a car for the day in Brasov, I worked my way around the Transylvanian countryside. Bran Castle, built 1377, eight years before Winchester College in England where I was working at the time, is a very pleasant place but, as a prison for Harker, it would have been very forbidding. The walls down which Stoker's Dracula scaled face-downward are indeed formidable. Hundreds of thousands of visitors come to Bran each year. Brogo Pass is not as bad as Stoker makes out and has a pub there now; let's call it a McDonald's to completely ruin the image. There is even a café on another pass which advertises itself as the café where Jonathon Harker had his last meal before going to Castle Dracula. People go there in droves. During the day it was snowing on the passes, so I did not exercise any heroics but went where it was convenient. I had a great Transylvanian meal at another roadside café, something you can't find if you live out of railway stations. Who has ever been to Transylvania? Well, I have now.

As I returned to the hotel in Brasov I noticed the temperature at dinner, varying between zero and plus one Celsius. It was pleasant sitting in the restaurant eating Romanian food as the temperature continued to drop. By morning the snow had taken over and there were several centimetres in the streets. I was able to spend the morning wandering the streets of Brasov in the snow. It had no business to snow so early in the winter, but it did. The cable car, the Black Church (built 1383, burnt in 1696), the White Church, the black tower, the white tower, the narrow street (1.82 m wide 95 m long), the old city and so on, are very pleasant to see. At 0900 next morning, Sunday, the streets were white, temperature minus two Celsius; by 1000 there were trails where cars were driving. By 1100 the roads were all slushy. The locals knew how fast to drive. Kids were making snowballs. People were towing goods and children around on sleds. Remember that this is a slight, out-of-season, Romanian snowfall. I'm told that the previous overnight temperature would have been heading for minus ten Celsius. This was November. Imagine the depths of winter.

The rail trip back over the mountains to Bucharest was not so much fairyland now, as the snowdrifts were thicker and cars buried. Only the main road was passable.

Language problems in Romania did not exist for me on this occasion. Where there were differences, they were usually fun. All of the hotel receptionists, hire car people, food shops, etc. I met spoke English. Of the railway station staff at Constanta, two ladies were able to help me in great English and show me where to find a hotel, etc. The other four were monolingual and a great charade of arm waving and passing notes ensued with the right reservations being issued and smiles all round. In one exceptional fast food store the momma was purely monolingual, so the customer in the line behind me translated. The lady selling tickets at Bran Castle was word perfect in English. Mind you, she deals with dozens of busloads a day in all languages. You can be sure that the beggars will understand English and will know all the most despicable words to throw back at you in any language you choose, if you do not contribute. There are a lot of street stalls run by old ladies. These women have probably lost their husbands by more natural causes than those in the streets of Moscow 20 years ago and have to resort to low level trading to survive. They are not begging or soliciting, other than to normal levels, but endeavouring to stay alive.

From here I returned to Bucharest. This city reminded me of Warsaw at its dirtiest, before 1989. It is to be seen for what it is but, after Brasov, it lacks any charm.

While in Bucharest I saw a book in English, with a title '*Sell-out to Stalin'*, or words to that effect. It detailed what the author saw as the worst outcomes of the Yalta conference in 1945 and its outcome.

***

In February 1945, Churchill, Roosevelt and Stalin met in Yalta and decided how Europe should be divided. It was hardly democratic and it influenced Europe for years to come, certainly directly until 1989, 45 years later. The definitive photograph shows the three men, with Uncle Joe sporting a great smile. Well he might have.

The outcomes were something like this.

Germany was partitioned roughly along the line of occupation at the end of hostilities, except that a large area of Germany around Jena was added to the Soviet zone in recompense for half of Berlin being added to the section administered by the Allies. Austria was occupied similarly. A corridor along the east of Germany was taken and added to Poland, while East Prussia, the enclave of Germany adjoining Lithuania and Poland, was divided between Poland and Russia. This latter included the Baltic Sea port of Königsberg, now Kaliningrad. A much larger corridor of Poland to the east was added to Belarus; at the time 'White Russia'. These latter changes were permanent and populations were moved to fit. Poland was pushed around with no consultation.

In addition to this, Estonia, Latvia and Lithuania, the tail of Slovakia and all of Moldova (once part of Romania) were added permanently to the USSR.

The USSR was given occupation rights over Poland, Czechoslovakia,

Hungary, Romania and Bulgaria, later called the Soviet Satellite States. Greece was in civil war (finally sorted out by Britain) and Yugoslavia, which had been liberated by the Allies, was set up with a puppet dictator, Tito. These details may not be 100% correct but if you are only briefly reading this, it will be enough.

The above gives an idea of the enormous land grab made by Stalin and its influence on the later Cold War. The Iron Curtain was to come down, separating the USSR and these Soviet-controlled nations from the West and to last for 45 years. At the time, to Roosevelt, this would have been too far away to be of consequence and Churchill had a nation in tatters to run. No wonder Stalin had a smile on his face. Marx and Lenin would have been pleased.

***

So I then hopped back on the train for the 17 hours back to Vienna. That is a long time in a sleeping berth, but extremely relaxing for me. What a delight to see clean Hungary and even cleaner Austria, the efficient Hungarian immigration service and the non-existent Hungary-Austria border. It was cold. There had been a little snow but nothing was as memorable as Brasov.

Except for passing through Bucharest on the train to Sofia, I've not been back to Romania since. I must return some day and expect to see it much cleaner and more pleasing.

20. SERBIA, MONTENEGRO, KOSOVO, MACEDONIA (FYROM), ALBANIA

Serbia

If Croatia is the naughty boy of the Yugoslav break-up in 1990, then Serbia is the bastard, using the Australian meaning of the word rather than the classic dictionary meaning. Serbia had the upper hand with Beograd in its midst and intended to maintain it, by hook or by crook. Its methods were more severe than using a crook. Eventually it was all sorted out with a lot of people dead and a lot of destruction, which there need not have been. Serbia, with Montenegro, retained the title of Yugoslavia, very much emasculated. Finally Montenegro broke away and later Kosovo seceded; more about those later.

Serbia has on its agenda to join the EU and it has been stated that it might be granted 'applicant status' by December 2011. Montenegro and Macedonia have this status and, while the application of Montenegro is proceeding, Macedonia is not advancing rapidly. That leaves Bosnia, Albania and Kosovo as the non-contenders of the area.

My host in Belgrade, Zoran, completed his graduate study in Canberra with the same supervisor as I had, but much further down the line, some 20 years later. The laboratory closed down as he finished and he was invited to take anything he could use. Since he had a container going back to Belgrade, he did so. Unlike me, he remained an experimental physicist and is of high world standing.

My first shock was to see a photo of me on the wall of Zoran's office, included in the chain of graduate students. Seeing all of my former equipment was another shock. Then he showed me a copy of our supervisor's book translated into Russian. There was my equipment and data, all described in Russian.

Zoran and Nevenka made me very welcome in their apartment in Beograd. Their very modest little flat on the sixth floor was of post-World War II vintage and, in its time, a very prestigious residence. In Australia one would not expect a couple to use it as their sole residence. It consisted of a not large lounge room, two small bedrooms, a very small bathroom and a galley kitchen. In this apartment Zoran and Nevenka had brought up two kids, while having his parents live there as well. Grandpa and grandma slept in one tiny bedroom, mum and dad in the lounge room and the two kids, boy and girl, in the other bedroom. Since the kids had been born and lived their formative years in Canberra, the return must have been a shock. Both children are now adults and have a bedroom each, as grandma and grandpa have retired to the country. Mum and dad still sleep in the lounge room. The kids doubled up to provide a room for me.

When she met me at the station all Nevenka had was a 30 year old photograph of me. You can never fail to find anyone in a railway station. Nevenka was standing in the crowd at the head of the platform and it was obvious who was my target. Waves were exchanged from around 100 metres. She was so pleased to see me, a complete stranger. People of international standing from small countries must tire of being wheeled around the large cities of the world and never having a chance to show others their city.

Nevenka first took me on a car tour around Beograd, the White City, after which she returned the car home and called a taxi to take us down-town where it was possible to walk to the places of significance and have lunch in the local style. It was here that the true recent history of the Serbs was unfolded to me. At the end of WWII the British came in through Greece, while the Soviets took possession of Hungary, Romania and Bulgaria. This left a rag-bag of little countries of different beliefs and the Allies lumped them all together into a single country called Yugoslavia and found a guy called Tito to run it. Slovenia was Western-leaning; Croatia ardent Roman Catholic; Bosnia basically Muslim, with Serbian and Croatian minorities; Serbia of Eastern Orthodox belief, but containing a region of Albanian majority called Kosovo; Montenegro was seemingly like Serbia and Macedonia, of Greek Orthodox leaning. This we have discussed briefly in earlier chapters. Tito was a communist autocrat but did not toe the Stalinist line. Once Tito died and the Soviet influence was waning, it all broke down.

Nevenka showed me around Belgrade and laid particular emphasis on the last days of the Milosevich regime. Milosevich was the boss in Serbia at the time of the first free elections there. He lost the election to a very popular candidate, mainly because Milosevich was one of the greater miscreants of those years. He refused to stand down. It is fairly clear why, because once he ceased to be the boss, others would be able to begin to count his short-comings. Nevenka took me to the square outside the Milosevich HQ and described how around half a million people had amassed outside, demand-ing peacefully that he go. Milosevich finally stood down and the episode was over. She was one of the tens of thousands of people who kept vigil in the city square on that fateful night to force Milosevitch to resign. There is cer-tainly history to be found there.

History aside, Beograd is clearly a city with a communist background in rather pretty surroundings on the Danube, but dominated by the bleak multi-storey apartment buildings, far more austere than the one in which my hosts lived. The Serbian people go about their business as in any other part of Europe. They are well dressed; the teenagers wear American T-shirts bearing meaningless names or advertising which no American would wear. Incomes must be low because prices are low, but there is no more evidence of poverty here than in Greece or Italy. The populace, having expended so much effort on internal turmoil, are making do with less and managing. They aim 'one day' to become part of the EU but that day must be very far away. People out-side the cities may be worse off but that cannot simply be seen. At an altitude of 500 metres, hot days like that one of 28 Celsius are to be expected, but tem-peratures of minus 20 Celsius in winter must make life hard. Beograd is truly a great place to visit but not a place which is high on your visit's shopping list.

Once again, the city must be seen to be understood.

There are day trains and night trains in each direction between Budapest and Beograd, between Beograd and Thessaloniki and between Beograd and Sofia. It is thus possible to structure a visit of any length to Beograd. There are around one hundred Serbian dinars to the Euro.

The train for Beograd originates in Budapest and is of Austrian stock and, although the train might not be the most up-to-date, there was nothing to complain about. The Eurail pass stops at the Hungarian-Serbian border so a subsequent fare is necessary, but this is only around €10. The couchette supplement was lower than the usual €20, as it is in places further west. Night trains in this part of Europe are run by the local railway authority.

Montenegro

Montenegro voted at a referendum in 2006 to break away from Serbia and go it alone. This was not a bad move, as Montenegro is now much closer to its aim of joining the EU than Serbia, for both monetary and political reasons. Montenegro uses the Euro as its currency although not officially. It traded in German marks before the Euro replaced them and continued after the change.

Zoran and Nevenka and family took me to the coast in Montenegro and we spent a very pleasant few days on the beach. As an Australian, I like wide open beaches and see no benefit in cooking oneself to the colour of a lobster within a few metres of a sweating stranger. The locals were the opposite and were quite astounded that I declined to take off my shirt and hat.

Montenegro possesses one railway line from Beograd to the coast at Bar, via the capital, Podogorica. On this line are the standard two trains each way per day, which gives enough time to explore Podogorica in a simple round trip. Since Beograd is high on the plateau, the train comes down through some unexpectedly magnificent scenery with valleys, waterfalls and winding passes.

No passports are required when crossing from Serbia.

Kosovo

Kosovo was a province of Serbia which the Serbs classified as the 'heartland'. Over the years its population has become predominantly Albanian Muslim and on 17 February, 2008 it proclaimed its independence from Serbia. Serbia did not like this but, as the EU still had forces stationed in the area, there was little they could do about it. The situation is currently a stalemate as around five members of the EU, most notably Spain, will not recognise the independence; nor does the UN. Spain in particular views this as a precedent which it does not want to see followed by its own dissenting provinces.

Time, and promises of other settlements, will allow the problem to be sorted out.

Kosovo does not lie on any of the trade routes so to speak, so inability to go there causes no problem. Whether it is safe to go there or not is uncertain and many nations will not support their passport holders going there. I have not been there and at the moment have no inclination to do so.

Macedonia

The former Yugoslav republic of Macedonia was, like Slovenia, not involved in the fighting between the other states. It has concentrated on building its economy and sees its target of joining the EU as closer than that of Serbia and Kosovo, or even Montenegro. Greece, however, will not countenance the name 'Macedonia' as this is the name of one of its provinces and it wants no misunderstandings. This gives rise to the name FYROM (Former Yugoslav Republic of Macedonia) that is widely used and must annoy the Macedonians. Australia, for one, uses this title and this is probably why (no evidence quoted) Australians were not welcome in FYROM without a pre-purchased visa. In 2009 this anomaly was rectified, probably as a step toward EU assimilation. I really can't comment on FYROM, as I have only seen it and its capital, Skopje, from the train while passing from Beograd to Thessaloniki in Greece.

Albania

Albania spent the years of the Cold War as a communist state, alienated from the USSR and cultivating China. When the barriers came down, Albania remained steadfast and remained aligned only with North Korea, Cuba and few others. Consequently, it was for a long time the poorest country in Europe and is likely to remain so for some time. It has possibly been eclipsed in that regard by Moldova, one of Stalin's creations, which has nothing going for it whatsoever.

Albania's policies on tourists change frequently and the best advice most governments give to their citizens is to stay away. I concur.

Once I met a young fellow coming from Turkey and disembarking in Sofia. 'It is alright for people your age,' he said. 'You remember the conditions in Warsaw, Berlin, Budapest, etc., pre-1990. To find the same conditions today, before they all disappear completely, I am going to Tirana in Albania, the only place like that remaining.' I wished him luck and have no idea how he was going to argue his way past the border police. We had to do those things pre-1990 to see Berlin, Warsaw and so on, and we survived. With his logic, he would next want to go to Pyongyang and I don't think his government would support that.

The Albanian rail system is completely isolated from anywhere else. Train tickets cannot be purchased in advance and are only valid for the next train.

It is reported that Albania has now relaxed its entry requirements and will allow passport holders of some countries, of which Australia is reputed to be one, entry without a pre-purchased visa. This I have yet to test. Thomas Cook shows a bus from Athens, but gives no details.

Through travel

To reach Greece overland from the EU countries of the north, the best route runs through Beograd, although via Bucharest is another possibility. Take the day train from Budapest to Beograd then change to the night train to either Sofia or Thessaloniki. Alternatively, take the day train from Budapest to Beograd and change to the night trains to either Sofia or Thessaloniki. There is a long enough connecting time in Beograd. The same applies in the reverse direction. Once these routes were plied by the fabled *Orient Express*. Today's trains are not as romantic and are not likely to be any more comfortable. The night train into Greece from Beograd has acceptable couchettes, but is still in the pre-WWII train category. Worthy of note, however, is the fact that there are through sleeping cars which continue on the next connecting train via Beograd to Budapest and Vienna.

The Budapest-Beograd-Thessaloniki route has only been available to me without a pre-purchased visa since FYROM liberalised its visa rules and brought them into line with the EU, thus saving 12 hours in not having to go via Sofia. Buying a ticket for the non-Eurail gap between Hungary and Greece is possible in Budapest or Vienna, but if you have the choice, buy in Vienna as the ticket offices there can discuss your needs with you and you can use a credit card, while in Budapest you will have more difficulty. The ticket to Greece should read *Subotica to Gevgeilja*.

Unfortunately with so many railway systems involved, these trains are quite often late and can be hours so in Beograd. Your train simply does not arrive before the appointed departure time of the connecting train. The connecting train receives the whistle from the Fat Controller and sets off on its journey. You are left with up to a 12-hour wait for the next connection, either all day or overnight. Hard luck.

On the first time this happened to me, the train from Sofia arrived too late at night to find any accommodation so I found a carriage in the platform with the heating on which did not leave until morning, curled up in a corner and had a good night's sleep. In the morning I sniffed out the correct train and was on my way.

On the next occasion I was more cunning. I booked a bed on the through sleeper car from Sofia to Budapest and Vienna. This was coming closer to the *Orient Express*. There were three of us in the car, each alone in our own compartment for four, plus the conductor. The first snow of the season came upon us and the train was repeatedly delayed. It was apparent we were not going to reach Beograd in time to be attached to the night train. No worries, explained the conductor in his best Bulgarian, we merely stay overnight and attach to the morning train. So we were shunted into the yard, the door locked, the coal-burning boiler stoked up and we spent a not unpleasant night at someone else's expense. Come morning, we were shunted into the platform, attached to the correct train, still with no dining car and no time to buy breakfast, and headed for Budapest. It really felt as if Hercule Poirot should have been in the next compartment, with Mrs Hubbard in the one beyond. But it was not all over. The car obviously now could not make the round trip to Vienna, so we were offloaded in Budapest to a fast first class train with dining car. What a pity!

More recently I travelled southward to Thessaloniki and had the same routine repeated. This time I had come prepared and had brought sufficient food and drink for the overnight stand. The car was warm, the bed comfortable, and stationary.

The moral of the story is then:

Bring plenty of €5 and €10 notes.
Buy your Serbia/Macedonia (*Subotica to Gevgeilja*) rail ticket in Vienna.
Take enough food and drink to last the journey.
Book on the through sleeping car if one exists.
Be prepared for any delay.
Don't bother with Kosovo or Albania.

All this now is to no avail. In the last few months of 2010 Greece decided, ostensibly as a money saving exercise, to suspend the trains from Thessaloniki to Sarajevo, Sofia and Istanbul. This is hardly surprising, as the Greeks need to save money and the patronage of the trains would not have paid for them. To reach Greece from Austria, it is now necessary to go via Italy and use the ferries.

21. BULGARIA

When I was in primary school in the latter half of the 1940s, we had kids arrive at the school who spoke no English. They were true refugees and we were told that they were *Displaced Persons* and *Bulgarians*. We did not know where Bulgaria was and they probably were not Bulgarians anyway. Our parents called them *dagoes*. Their fathers grew tomatoes and the families lived in conditions which we, even immediately post-war, would not have tolerated. Most of these kids were bigger than we were and we thought they were just big kids. In truth they were under-nourished and small for their size, but a lot older than we were. They had to be, because they had no English and could not be placed further up in the school system. In retrospect, one of the boys would have been shaving when the rest of us were only about ten, but we did not see things like that. They soon learned Australian Rules Football and we beat a lot of the other local schools.

This was my introduction to Bulgaria.

On my first visit to Bulgaria, the train to Sofia was of true Eastern stock and not the most amenable. The sleeper made it acceptable but the pervading smell of urine from the WC could not be forgiven. One luxury was the *en suite* in the compartment. Behind a little door at the side of the washstand was a potty, shaped a little like a household dustpan, with the opening facing down. Once you used the potty, you replaced it in the holder and the contents went straight down onto the track. The communal WC at the end of the carriage had the same type of disposal.

In the days before welded rail, books described the noise of trains as 'clicketty clack'; this being caused by the fact that the expansion joints in the two rails were offset and the wheels met the gaps out of phase to make the traditional sound. Some still make this noise. Welded rails, as installed today, have no expansion joints and are held under tension and thus there is no 'clicketty clack'. It is said that if the tension was relaxed on the Alice Springs to Darwin continuous welded rail, it would extend 2.5km into Darwin harbour on a hot day. The Russians, however, place their expansion joints differently and have the gaps in phase so that the motion of the train is more like 'ka thump' as both wheels cross the gap at the same time. Well, the Bulgarians do the same; the train leaves Serbia with a 'clicketty clack' and one wakes up in Bulgaria to a 'ka thump'. The noise disappears into the subconscious after a short while, but is ever-present.

Arrival in Sofia for the first time was more of a shock than at any other place I have been in Europe. Bulgaria, like Serbia and Russia, uses Cyrillic script, which was put together by St Cyril centuries ago. Not being content to use Latin script, nor Greek script, Cyril came up with a hybrid compromise, which is relatively easy to read after a little thought but a horror for the uninitiated. The court of the Tsars in St Petersburg spoke French, while Russian with Cyrillic script was the language of the plebs, so Russian remained a very simple language with not a huge vocabulary. After the revolution in 1917, Russian became universally spoken and written, of course, and the growth of the language brought with it the adoption of words from English and French, in large quantities. Almost all non-simple words and almost all names in Russian are adapted from one of these languages, but in Cyrillic script. Making your way around Moscow is a cinch. 'PECTOPAN' is obviously 'restaurant', and so on. Not so in Sofia, where the language has grown at its own pace and Bulgarian words are what they are: Bulgarian words. My time in Russia in the past was enough to allow me to translate the Cyrillic script, but not to do so quickly enough to be either comfortable or communicative. But the Bulgarian words were meaningless when written in Latin script. Why would a Bulgarian speak English? English would be about as useful to a post WWII Bulgarian as Bulgarian might be to an Australian.

My first reaction in Sofia railway station was to seek the first train out but, once the fear of the unknown disappeared, it became easier. Everything was written in Cyrillic characters but furthermore unrecognisable. Nobody spoke English; there was always someone in Greece or Serbia or Romania, but not here. The arrangement of the departure boards was such that nothing appeared to make sense and I almost despaired. I had no idea which way the city centre was, nor how to reach it. I stood in the middle of the concourse, now nearly deserted, and gazed at the unintelligible departure board. Eventually a local materialised and asked me, in good English, whether I was in trouble. I explained my problem and he pointed out that it was all easy. You are going tonight to Thessaloniki, which is obviously Slonik, Σλονικ, is it not? There was my train marked Σλονικ and that was the train for Thessaloniki, quite simple. Of course it was, especially when I recognised that the appended time was the one on my travel plan. 'That will be €2, please.' Of course, I was happy to pay him, but here was my first example of exploitation by the Bulgarians. I was to see many more incidents. One contact explained that the Bulgarians were essentially honest and would hand back your wallet if you dropped it, but they would take any opportunity to have you extract some of that money and place it in their hands.

One piece of advice I can offer here. If you are about to embark on travel in Europe, don't waste your time learning a few words of another language to use on someone who already speaks English, but **learn the Cyrillic and Greek characters** so that you can read the signs in Bulgaria, Russia, Serbia, Macedonia and Greece.

Eventually it came to me that the young lady in the Avis office must speak English, and she was happy to explain to me where we were in relation to the city, how to buy a day pass and how to catch a tram. I could not remember that now, but if I were placed in that situation again, most would come back to me and I would know whom to ask.

Bulgaria joined the EU along with Romania in 2007, in what some still believe was premature action and certainly unwise. The management of the Bulgarian economy is still under question and corruption is alleged to be rife.

Sofia is a beautiful city without a doubt and contains monuments of considerable importance. The St Alexander Nevski church, for instance, built to commemorate those who fell liberating Bulgaria from the Ottomans in 1820 or so, is one of the more exciting Eastern Orthodox churches to be seen. I spent a full day in Sofia, sitting in cafés, drinking coke and wandering off to the various sites in the guidebook as the mood took me. For me, this is very unusual as I usually run from place to place to see as much as possible, regardless of its importance.

So I returned to the station to find my train to Σλονικ and so on to Greece.

On another occasion in Sofia I had no onward booking and, as it was already after dinner, the booking office had passed the manifest for the train on to the conductor, so I should try there. €9 was the quoted price. I tried banging on the door of the sleeping coach but the conductor was not wanting to hear me. Ultimately a security guard, with no English, took pity on me, banged much more determinedly and confronted the conductor on my behalf with much more confidence than I would have had. Yes, he had a berth at €12 and I should come back in ten minutes, all by arm waving of course. Such was the bargain struck and after the allotted ten minutes I returned, alone now of course, to be told €15. Well, he had the ticket in his hand, so I presented him with a €20 note, was given the ticket and the conversation was over. You have the ticket so go away, was the attitude. Once in the compartment a man comes in demanding €10 from each berth, arms waving and a lot of noise. Once more €20 was produced and he was gone. Later I saw him on the platform with a colleague counting his ill-gotten cash. That berth cost me €40 instead of the prescribed €9. This is, of course, still exceptionally cheap and €40 is much nearer the real value to me. It does confirm my entreaty to carry lots of €5 and €10 notes.

In the bottom end of the Balkans, the carriages look familiar even though they are painted in the colours of the respective railway companies. Only on closer inspection will you find 'DR' in irremovable places, such as etched into the mirrors, indicating that these were once cars of the DR, the old East German railways, the *Deutsche Reichsbahn,* and passed on by the new regime in favour of newer and more hygienically conforming trains through DB, the *Deutsche Bahn.*

Another entry to Sofia and on to Greece, other than via Beograd, is from Bucharest in Romania. This is also a very long way and will require an extra night from Budapest to Bucharest. It has the advantage, however, of being entirely in global Eurail pass countries and requires no train tickets. Ultimately, when Bulgaria and Romania implement the Schengen Treaty, the journey will be able to be made without producing a passport. The saving from this route is given away in the extra overnight journey. Of course, if you were out to save money or time in going to Greece, you would never come this way but go instead via Italy.

To do something different, I diverted through Varna on the Black Sea coast of Bulgaria. It is a fairly daunting experience to climb off a train with a known destination at a small town in provincial Bulgaria, where the signs and language are anything but reassuring, to take a train to a relatively unknown destination even further from home.

Varna proved to be a very clean coastal city, a fairly strategic one at that, with a much more modern and more prosperous feeling about it than Sofia. After a brief excursion about the city, the onward journey to Sofia was quite simple.

From Sofia the train can take you on to Thessaloniki either overnight or by day, in my case preferably overnight. This allows a full day in Sofia flanked by two night sleepers, which, at that price, are no problem. Note, however, that the train service no longer operates.

My main thoughts related to those who joined my class in Grade Six in 1949 and who were displaced persons, *dagoes*, from Bulgaria. In particular I think of Victor, who is now a reputable and upstanding Australian citizen. They, like the Italian immigrants of those days, became good Australian citizens and Australia learned much from having them join us.

22. TURKEY

A speaker once explained to his audience that no-one was wrong about the way they behaved, it purely depended on the point of view. He showed a slide of an old Muslim couple sitting on a park bench. He was in black robes and sported a long white beard, similar to the prophet. She was also in black, wearing a burka and headscarf. But look more closely. He was pounding away sending text on his cell-phone and wearing trendy sneakers and she carried a Gucci handbag and was wearing name-brand shoes.

Then the speaker showed a photo of a couple of teenagers dressed in T-shirt and jeans with reverse baseball caps and a hoodie over that. The boys are passing a Muslim lady in black with burka and saying, 'Gee, some people wear weird outfits, don't they?'

Roman Catholic nuns of no more than 50 years ago, and some elderly ones today, wore mediaeval dress and were likened to penguins. One order was called the 'Flying Nuns' because of their head-dress (hardly a hat). This we all accepted. Even today the young men who are Mormon missionaries wear the white shirt with tie and black trousers of the 1960s, and stand out in a crowd. Now we are confronted with another style of dress coming from a different religion which we do not understand, and some folk are militant about it.

We accept Christian church spires, but they question minarets. We tolerate church bells ringing at all hours, but they object to a Muslim call to prayer.

It all depends on your point of view.

Istanbul demonstrates this to anyone who has not been exposed to this way of life before.

Kemal Attaturk, back in the 1930s, was determined not to have Turkey left out of this universe and carried out, imposed would be a better word, a series of reforms to come closer to the West. As an example, the Turks moved in one fell swoop to use Latin script rather than Arabic. This meant that seven million people were not able to read the morning paper on the first day of the change. Such changes make our small changes to metric measurement and decimal currency appear trivial. In Turkey, at least in Istanbul, the women wear what is decidedly Muslim dress, there are very few women with their faces covered, certainly in the city, and quite a few without the scarf. Some even wear complete Western clothing. Christian worship is allowed in Turkey and many of the confiscated Christian churches of the past have been returned to them.

Turkey applied to join the EU as far back as 1987, but progress in reaching its membership has been very slow. Its record on civil rights, particularly in regard to the Kurds, has not been good. Turkey's population is large and its entry would cause a big shift in the demography of the EU; greater perhaps than when the last 12 were admitted, but certainly far greater than the change which might follow if any of the six 'Western Balkan' nations were to join. Turkey has boundaries with Iran and Iraq, which must frighten anyone. Finally, when the referendum on the EU constitution was lost by the citizenry of France and The Netherlands voting an overwhelming 'Non', the chief suspect for the decision was the potential admission of Turkey to the EU.

On crossing the Turkish border by train, and supposedly by road, one can be forgiven for believing that the rules of Europe are far in the distance. They are not all that distant because many EU countries of today once had border checks far more exhausting than this.

For Istanbul, direct trains come once daily from Thessaloniki, Sofia and Bucharest. The train arrives at the border in the middle of the night, whether from Greece or Bulgaria. Everyone is told to bring their passports and report to the immigration office. To do this means crossing the platform, climbing down onto the tracks and climbing once more back to the platform to enter the office. This is an activity which is forbidden anywhere else in Europe in more languages than one can count. On arrival inside the office, everyone lines up. Locals are admitted with the usual identification card, those from the EU and chosen nations (probably including the US) receive a stamp in the passport, while those from heretic nations like Australia are simply told 'visa' and dismissed. This means a 100 metre trek to the other end of the platform to wake a sleeping visa official who makes you fill out the appropriate forms, relieves you of €15 and adheres a visa the size of a postage stamp. Notice that this is in Euro, many other nations want their own currency. Now you must go back to the first line and go around again. When all are settled and everyone has climbed back over the tracks, the officials, another group perhaps, go through the train and check all passports.

It could be worse. *To enter Turkey is not anywhere near as difficult as entering the United States.*

The train arrives at the Istanbul railway station, which was once the terminus of the legendary *Orient Express*. Nearby you can see the hotel where Agatha Christie is alleged to have stayed while she wrote about the murder. When the last traditional *Orient Express* ran, about 30 years ago but from Paris only, railway buffs from all over the world assembled for the final run, expecting all of the splendour. They were greeted with a miscellany of assorted carriages very much out of keeping. Naturally, none of the railway companies of the West were going to send their good cars on the last journey with little chance of ever seeing them come back. The old train has long since disappeared but there is a private luxury train made up of the vintage cars, called the *Venice Simplon Orient Express* which ventures from London every few weeks and takes passengers to Venezia through the Alps for an enormous sum.

It was interesting to watch the progress of the tour groups, whether from the cruise ships or otherwise. The participants are herded from museum to mosque to cathedral. The locations that are shown to them are indeed worthy of the trip to Istanbul, the greatest of these being the Blue Mosque. Finally they are taken to the inevitable carpet emporium and the greatest display of carpets of all time is revealed unto them; all they need is a credit card of the right proportions. To carry a large carpet around on trains was hardly appropriate, so this did not interest me.

The escape was then to the Grand Bazaar, which really does live up to its name. Once it must have sold everything to anyone but now it concentrates on selling the inevitable junk to the tourist.

Many tourists, particularly from Australia and New Zealand, make the trek down the coast, the tour companies being anxious to help, to ANZAC Cove, the scene of that military tragedy on 25 April, 1915.

Sunset over the Bosporus from a high vantage point is a delight, with all of the floodlit mosques and public buildings slowly coming into view. The wailing of the Imams at prayer time can be heard very clearly, beginning as each gauges the time to be sunset.

Once the Imam had to climb the minaret for each prayer. Then he discovered the virtue of what the British would call the 'tannoy' and called into the microphone. Next he moved to recorded sound which made the task much easier for him. Today the whole system is probably computerised with the times preset and the sound from the best recording available. It does reduce the value of the whole issue. One wonders whether the Roman Catholic alternative would be to have a common sermon from the Pope broadcast concurrently in every church in the realm each Sunday morning.

According to one theory, the Black Sea was once not connected to the Mediterranean and was a landlocked sea, about 200 metres below the level of the Mediterranean, receiving fresh water from the huge rivers that flow in from the north. Marine deposits at this level show this clearly. Ultimately, and there is always an ultimately, the seas broke through with, as you can imagine, a great rush, and the inhabitants of the lower shores would have seen this as a flood to end all floods. Only the ready were able to be saved. One of these was our friend, Noah, with his wife, his sons and their wives, and whatever animals he managed to collect. He had a well prepared, seaworthy craft which was called an 'ark'. It is often asked where Noah's daughters were. They, of course, lived elsewhere with their husbands. Old Noah would have had a rough time for those 40 days and nights, the expression in those days, for 'a long time', in these waters, but eventually he came on shore, much higher up than he had left (200 metres we said) and, to him, on the side of a mountain, not far from Mt Ararat. It may have been so!

There is a road bridge across the Bosporus linking Europe with Asia. A railway tunnel is planned, but so are a lot of things in this type of economy. It is easy to locate the ferry across the Bosporus to the Asian side. This is where the toffs of Istanbul live and has no natural or other beauty, except for the view across to the old city, and the ships, on the European side. That makes the trip worthwhile.

Near the ferry on the Asian side is the quite substantial railway station of Haydarpasa, with track and trains leading across Turkey and perhaps beyond. This would be a new world to a Eurail pass user.

Thomas Cook has tables giving times on the line east from Haydarpasa. This gives me reason for contemplating an out-and-back trip to Ankara. The furthest destination is Teheran and that is *not* under consideration.

Many of my friends and family have visited Anatolia, that part of Turkey on the Asian side, and most have stated that they enjoyed it. Many of the locations unfortunately only reproduce what can be found on the Greek Islands and do nothing to introduce one to the local customs, culture and history.

My only incursion into Anatolia was to Ephesus on the Mediterranean Levant coast. St Paul resided in Ephesus for about three months, but he eventually found it necessary to move on due to the fact that the local manufacturers of graven images were losing business and putting pressure on him. Apparently St John wrote his gospel in Ephesus and his church still stands, with four new handles and three new heads. Even more, apparently St John brought Mary, the mother of Jesus, with him and she lived her last days in a house on the hill. The 'proof' of the latter is that a lady in Germany dreamed of the location of this house, told them where to look, and behold, they found it. Proof or not, the Roman Church subscribes to the idea and the tourist potential of the area has risen because of it. Ephesus was once a port, but the meanderings of rivers and the lifting of the land has left it many kilometres inland and the arrival location of the cruise ships is now at Kusadasi, a rather modern port on the Mediterranean.

The old town of Ephesus was unearthed a few years ago, and the result of extensive diggings gives an amazing picture of the way people lived over 2,000 years ago. Progress is slow and one estimate is that at present rate of progress, the job will be finished in 750 years. The area in general is very hot indeed, but the tramp around in the heat is well worth the effort. Our guide was very careful to show us the markings in one street which indicated, in a simple code, the direction to the brothel. The obscured rectangle at the bottom, she had been told, once contained the phone numbers of the ladies. Not so, she said. She preferred to believe that it was a simple signal to indicate that the establishment accepted American Express. Of course in this city we once had the Temple of Artemis, one of the seven ancient wonders of the world. Reference to the other wonders is in the chapter on the Greek islands.

Hornblower also visited the coast of Anatolia, searching for lost gold in a shipwreck. Of course, being fictional, he found it.

23. GREECE

When Greece joined the EU back in 1999, my thoughts were that the EU was diluting its standards. Perhaps they were at the time, but the expanded market, coming from the addition of Greece and countries of the same size, has brought greater prosperity to the EU but mainly to the added countries.

Put in simple terms, before those days the Greeks managed their own currency, the drachma, and if they overspent they merely devalued the drachma. Their creditors were furious but they accepted that this was part of the risk taken.

Then Greece applied to, and was allowed to join, the Eurozone. The Greek currency is now fixed to that of the major nations of Europe. In household terms, Greece began writing cheques without filling in the butts and life was great. If there was a problem, borrow a bit more and keep going.

Then in 2009 the boom dropped. Money became tight and Mr Moody and Messrs Standard and Poors decreed that Greece was in trouble. Germany came to their rescue and stood behind them, but not before some rather stringent conditions had been placed on the Greeks which they are not enjoying. They were told to take the scissors to their credit cards and to pay cash.

Of course, most of the changes required should have been part of the Greek agenda years ago and involve stemming corruption, tidying up trade practices, throwing out unreasonable union agreements, selling state assets and so on. The Greek government has taken on the task with diligence, even if not with enthusiasm, and it should all work out.

The Greeks are not alone. The same problem happened in the Baltic States, but they have found enough friends to avoid a crisis. Estonia has managed to persuade Brussels that its finances are in such good shape that it has been admitted to the Eurozone.

The next to topple were the Irish and very large sums of money are needed and will probably be found. No-one likes to see the Irish hurt. As a result, the population voted for a change in government and the new leaders will have a large task on their hands. Of course Iceland actually fell off the shelf, as it did not have the EU as a buffer. The Icelanders are now hell-bent on securing membership of the EU before the tide goes out completely. Portugal followed, and is hopefully the last.

***

One can reach Greece from the north, from Turkey, Bulgaria or Macedonia, coming by train into Thessaloniki, or from the south and west from Italy. We will arrive by the former and leave by the latter, remembering that the train service is currently suspended.

There is generally not time to venture far from the station in Thessaloniki, even with a very early morning arrival. Thessaloniki is the second largest city in Greece after Athens but apparently stands behind Melbourne in the size of its Greek community. Doubtless there is an attractive city to be seen, but if you are only changing trains the area around the railway station looks as bad as any you have seen, so we let that one pass.

The Greeks are upgrading and electrifying the main railway from Thessaloniki to Athens but the progress is very slow. Electrification is not effective until the last kilometre of wire is in place and that is a long way off. It is most likely that this project will be halted or at least slowed by Greece's monetary problems, so it could be a long time before the first electric train from Athens rolls into Thessaloniki.

The Greek trains are quite good and they make you feel better by giving you a seat reservation at no charge and, as I found in Thessaloniki, with a smile. That is a good start. Their overnight sleepers are inexpensive; I was given one for €20.

After a comfortable but seemingly endless journey, the train arrives at Athens Larissa, the central station for Athens, which is a few stops on the subway from any of the main sites. Across the road is the Ariston Hotel, a simple, clean and inexpensive hotel. If the Ariston is full, they will find a bed for you elsewhere.

The map of the Athens suburban rail system makes it look very extensive until you read the legend and find that towards one half of it is 'proposed (funds allocated)' and much of the remainder 'under construction'. Even so, the system is a good one and very cheap. A day ticket will take you anywhere you wish to go in Athens. Beware that the green line is not operational (2011) between Monastiraki and Attiki.

For your first vista of Athens, the first call is definitely the Acropolis.

The subway, red line, will take you directly to Akropoli for the Acropolis, high above Athens. After a short walk, an admission fee and lots of steps, you are in one of the most amazing ancient monuments of this world. The Greeks are endeavouring to restore the main building and have quite sensible plans in hand. They have two problems. The first is that the atmosphere of Athens, which is every bit as bad as claimed, will reduce the stone to rubble before the restoration can be completed. The second is that huge pieces of the construction lie in the British Museum, taken there by Lord Elgin, British ambassador to Greece, over 100 years ago. Of course, these are the best bits and the Greeks know precisely what the Brits have and where. Tony Blair promised to give them back but one cannot see the ancient custodians of the British Museum being enthusiastic about giving back their priceless collection of Elgin Marbles.

After you have done your time there, you will have been acquainted by chit-chat with all the other fabulous, in the true meaning of the word, sights of antiquity available in Athens and will plan your journeys accordingly. The main squares of Athens, which are written into in everyone's novel about Athens, are Omonia and Syntagma, both on the red line. You have not been to Athens until you have seen both. For a Greek meal, check out the restaurants and cafes around Monastiraki. My guess is that they could not be beaten in quality. Remember that the Greeks eat very late.

Most of us have heard at some time of the legendary monasteries somewhere, where women were forbidden with such enthusiasm that they would not even keep chickens or cows. These monasteries do exist, although perhaps not as extreme as is suggested, and the best examples are at Meteora in the centre of Greece. The word Meteora has nothing to do with meteor. Take a train from Athens heading for Kalambaka and you are in the right area. Most visitors to the area must come by coach or car, as there was nothing at

Kalambaka station when I arrived, so I contracted the only available taxi to take me to Meteora for a few tens of Euros.

The first source of amazement is the geology of the area. The drive was hair-raising but the view unforgettable. Huge pillars of rock stand between cliff faces of the same height, defying anyone to climb them. This, indeed, is why these monasteries are secure, because they have been built on the tops of these pillars and are only then accessible with the assistance of those at the top. These places are absolutely impregnable and hence have remained in place for centuries. Some of the more resourceful ones, however, have recognised the value of today's tourist market and have invested in bridges and catwalks which allow those with money to enter and inspect the residences of the faithful. These must be the more broadminded, as women tourists are permitted. The monasteries were, naturally, of Orthodox faith but usually far stronger. The old ways of the Orthodox Church are made very clear. This did not stop one of the priests from driving away in his Mercedes in front of us.

Place Meteora on your list of places to visit. There are not many places in Europe more difficult to reach.

Don't be misled by thinking that the small gap on the map between Kalambaka and Igoumenitsa on the coast may be easily traversed. The distance is not small but, above all, the terrain is extremely harsh and mountainous. Thomas Cook, prompted by yours truly, tells us that 'an irregular bus service exists to Igoumenitsa'. The journey to Igoumenitsa takes six hours to cover the 250 kilometres from Kalambaka via Ioannina. This journey was revealing, because it gave some idea of the money being spent, presumably by the EU, to open up the road from the port of Igoumenitsa to Thessaloniki and northern Greece, and thence on to Bulgaria and Macedonia. It also showed how mountainous and rugged was this section of Greece.

North of the Gulf of Corinth, that long strip of water with an estuary-like appearance on the map, is the area of Parnassos. To reach this area, one must take a bus from the second of the Athens bus stations located to the north of Attiki underground, about 30 minutes easy walk. The trip to Delphi and Itea is well described by Mary Stewart in her book, *My Brother Michael*.

Delphi comes first, the home of the legendary Oracle of Delphi who predicted so many of the tragedies of the ancient world, analysed after the act, of course. Not to be missed are the theatre with its amazing acoustics, and *The Charioteer* (474 BC) in the Delphi Archeological Museum. Visitors to Delphi must come by tour group because there were very few itinerants on our bus, but lots of coaches parked nearby. A little further along the road is Itea, generally the terminus of the bus and an important port for the area. The promenade abounds with cafés filled with men drinking coffee or the local liquor. They are obviously content with leaving the work at home to Mother.

To reach my destination, a further bus ride of perhaps 30 minutes was required.

Galaxidi, which sounds something like Galack-city, is a one-time important fishing port but now the houses are mainly in the possession of absentee owners as summertime residents.

My first experience here was with the family in the cooler part on 1982, when the fisher-folk still plied their duties. Almost every morning there would be one such person pounding an octopus on the concrete of the dock. An English Australian colleague, known locally as Mr Rex, had bought a cottage there and was happy to lend it to any of his friends. It had once been a fisherman's cottage with the front door opening on to the water, Venetian-style, but the local city fathers had since built a promenade along the dockside. He alleges that he paid £1,100 for the house. The water coming from the taps was very little different from that in the sea out front, but one could buy drums of clean (?) water from the truck which visited irregularly. Mr Rex was still there when I called in 2010, spending a Greek summer as usual in preference to an Australian winter. He estimates that the house is now worth £500,000. Mr Rex still speaks no Greek and was, at that time, 89 years of age.

The Gulf of Corinth is separated from the Aegean Sea by a narrow neck of land with the ancient name of Isthmus, a word that has been carried into our language today. The Corinth Canal has been cut through this isthmus and allows shipping to reach Piraeus, the port of Athens, without going around the Peloponnese peninsular. In contrast to the Kiel Canal in north Germany, or the Noordzeekanaal in Amsterdam, the Corinth Canal was cut through solid rock but the Greeks have had a few more centuries to build it.

On one occasion, many years ago, I took a complete trip around the narrow gauge loop of the Peloponnese. This passes by Mt Olympus, which I must revisit someday while the line still exists. This is a worthwhile journey for the adventurous.

One could pause here in Piraeus and take trips to the Greek islands of the Aegean, to Crete and to Cyprus. These journeys can be found in the next chapter.

Patras is the departure point by ship for Italy. The ferry companies provide a bus connection from Athens with an appropriate charge.

The train service to Patras, on the new standard gauge link, starts with a modern clockface departure from Athens, crossing the isthmus and on to Kiato. From Kiato as far as Diakofto (50 minutes) the line is being 'converted to standard gauge', but the sad part of the story is that parts of the track are lifted and nothing is being done; so this leg must be by bus. A narrow gauge, loco-hauled, graffiti-covered, slow, non-air-conditioned train once completed the journey to Patras, but it appears that the whole journey from Kiato may now be by bus. Since this link is a key to access from Athens to the Adriatic Sea, its lot is to be completed, but perhaps Greece is waiting for EU money.

A noticeable feature is the bridge across the Gulf of Corinth from Rio, on the Peloponnese side, to Anti-Rio, on the north, Parnassos, side. This gives the Gulf of Corinth a road across each end and shipping access from both ends.

In Patras the Eurail pass holder only needs to walk into the *Superfast* office across the road and along from the station to be issued with a free passage to Ancona, departing at 1430, port taxes, about €15, not included. The second class pass holder sits in sleeper chairs, first class in a designated berth in the dormitory at no extra charge. *Superfast XI* and *Superfast XII* are car-carrying ferries of about 30,000 tonnes. This is about the same size as the ships that brought all those migrants to Australia in the late 1940s. They ply the Adriatic on a daily schedule like a railway train, similar to the ferries in the Baltic. One of the sights to be seen on this ferry is the loading at Igoumenitsa, around dark. In 30 minutes, from touching the dock until leaving it, I saw about 25 articulated trucks and about 50 cars driven onto the ferry; that is between two and three vehicles a minute, almost faster than city traffic. Within a few minutes of us pulling away, the last of the cars and pedestrians had left the dock which was now in darkness. Igoumenitsa? Where?

When Heather and the boys were with me on the old shipping line in 1982, they gave us aircraft-type seats in an old tub which should have long been on the scrap heap. It still had to do the same job as the new ships do today. In the washrooms there were 'sinks' with water continually swirling like the basin you have next to the dentist chair. 'Spit, please.' In the middle of the night when a storm hit, it became obvious why they were there. A woman never leaves her handbag behind for anything, but Heather did in her rush to the washroom.

After partaking of three substantial and relatively inexpensive meals on this Greek ship, you are now free to think Italian.

24. THE GREEK ISLANDS

Before leaving Greece, it is customary to visit a sample of the islands. Here Thomas Cook devotes a whole volume on 'Greek Island Hopping'. Needless to say there are no trains to or on these islands.

Cyprus, while not being part of Greece, is included here and can be reached by a once weekly ferry, but taking two or three days. This country, like Iceland, is going to require an air ticket.

Ferries to anywhere can be found in Piraeus, the port of Athens, about 30 minutes away by train or Metro.

Mykonos

One of the nearer islands is the island of Mykonos. One can spend a day wandering around the principal town to see how exaggerated the tourist brochures are.

At the end of a day's walking someone offered us motor scooters at ONE Euro (€1) per day. This would have changed our feelings about the island. These guys are smart enough. You have to leave your passport as deposit and there is very little you can do to hurt a motor scooter on their island, short of dropping it into the sea. Since you want your passport back, you are not about to do that.

As I have said elsewhere, I am past the time when I wanted to imitate a lobster in front of countless others doing the same nor am I a partaker of the nightlife, so the island does not hold much attraction for me.

The principal inhabitant of Mykonos is Petros the pelican, who has full rights of the esplanade and foreshore, and knows it. If he does not want his photo taken with you, then he won't let you. There has been a Petros on Mykonos for over 50 years.

Rhodos

There are seven recognised wonders of the ancient world, all but one long since destroyed:

Two in Greece: The statue of Zeus at Olympia and The Colossus of Rhodes
Two in Iraq: The Hanging Gardens of Babylon and The Mausoleum of Maussollos at Halicarnassus
Two in Egypt: The Great Pyramid of Giza and The Lighthouse of Alexandria
One in Turkey: The Temple of Artemis at Ephesus

The Colossus of Rhodes was a bronze statue of a warrior, standing 33 metres high, with a foot apparently on each side of the harbour mouth. He was brought down by an earthquake in 226 BC, lost for ever, and can never be rebuilt as it is said that it would bring bad luck to the populace. They don't seem to have had much good luck in this part of the world over the centuries, so maybe they could try some bad.

After the Knights Templar were kicked out of Jerusalem, they wandered about a bit until they finally made their home here on Rhodes in 1309. After a couple of hundred years, they were kicked out of Rhodes in 1522 and made their way to Malta.

The Ottoman Empire of the Turks collapsed over the last part of the nineteenth century and Turkey gained its independence as 'one of those Middle Eastern countries'. The Turks had the misfortune to choose the wrong side to support in WWI and, after the war, were reallocated their boundaries by the victorious Allies. Accordingly, all of the islands in the Aegean Sea, right up to the Turkish coast, including Rhodos, became part of Greece, who had sided with the winners. Is it any wonder that the Turks are not good mates with the Greeks?

Given the above, Rhodos is a pleasant place to visit.

Santorini

To the geologist or vulcanologist, or even a physicist, Santorini is the gem of the islands.

Santorini is one of a part circle of islands, about 10km across, with a bare, black island in the middle of the circle. The island of Santorini is a ridge with very steep sides of about 500 metres, with the towns on the top like icing on a slice of cake. This is all very straightforward if you do not consider the geology of the situation which shows that the Santorini group is a huge volcanic crater, not all of it above sea level, with a volcanic mound in the centre which is still active, but dormant at the moment. Krakatoa, in Indonesia, gave us the world's biggest recorded natural explosion, back in the 1880s. It is claimed that two cubic miles, four cubic kilometres, of seawater broke into the crater of Krakatoa and were instantly vapourised. James Watt could have revelled in the explanation of the amount of mechanical energy that would become available as that water vapour expanded. Several hundred years BC the same happened to Santorini except that twenty cubic miles of seawater were evaporated, a factor of ten greater. It must have been some bang. The resulting tsunamis in the Mediterranean, which would have bounced around in the enclosed seas for weeks like waves in your bathtub, would have made the more recent events in Indonesia and Japan look like a small splash. At about this time the Minoans were enjoying their supremacy on the northern coast of Crete. For some reason the entire Minoan civilisation disappeared, almost instantly. It is possible that Santorini was the villain and that the Minoans were wiped out by a tsunami of unprecedented proportions. A small Minoan community actually lived on Santorini. Excavations show that the village was abandoned and not a soul remained. This would indicate that there was some warning and the locals did not die in their beds, but died just as thoroughly.

The principal feature of Santorini, after the geology, is that the houses are all white with a secondary blue motif. Apparently during the Nazi occupation, Hitler forbade the flying of the Greek flag. The locals accepted this, but instead painted their houses in the Greek white and blue.

To reach the principal town of Santorini it is necessary to climb, from the harbour, up a ramp which takes you up over 500 steps. This is a steep walk by anyone's standards. Donkeys can be hired to carry you to the top at a modest fee. Never forget the skill of the local entrepreneur. The alternative is a rather steep cable car from the same point. The coach tours, of course, go up by a roundabout way. It is possible to hire a car on the island for around €50 for the day but you are warned by the proprietor that, since most of the drivers on the island are tourists, driving on the island is very dangerous!

Crete

Crete is an integral part of Greece, but has an interesting history of its own. Stories of banditry abound, but in general the island is made up of local people going about their day's work and minding their own business.

Crete is quite a way off from Athens and requires a night ferry from Piraeus to Iraklio. Since it is a bigger island, more time needs to be spent there than on the traditional Greek islands.

Mary Stewart explains the logic of the island well in her book, *The Moon Spinners*.

Having stayed three days and hired a car, I can claim to have seen a little of the island, having driven from the western to the eastern extremities.

One factor remains in my mind more than anything else. The beaches are beautiful and unpopulated. They are, however, littered with rubbish, mainly of the plastic variety, which has been washed up by the sea. Apparently another 'sink' for this type of non-biodegradable junk is in the centre of one of the circulation patterns in the Pacific Ocean. Doubtless there is less junk per cubic metre than in the seas around Crete, but the effect is the same.

These two features alone are very poor reflections on the way in which we are caring for our planet.

Cyprus

Cyprus came under British 'protection' in 1914 and remained a protectorate/dependency/colony until 1960, when it was granted its independence. Very little evidence of British rule remains except for one factor. In Cyprus they drive on the left. This is to be compared with Malta, which received its independence at around the same time and still retains the British atmosphere.

After independence the nation was attacked (the use of the word depends on the point of view) by the Turks, who set up the independent republic of northern Cyprus, which is recognised by no-one but Turkey. For many years the boundary, which runs through the capital, Nicosia, was a wall, copied no doubt from Berlin, with the UN guarding the peace. Ultimately the boundary was opened, at least to the locals, and replaced by the 'Green Line' which is administered by the UN. From within Nicosia it is possible to see the large and high Turkish flags on the other side of the line, and assuredly the Turks will describe the converse. Crossing the line is not likely to be a simple matter without a Cypriot, or at least an EU, passport or identity card.

Cyprus joined the EU in 2004 and signed the Schengen Treaty in 2007 but the latter has not been able to be implemented, due firstly to the Turkish 'occupation' and secondly due to the presence of British 'Sovereign Bases' on the island. The lease of a base on foreign territory one can understand but these bases are British sovereign territory and seem to have as much right to be there as the US in the base at Guantanamo in Cuba.

The nation of Cyprus is not part of Greece, although one can be forgiven for thinking so. There are more Greek flags to be seen here than in Greece, and very rarely a Cypriot flag. Much of the expensive property in Cyprus is owned by the wealthy Greek absentee landlord who uses this as his holiday resort.

Flying from Athens is very simple, as the mainline railway can take you to the airport. It is only when on the flight that you realise how far Cyprus is from the rest of the EU.

As in Crete, I spent three days in a hire car driving around Cyprus. This took me from the airport at Larnaca to Agios Georgios at the western end of the island, through the mountains in the centre and to Cape Greko at the eastern end. This gave me time to wander about both the old town of Nicosia and the modern sector. All of the city is dominated by the presence of the huge Turkish flag in the distance.

Corfu, *Kėkira*

Alone of the islands discussed here, Corfu is in the Adriatic Sea on the western side of Greece. The ferry will not take passengers between Patras and Igoumenitsa, hence a bus to Igoumenitsa is necessary and I chose the route from Kalambaka via Ioannina. A bus from Patras would make more sense.

Ferries to Corfu leave frequently from Igoumenitsa and I then made the best of a two-day stay by hiring a car and driving to each end of the island. Once more, Mary Stewart in *This Rough Magic* gives a good account, if somewhat idealised, of the island. Perhaps it was the island of Shakespeare's *Tempest,* but who is to know?

From Igoumenitsa, the daily ferry will take you to Ancona in Italy.

25. VENICE, VENEZIA

Mama, I spent six hours in Venice and could not get out quickly enough; it was dirty, smelly, hard to move around, crowds of tourists and very expensive.

***

Mama, I spent six days in Venezia and could have stayed longer.

***

The second speaker was able to see below the surface and glimpse the soul of Venezia. Of course, Venice is all of the things noticed by the first speaker, but they are only superficial; below them is the real Venezia.

Venezia has more unique qualities than any other city in the world. Cities of the world can be classified into two: Venezia and all the others. To recognise this you must spend time in Venezia, and you will not regret it.

Venezia is thus a good place to begin a tour of the major sights of Italy.

Trains arrive first of all at Venezia Mestre, which is on the mainland. Don't leave the train there. The industry and commerce of Venezia is centred here, and that you can find anywhere. The train continues forward and crosses the lagoon to Venezia Santa Lucia, the terminal station.

Arrive early in the morning in Venezia, or start your day from your lodgings equally early, around 0600.

Crossing the causeway you will see the extent of the lagoon, very shallow and surrounded by flat countryside. The road crosses alongside but goes no further than the train, to an enormous, expensive parking lot with a bus station. If you are only on a day visit then dump your bag at the baggage room, *bagaglia*, at Santa Lucia, then check your departure time before you walk away from the station. Since the fast train out requires reservations, it might pay to secure them now at about €10 a seat. If you are staying overnight, you will find a collection of non-spectacular hotels near the station.

Venetian history began in the fifth century AD and survived because it was isolated, in the middle of a shallow lagoon, and placed so that any attempts at an invasion could easily be detected and quelled.

The first settlers would have found a high point, dug some mud from the lagoon and built on it. Their neighbours would have done the same until ultimately a string of islands, now seen as one island, would have been built up, separated by numerous canals and all at a large distance from the land. Their existence would have depended on boats, later ships, and Venezia was born.

From this humble beginning developed one of the greatest trading nations the Mediterranean has ever seen.

With an early start you have plenty of time to amble through the lanes of Venezia to San Marco Square. As you leave the *Ferrovia*, the railway station, take note of the sign saying *per Rialto*, the Rialto Bridge. You have no need to follow the signs always, nor for any haste, just keep that direction in mind. Wander as you wish, head for the food markets, the fish markets, the small residences. Arrive at a dead-end, staring at only water. This is Venezia.

Most of the food shops do not open until about 0800, so you may need to wait a little for your breakfast. You will see the deliveries coming on barrows, from boats. All of the mundane services like taxis, police vehicles, fire vehicles, garbage collection, mail delivery and food distribution are by boat.

Ultimately you will come to the Rialto Bridge, across the Grand Canal. This is perhaps the most photographed spot in Venezia. Look at its magnificence before the tourists and the hawkers take over.

Now your destination is *San Marco*. Continue to diverge as you see fit. Here is the more commercial side of Venezia. By the time you reach Piazza San Marco you will be filled from the mouth-watering food you've been passing. Remember to buy food which has been cooked, where possible, and try a real, non-American, pizza. Pizza from Italy is quite different.

If you are still sufficiently early, wander about the square and the waterfront before the tourists arrive. The focal point is the Basilica of San Marco with mosaic as you have not seen anywhere, perhaps, in the world. Near it is the bell-tower which dates back to the ninth century. In 1902 the bell-tower collapsed, in slow motion, in front of the watching residents and has, of course, been rebuilt. Looking further around the square you will see the clock-tower built in 1499, with the time in Roman numerals and the two 'giant moors' striking the hour. On the basilica you will see four bronze horses which were allegedly cast in the 4th century BC as part of a quad-riga and placed on St Mark's in 1254. Napoleon took these to Paris in 1797 and they were returned in 1815. The horses you see are exact copies, as the present day atmosphere was found to be corroding the originals too much. Next there is the Duke's Palace (*Palazzo Ducale*), with fine sculptures and paintings, the library, the Bridge of Sighs (*Ponte del Sospiri*), the restaurants, the orchestras… Need I go on? Of the columns on the waterfront, one has the winged lion of St Mark, the other has a symbol of a gentleman with his foot on an alligator, which is purported to represent St Theodore, one of the ear-lier patron saints of the city.

A replica of the winged lion of St Mark once stood in the Südbahnhof in Vienna to commemorate the railway between the two cities. Not only has that station been demolished to make way for the construction of the Hauptbahnhof, but the direct day train services between Venezia and Vienna have been dis-continued and replaced in part by a bus.

At the time of the Spring and Autumn tides, the high water rises above the level of the square, perhaps by over half a metre. You may be lucky enough to see it happen. In the square are tiers of duckboards ready to put out in advance of the tides, to give the locals and the tourists access across and around the square, and indeed the various parts of the island. Under construction at the entrance to the lagoon, out of sight, is a pair of lock gates which will be used to prevent the entry of these high tides. Regardless of such efforts, the city is still sinking into the lagoon, possibly due to the pumping of ground water from beneath the surrounding land and from beneath the lagoon. This has nothing to do with the 'rising of the oceans'.

The Church of San Marco and the bell-tower open at about 0930 and 0900 respectively ,depending on the time of year, and, as you see the line beginning to form, you should join it. You need long trousers and covered shoulders to go into San Marco, so take a pair of track-pants to pull over your shorts and a scarf or similar to cover your bare shoulders. Be amazed at the size and beauty of San Marco. It is all mosaic. If you are lucky you may be able to climb up to the balcony or into the treasure house (the latter for a fee).

Once you emerge, at perhaps about 1030, you will see a different world, because the square will now be shoulder-to-shoulder with about 50,000 American tourists and you will definitely want out. They have come by bus, by train, by cruise ship and even by car and want to see all the things you have just seen, all in two hours. You should by now have seen all the things they have come for so you can leave the 'beaten track' and see things away from the square.

Don't, whatever you do, sit in the square to eat, or any other such villainous thing prohibited by the city fathers and shown on signs around the square.

The vaporettos of Venezia are the local form of transport. They play the part of the local bus service and run about all canals and neighbouring islands. They look as if they should hold about 100 people and probably carry 400 at peaks, which is most of the time. They will sell you a 24 hour ticket which costs less than three single journey tickets, and so is worthwhile.

The gondola is today a romantic, flowery-painted vessel with an extravagant charge, which is used to extract large quantities of money from people who have somehow set their mind to thinking that is how one travels in Venezia. There are a couple of old traditional gondolas which ply across the Grand Canal near the Ca d'Oro market, which will tote you across the canal for less than a Euro, starting from about 0700. Be content with one of those.

Shopping in Venezia is fascinating for many people, although it does not interest me in the slightest. Shops generally open from 0900 to 1230 and from 1530 to 1930 but not always on Sunday. The well-known brands of any fashion items are shown at the various stores and the discerning will be able to compare prices here with those on any city high street. The glassware, ceramics and lace are second-to-none in the world, and they will pack and deliver anywhere in the world at prices you possibly cannot match anywhere. But did you really want that, nice as it may be? Granny might like the lace. The junk is another matter. Most of the junk is, as they tell, unique to Venezia and for this we should be grateful. The stuff is mass produced, has no value and all they want is the money from your pocket. Note, when you see €5 per item with three for €12, what must the wholesale value of the item be? The silly hat, T-shirt, mask, etc., must be bought with the knowledge that it will almost certainly be thrown out at your next re-pack.

Further afield:

The vaporetta can take you around the various canals of the city to see the remarkable array of buildings, homes, museums and churches that Venezia can offer. Jump on or off the vaporetti at any stop you wish. Choose your museums as you wish. There are any number of them, many of world renown. Note that most buildings have water over their front steps and the residents have retreated to higher floors.

The island of Murano specialises in glassblowing. Take the vaporetto for an extensive visit. Prices there are even lower.

On the island of Burano is a centre for lace-making.

The Lido is across the lagoon where you can see the beaches on the Adriatic.

One of the more interesting technical feats is that of the cruise ships leaving, generally late in the afternoon. Ships must leave along the narrow shipping channel past the esplanade of St Mark's Square. Each one is accompanied by two tugs, otherwise unnecessary with today's bow-thrusters and the like, presumably because the ship must do some very sharp turns and most likely because the ship's engines will stir up too much mud in their carefully dredged channels. The ships are watching you too. The cruise ships call their passengers out on deck and play tear-jerking operatic themes as they cruise slowly past St Mark's Square and elsewhere.

Spend the evening in Venezia and eat a wonderful meal on the bank of the canal. Spend your time in St Mark's Square, which is filled with restaurants with spectacularly good food, most with some musical item to entice you in. The two adjacent orchestras play ten minutes on and ten minutes off. The most memorable item for me one evening was a string trio plus grand piano playing a very well-orchestrated version of *Waltzing Matilda*. Dean Martin imitation songs do NOT feature. Alternatively, there are more restaurants on the waterfront away from the square. If you are leaving by train there is a superb restaurant on the Grand Canal near the station, *Povoledo*, which will allow you to adjust your timing for departure more precisely.

You can now see why you could spend many days in Venezia.

If you are only in Venezia for the morning, ride the vaporetto back to the Ferrovia, St Lucia, taking about 45 minutes, and you'll now be at St Lucia in time for the high speed train from St Lucia to Firenze SMN at about 1145. This requires reservations, but if you are really late they tell you to get on anyway and find a seat. After a hot morning in Venezia, this is heaven. You should plan to arrive in Firenze SMN at about 1430 in time to see as much as you want there. If you take a later train, most of the attractions in Firenze will be closed when you arrive. There are night trains from Venezia to most places, so you can book a berth or a seat from Venezia to somewhere and, after your afternoon nap, be ready to see Venezia in the evening before departure.

Of course, you may have a hotel room and are staying the night. In this case, you retire to your room and have a good nap during the heat of the day and emerge for an evening in Venezia.

26. TUSCANY

Italy has a spine of high speed railway, which runs from Torino in the north west through Milano, Bologna, Firenze, Roma to Napoli, with additional services coming from Venezia via Bologna. On these tracks run the superlative AV (alta velocita) high speed sets of TrenItalia, which command a premium which is well worth paying. The time taken by these new trains may be less than half of that taken by conventional trains.

The next trains down are the 'Eurostar Italia' sets which are equally well-appointed. Don't confuse these with 'Eurostar City' which are conventional trains branded to attract attention, also with a surcharge but nothing like the speed and comfort. Wherever you want to go there will be a conventional train which will take you there without premium, in the same times as one would have taken for granted twenty years ago.

By comparison, a high proportion of the local Italian trains are terrible, but that is another story.

Be sure you drink plenty of water as you travel about Italy. You should carry at least one litre per person when you are on the train or walking about. You can buy 'Frizzante', with gas (a blue top), or natural, with no gas (a pink top). As your water level goes down, you become cranky and irritable and your day is spoiled. In this climate, you should drink at least two litres of water a day.

Firenze, Florence

Most train trips travelling north and south will pass through the station of Firenze SMN so, apart from being an absolute necessity for a visit, Firenze is easy to reach.

The city of Firenze must contain more valuable works of art than any other place in the world, bar none.

All of Firenze is within walking distance from the station but you do need your good walking shoes. Bags can be left at the station *bagaglia*, so don't carry any, but wear your hat.

Drop down into the tunnel as you leave the station and save the problem of crossing the square and several roads. Keep following the flow, passing many pizza and ice cream shops in which you might as well indulge.

Walk forward from the station for about fifteen minutes and you come to the cathedral square and are pinned to the wall by the enormity and grandeur of the Duomo (the Cathedral of Santa Maria del Fiore). Unfortunately, the Baptistry at the front blocks the view somewhat, but it can be forgiven.

The line for entry to the Duomo is not usually very long but can be tedious in the sun. They allow one-for-one entry for each exit, so the speed depends on those inside. Normally the guardians are not fussed that the Lord does not see your knees and shoulders, but you can never be sure.

Once inside, the enormity and beauty of the dome hits you. All you can do is wander about with your mouth open. Standing under the dome is breath-taking. The Duomo is one of the three largest domes in the world, the others are St Peter's in Rome and St Paul's in London. It was begun in 1296 and took 140 years to complete. Brunelleschi did an amazing job, since he had to design a new way of holding up the dome, rather like Utzon did in the Sydney Opera House. The Duomo is magnificently painted, as are the adjoining buildings, thanks to Michelangelo and others. Go to the top of the dome to the cupola, up 463 steps, for which you must line up in the street outside, for an amazing view of the city and the valley. Beware that the dome closes at about 1600, well ahead of the other buildings.

The adjacent bell-tower is 90 metres high and dates from the 14th century. It is reputed to be one of the most beautiful in the world. 414 steps lead to a vista across the Arno Valley, which is not to be missed.

Finally, you return to the Baptistry. This octagonal building obscures the view of the Duomo and one would imagine that moving it away would be a priority. Hardly so, since this was created in the 11th century, contains many works of art dating from the 13th and 14th centuries and, by anyone's standards, would outrank any work of art, architecture or artistic history that one could find anywhere in any other part of the world. You can be excused if all you do is crane your neck around the entrance to see more of the inside. The external doors, seen from the outside, are something again.

Be aware of the pedlars! Most of these must be working outside the law, as they display their wares on a blanket and at a moment's notice they grab the four corners and are off. I was taken by the guys who sell wooden railway trains with each car in the form of a letter. They will put your name behind a loco for one Euro per car, if the law does not spot them first. It makes a good talking point on your kitchen windowsill. 'Granny' would be too many letters.

Follow the crowds down toward the River Arno and come to the main square, the Piazza della Signoria. On the opposite corner you can see Michelangelo's statue of David, or at least a copy of it. The original is in the Accademie Museum further back in the city, which is worth a visit. David is not alone in the square, as there are many other statues of lesser repute but on different themes. Perseus (by Cellini) stands naked holding the severed head of Medusa. Why you would want to go after Medusa in your birthday suit bothers me, but this is artistic licence. Now proceed down the galleria toward the Arno. On both sides you have statues of famous Italians of history, and a lot of them there are. Try to recognise what each one stands for. The Uffizi Gallery, which you pass on the left, contains Italy's most important art collection.

You have now reached the River Arno.

The most notable event associated with this famous river was in 1965 when it flooded the city and covered untold numbers of works of art in glorious mud. Some items had been in basements for centuries and had to be rescued. Much has probably not been rediscovered.

When the Germans visited Firenze back in 1943, because they were confronted by the advancing Allies, they carelessly knocked down all the bridges. Only one remains, the Ponte Vecchio. As you walk across the bridge you could be forgiven for wondering if you were on a bridge, since you are flanked with jewellery shops, etc., for all but the central few metres, where at last you have a view both ways along the river.

Back a little from the river is one concentrated market which sells fair quality items, in particular leather goods such as handbags and wallets. Of course, they are all mass produced but they look good, especially to those who don't know their origin. Granny would like a leather wallet? In front of this market is a bronze pig, a rather large one. Legend has it that if you stroke the nose of this pig you will return to Firenze. In consequence the nose of the pig is well polished. I once believed that this pig and his brother (quite clearly his brother and not his sister), who sits in the main street of München, were unique in the world until I saw yet another brother in the Butchart Gardens on Vancouver Island in Canada. It took a German friend to tell me that there is a fourth in front of the Parliament House in Sydney.

No visit to Firenze is complete without a visit to the Church of San Croce, a kilometre or so to the south on the Piazza Santa Croce. This comparatively bare church, built in 1294, contains, *inter alia*, the graves of Galileo, Michelangelo, Machiavelli and Ghiberti. All in one church!

Enjoy Firenze at dusk; a beautiful city. Then make the big splurge and order a fixed menu dinner for not much over €20 in the town square. Meals are even cheaper one street back, but don't have the atmosphere.

There is far more to Firenze than I have listed here, but if you see those which I have described, you will have done well.

Pisa

Pisa is an hour in a local train from Firenze, so a gap of four hours in Firenze is enough time to visit there. Pisa, like Livorno, the port for both cities, lies on the coastal railway from Roma to Torino, but this has not the same fast trains as on the spine of Italy.

Pisa railway station is on the opposite side of the city to the Piazza del Duomo and so the latter requires a fair hike to achieve. A taxi will take you across town for less than €10 and can be persuaded to wait and bring you back if time is short.

Here you will find the Cathedral, the Leaning Tower, the Baptistry and other significant buildings. The ticket office is located across the Piazza from the road entry and sells tickets to some or all locations. A word of warning. One can only climb the Tower in organised groups, for which tickets are sold in advance. At any time you may find there is a wait of one or more hours for the next tour. Don't expect to arrive and be able to climb the Tower at will.

First the Cathedral. This is so different and yet again breathtaking. This was built in 1063 to a very simple geometrical design. The main interest to a physicist is the lantern which swings from a point way up in the ceiling. It is alleged that it was this lantern which Galileo timed, using his pulse, when he should have been listening to the sermon. The things folk do to avoid going to sleep. Galileo found that the period of this pendulum (the time for a complete swing) was independent of its amplitude (how far it did swing), a far-reaching discovery and one which would lead him, and Newton after him, to revolutionise the understanding of Physics. The lantern is doubtless the original but probably with four new bodies, six new chains and three new mountings, like George Washington's axe. Words cannot explain the age and beauty of the cathedral. Like many others, it is a 'see-it-yourself' wonder.

The Baptistry comes next, commenced in 1152 but not completed until 1284. I leave it to you to discover the beauties here.

Then there is the bell-tower, the famed Leaning Tower of Pisa. The bell-tower was begun in 1172 but after three floors of construction it was found to be leaning, due to the poor foundations. Later construction was resumed except that, like a tree, it went straight up from this point. It was completed in the mid-14th century. It still, however, continued to lean and back in the 1980s it was considered unsafe and access was banned. Then it was found to be in danger of falling completely. In recent years extensive engineering action has pulled the tower back and the foundations have been reinforced, so that its tilt is only 14 degrees from vertical and the increase has been arrested. The tower is 60 metres high, built in white marble, recently resurfaced.

Health and safety people have stepped in and it is now possible to climb the 294 steps of the Tower, but only in an organised group and only to one specific level where the Tower is hemmed in with chicken wire. We were allowed to scramble all over the sloping marble balconies in the 1960s and no-one fell off; well, I certainly did not. How come we can't do it today?

A walk back to the station through the city is a worthwhile exercise. A living Italian city can be seen, unspoiled by zillions of camera-toting tourists.

Proceeding north from Pisa, you reach the National Park of Cinque Terre. This area includes five (cinque) unspoiled villages (towns?) with no roads linking them and thus no traffic. Paths link the towns along the coast and also further inland. The railway threads through a series of tunnels and services all towns. You could spend a day here or a week. My brother and his wife chose to take a room in each village in turn and walk along the sequence.

I arrived by train and chose to walk some of the coastal stretches, and finished up at an amazing little restaurant on the beach of the northernmost. Horses for courses, but don't miss it, even if you do not intend to spend a lot of time. At least hop off one train, walk along the coastline a short way and back then pick up the next one.

27. ROMA, ROME

THE ETERNAL CITY

'I've been to Rome.'
'Really? How long did you spend there?'
'About a day and I saw St Peter's and the Coliseum.'

***

To spend a day in Roma will show you about as much in proportion as an hour in the British Museum, the Smithsonian or the *Deutsches Museum*. The grandeur of Roma, of its past, goes on and on.

According to legend, Roma was founded by Romulus, one of twin brothers who were brought up by a she-wolf. From that story you find the statue of the wolf suckling the two boys and carrying the city's title in the letters SPQR, *'Senatus Populusque Romae'*, the Senate and People of Rome. I have a replica of this in my lounge room.

Octavius became the first Emperor in 27 BC and during this period many famous buildings were erected, some of which survive today. The Roman Empire declined, the Roman Catholic Church became the supreme power and then Napoleon arrived in the early 1800s. In 1870 the Kingdom of Italy included Roma. Mussolini became the power from 1922 until 1942, when Hitler took control. Finally in 1946, Italy was declared a Republic.

Italy was one of the six founder members of the European Common Market, now the EU, and then became a foundation signatory of the Schengen Treaty. Italy gave up the lira, a currency which had around 1,000 lira to the dollar (anybody's), and was a foundation member of the Eurozone, using the Euro.

You will arrive in Roma at the Central Station, '*Termini*'. Trains bring you there from the ships, the airport, the remainder of Italy and of Europe.

Strangely enough, the logical meeting place is the head of platform 29, where the trains pull in from the city of Civitavecchia, the port, and the airport at Fuminico, Leonardo da Vinci. This platform is a considerable distance through a tunnel from the main concourse. With only one point of entry, this provides a unique location in this otherwise huge station. I once agreed to meet my meteorologist colleague, Andrew, here as he came from the airport and, as the doors of his train opened, he almost fell out at my feet.

Step out from the front of the station and see the traffic of Roma, hidden in part by the inevitable road construction, and take a deep breath.

If you are an early morning arrival, then leave your bag in the *bagaglia*. Regardless of your category, take with you your lip balm, a hat, plenty of water and a covering for your shoulders and knees. The Lord objects more to seeing arms and legs here than in other cities.

Your first port of call must be the Vatican and the Sistine Chapel. The most effort-free way of reaching there is to take the same Civitavecchia train from Termini, and hop off at San Pietro, in sight of the dome of St Peter's; the fourth station. After a short walk in a non-crowded area, you are in the famous St Peter's Square, Piazza San Pietro, which is said to hold 400,000 people. Don't expect me to be one of them! If you choose to come by a bus, don't say you weren't warned and don't even consider hoofing it. Cross the square and take a five minute walk to the back of the line for the Vatican Museum. Arrive there at the latest by about 0800, when the queue is of only minor proportions. At around 0900 the doors to the Vatican open, by which time the line is a couple of hours long. Hold your temper as you watch the tour groups at the entry door jumping the line ahead of you. Remember that they paid more than you did, especially the ones from the cruise ships.

You are now in the most amazing museum in the world. I did not say the greatest. The value of the artefacts is beyond belief and they are all there as a result of gifts. Gifts to the Almighty over the centuries, received and hoarded by subsequent popes. It is all 'loot'. This contrasts very much with the Louvre, the Hermitage or Buckingham Palace, where everything was legitimately bought, or so we are told.

What could be done if this was all sold in the name of the Almighty and the proceeds invested to care for the flock in need? The price of gold, jewellery and antiquity in the world would crash. My apologies to His Holiness, but it is a great and unnecessary display of supposed grandeur.

> *'When every blessed thing you hold*
> *Is made of silver, or of gold,*
> *You long for simple pewter.*
> *When you have nothing else to wear*
> *But cloth of gold and satins rare,*
> *For cloth of gold you cease to care –*
> *Up goes the price of shoddy.'*
>
> W. S. Gilbert – *The Gondoliers*

There are parts of the museum which really are of beauty, make no mistake.

The establishment makes sure that you see the lot. You travel via never-ending passages and staircases with not enough time, nor by then enough enthusiasm, to see everything and wondering how long it will be before you reach the ever-signposted Sistine Chapel.

The irony of the situation is that the tour groups are taken up the back stairs and don't need to be shown the treasures.

Finally, there it is. Perhaps the greatest work of art in the world. The Chapel ceiling was painted by Michelangelo over a period of five years from 1508 to 1512. It tells the history of the world as known in those days. The most memorable part is the depiction of God extending the finger of life to the naked Adam. It is a chapel, but the movement of humanity makes it more like the Temple of Jerusalem as seen by Christ. Observers are craning their necks, lying backwards over chairs or even lying on the floor with their cameras, despite the fact that cameras are not allowed. There are better shots available on sale and the establishment wants you to buy them. The hubbub slowly increases until a voice calls out 'Silence!' Folk hold their heads in shame and the cycle begins once more.

Think of the times when a group of about 100 cardinals, all in their red hats, is walled into this chapel until they can finally burn the voting slips producing white smoke to announce that they have appointed a new pope.

You are out. Now you are in the inevitable gift shop. This one is a little unusual, as it has a special appeal to the true believers and makes a point of telling you so. Then there is the post office where you can buy Vatican stamps and send unwanted and expensive postcards, here and now, home to your loved ones. Granny would be pleased. Call me a cynic, but where there is money to be made there is always someone there to make it and these people have one of the best reputations in the world for making it.

Finally you descend the great staircase (however did you climb so high?) and emerge into the street and the sun. Once more you are set upon by the street sellers, this time the independent ones. Follow the line back, it is now several hours long, pass the gate with the Swiss Guards and finally re-emerge at St Peter's Square. In case you are thinking of choosing a later time, the museum closes at 1300, so much of the line must be frustrated.

Here it is, the centre of Christendom. The square where 400,000 people can, and do, gather at one time to hear words and take blessing from a frail old man who carries the franchise of the Almighty.

The line for St Peter's is not as long, but every bit as annoying. Men must wear trousers, no bare women's knees are acceptable and women must cover their arms and shoulders. The latter can be achieved with a sizeable scarf, but for men's legs it is often not so simple. Commerce comes to the rescue and, for the trivial sum of perhaps €10, you can purchase a pair of paper tissue over-trousers which are acceptable to the clergy on the door. The Temple in Jerusalem immediately comes to mind once more.

Choosing to exploit this, I stood at the exit and offered to buy second-hand trousers. For €4 I was appropriately kitted and followed the line inside. On exit the tissue was unbroken and I proceeded to sell the items at the entry to a willing purchaser. The buyer saved €4 when he paid me €6.

St Peter's is indeed the Centre of the Universe. See the most marvellous cathedral in the world. It is also one of the four largest in the world. Make sure you see the main altar, go to the top of the dome and go to the crypt to see the graves of the past popes including St Peter. In the crypt one can see the locations of the mortal remains of the previous popes and hold back a chuckle when considering the musical chairs which must be played when a new resident arrives to ensure that all priorities are preserved. Karol Wojtyla is in a simple tomb, not far from St Peter. Some poor unremembered pope (no, popes were never poor!) had to be shifted a few rows further down to accommodate him.

By now it is mid-afternoon and you have not seen Roma. You have not seen any of Roma, but merely the Vatican City; that micro-state which exists inside the city boundaries of Roma. Its head of state is the Pope, it has a population of about 1,000 and has no problems with immigration or commerce. It is not a member of the EU, nor the Schengen Agreement, but it is by default both. The Vatican uses Euros. Pause a moment to think of the task of their accountants.

If you have lodgings in Roma, it is very likely that your feet will tell you to give up for the day and resume next morning. If not, we continue.

Now you have to go back to the city. You have four alternatives:

1. Return the way you came to Termini on the train, but you won't see anything.
2. Take the underground back to Termini from Ottaviano station nearby (10 minutes along the Via Ottaviano), change at Termini and continue by underground to Coliseo for your next venture. You won't see much this way either, but it will take you to your destination. Entry to the Metro is by a coin in the slot.
3. Take the bus and see traffic of Roma.
4. Walk and really see Roma.

Let's take the Metro now to Coliseo and alight there. Here is a different Roma. Across the road is the Coliseum, one of the most famous monuments in the world, built in 72 AD. Next to it is the Arch of Constantine erected in 315 AD. Then there is the Forum, where Brutus started with '*Friends, Romans and Countrymen*'. Here you could easily spend another day.

From this point Roma is what you choose to see. You have now seen about 60%, perhaps 80%, of what people come to Roma to see. If you are on a time ration, then that is enough. Otherwise now is the time to see the Pantheon, the Spanish Steps, the Via Venetia, the Fontana di Trevi, the catacombs, etc., etc. I'm sorry, but you do need a map and a guidebook.

When all is done and the hotel bill is paid (or your feet are ground down to the ankles), let us return to Termini and resume our trip southward

28. NAPLES, NAPOLI

Without apology to the good Burghers of Napoli, I will state that you do not want to go to Naples.

Yes, there are some aspects of the city which are novel and lots of good things to do in the hinterland, but the city holds little appeal.

A walk about the area in front of the Central Station will confirm my view. My most recent memory of here was when I had a couple of hours to wait for a connection and I had hurt my back. Even a pack of about five kilograms was providing a pain level I could not stand. I stumbled across (in both senses of the word) a store in the square which sold suitcases. Within minutes he had sold me a wheelie suitcase for €10 into which I flung my pack. He was satisfied and so was I. The case survived only a few weeks, but long enough for my back to repair itself.

On another occasion I was travelling with the family and we had boarded a bus which was several hundred per cent over capacity. All of our passports and documents, credit cards and our base-load cash were under my shirt, but our day's cash allowance was in my overcoat pocket, supposedly with my hand to shield it. In such a crowded bus, I had no option but to hold on and keep the kids from being crushed. As we left the bus, I said to Heather: 'I'll bet he's taken it.' Sure enough, the cash was gone. Heather was mortified and wanted to leave Napoli there and then. We stayed, but not for too long and not in the city.

As suggested, the hinterland is another story.

A private railway, *Vesuviano*, proceeds southwards in the direction of Sorrento, the town to which you are urged to come back, and so you might.

The railway travels along the ridge at the top of the cliffs and the town is at the end of the line. The map shows a short distance to the port. Great. What the map does not show is that the port is nearly as far down as it is away horizontally. The pedestrian paths are stairways, for ever and ever, until finally reaching the port. Fortunately my problem is *avoirdupois*; lifting my weight is the difficulty, so going down is not as bad as coming up. After an eternity, I reached the bottom to be greeted by a delightful little port with all the pleasant aspects one could want.

From Sorrento port the ferry goes to the Isle of Capri. Everyone has a different reason for hearing about Capri, one of the better ones being of the Emperor Tiberius who lived and ruled Roma from the island in about the fourth century AD. Former Australian PM, Gough Whitlam, at the time leader of the opposition, was very quick when the PM of the day, Billy McMahon, worked through a government crisis while on an island resort. 'Tiberius on the telephone', was Gough's biting assessment.

On arriving at Capri, you find that the town is at the top of the island and that the very attractive esplanade and port is still not all that you have come for.

The cable car will take you to the top and just short of the town.

From there the view is breathtaking; the full extent of the Bay of Napoli with Vesuvius in the background. In your vista lies the home of 1.5 to 2 million people. Slightly to the left of the mountain is that not-so-nice city that you left this morning.

After the ferry back to Sorrento, there is an identifiable bus which will take you up to the station.

It was on a Monday morning, or some such day of the week, in 77 AD that Vesuvius, after a long period of rumbling, suddenly belched forth unbelievable quantities of highly toxic gas. Most volcanic gases are sulphurous, so the toxicity is not in question. Every living, breathing thing in the area, specifically in Pompeii, was immediately overwhelmed and died where it sat or lay. Nothing lived. The mountain then proceeded to bury everything in ash and dust. Everything was covered. This is *The Sleeping Beauty* without the happy ending.

So, on the way back is the city of Pompeii, at which you should most certainly stop. The conservators have done a marvellous job in restoring the city to its previous format.

Pompeii was a reminder of Ephesus, but the history could not have been more different. While Ephesus decayed after the seas retreated, Pompeii was buried as a working city with the inhabitants intact. Archaeologists have discovered the forms of people lying in their beds or dropped where they were when the cloud hit. All persons were buried as they lay. To recover the 'bodies', a plastic was injected into the space where the decomposed body had been, was allowed to set, and then the dirt was cut away. In this way an exact form of the body could be obtained from the 'negative' left in the surrounding rock, soil, ash or what have you. The houses, streets and public buildings of Pompeii still stand, exactly as the archaeologists dug them out. The timbers of the buildings have long gone, but the walls and solid roofs are still present. The ash permeated everything but did not have the overwhelming destructive power as would a lava flow or a tsunami.

Then take a guided trip to the top of Vesuvius. A bus will run you to a point well above the tree line where you are passed through the gate and told to hike to the next gate, about 30 minutes and all uphill, where your next guide awaits you. These guys are not silly. The hike is 'strenuous' as the guidebooks state, but not beyond a guy with a bad back and too much weight. The reward is enormous, like the mountain.

Apart from anything the view from the top of the mountain over the surrounding countryside is breathtaking. Here live 1.5 million people, all of whom could be buried, or at least rendered homeless, by a major eruption. They may have up to seven days warning of the possibility, but where would they go and what is the certainty? The last major eruption was over 60 years ago and the resultant lava flow, down into the valleys, can easily be seen. Vulcanologists are satisfied that they can predict the next eruption and can warn the surrounding citizenry with enough time to allow them to escape. But what do you do? Do you tell one and a half million people that the mountain might go up next week, or the week after? Does the government order that they must go somewhere else, leave their homes, their properties, their forms of sustenance, their jobs, etc. and wait? It would be very surprising if many took notice until it was too late.

One of the casualties of the 1944 eruption was the funicular railway going up to the summit. Its top station can still be seen. Apparently it was going broke, but this is one instance where foul play cannot be considered. The reason for mentioning this is that this railway was allegedly the origin of the song *Funiculi, Funicula*. The first refers to the trip up, the latter down.

There are some nasty disasters waiting to happen in our biosphere, like the Los Angeles earthquake to come, the eruption of Yellowstone, the landslide in the Canaries, not to mention all the ones without a warning sign. Vesuvius is one of the largest recognisable threats.

More amazing was the crater. Inside the mountain is a vertical pipe, around a kilometre across with sides stretching down hundreds of metres. Through this pipe came the devastation of 77 AD. Vesuvius is only dormant and rumbles away. At the top you gaze down into the crater, and recognise the potential it has to blow again. Fumes are emitted from holes in the rock and your mind wanders to Tolkien's Mt Doom. Here it is not as hot nor as imminent, but still worrying. Apparently it is changes in the content of these fumes which can signify the advent of an eruption. Our guide stated that we had not paid for an eruption, but if one did occur then there would be a surcharge, payable when we arrived back.

And so, back to Napoli.

29. SICILY AND MALTA

While Milano represents the industrial and business north of Italy, Roma and Firenze the classical area, Calabria and Sicily are the agricultural and self-sufficient areas of the country. The money in the north is what is missing in the south.

Here is an example of where the Eurail pass can be useful. Napoli is the southern end of the spine high-speed railway in Italy, as discussed earlier. If you proceed further south you will be using conventional trains, not so good in Italy, originating in Roma.

To proceed to Calabria and Sicily, it is convenient to use a night train. As the train leaves Roma for the south at a respectable hour and goes through Napoli late at night, what could be more sensible than back-tracking to Roma by fast train to pick up the night train from its point of origin. To double back from Napoli to Roma on a fast train to take possession of a compartment, or buy a sleeper or couchette, is a worthwhile exercise. Sitting all night in the middle seat of three is not a nice experience, exceeded only by doing the same thing in a 747 from London to Hong Kong, or Sydney to Los Angeles. The toilets, however, are cleaner on an aircraft than in an Italian train, by a long way!

From Roma such a train can take you to Palermo, or to Catania and Syracuse.

Trains are still carried from the mainland to Sicily by ship, operating about once an hour, day and night. Your train halts, shunts and fiddles about for about 30 minutes, and is shunted, without locomotive, on to the ferry. It is then transported across the Straits of Messina. After an hour the ferry arrives in Messina, fiddles for another hour and continues to its destination. You will not notice this in a couchette or sleeper, but in a seating car every bang is emphasised. Fortunately it is possible to go up top on the ferry for fresh air, a drink and a meal. Another loco hitches onto the front in Messina and the train continues on its way

You have now crossed the Strait of Messina into Sicily.

This must be one of the busiest waterways in the world with ships passing, with pilot, in both directions almost continuously, while the ferries operate across their path. Italy would dearly love a tunnel or bridge and is no doubt waiting until the EU will pay for it. The dominating part of the skyline on each side is a huge pylon for power lines, already painted and in place for about the last ten years. Alas, not a wire is evident. This is Italy.

More dominating is the shadow of Mt Etna to the south west, on Sicily. Mt Etna is an active volcano but has not caused much trouble for many years. To the north, in the Tyrhenian Sea, is Stromboli, which is also active. A small village nestles at the foot of this island mountain. Some folk are fatalists.

Try going south first to Syracuse. This city was the home of Archimedes, one of the world's greatest physicists and mathematicians. Apparently, when Syracuse was besieged by the Romans in 212 BC, it was Archimedes who put forward all the ideas for defence of the city, and they very nearly worked. Finally the city was conquered, with the invading general being instructed to recover Archimedes at all costs. There was a mistake in transmission and Archimedes was killed.

You can wander around the town and see where Archimedes lived, where he went to school, where he took his laundry and where he took his computer to be serviced. For a physicist, this means quite something.

The *Virtu* catamaran for Valetta in Malta operates six days a week in 1.5 hours from Pozzalo, about an hour by train to the south of Catania; departure times vary.

Malta has a more speckled history than most places its size and revels in the fact. Archaeological remains indicate that people were there 4,000 years ago. Like the Minoans, they all disappeared but this time no-one knows why nor has any ideas. Malta was subsequently the property of, or at least under the influence of, almost every power in the Mediterranean for the last couple of millennia. Even the Normans turned up in the eleventh century. Ultimately the Knights Templar of Jerusalem arrived, unheralded and unwelcome, in 1530 and took possession with about as much 'by-your-leave' for the locals as

Columbus had for the New World, the British and French for North America or the British for Australia.

There they resided without the consent of the locals until Napoleon arrived in 1798, disbanded them, chucked them out and took possession of the islands for France. Exactly two years and two days later, the British arrived in the form of the Royal Navy, ticked off Napoleon's adherents and Malta remained British for over 150 years. The Island of Malta was awarded the George Cross by King George VI for 'heroism' in World War II and this is a contributing factor to its flag.

The Maltese are alleged to have the second highest voter turnout in the world, of 94%, after Australia at 95%. The astounding part is that voting is not compulsory, as it is in Australia.

The latitude of Malta is 35 degrees north and this is roughly the most southerly point in Europe, comparable with Cyprus and Gibraltar. This corresponds with Atlanta or Los Angeles in North America and Canberra in Australia.

The Maltese were granted independence from Britain in 1964 under amicable conditions. This has to be compared with Cyprus, where there was no agreement. Like the Hungarians and the Poles, the Maltese passed power back to Brussels and became one of the ten new members of the EU in 2004.

Malta has a very much get-up-and-go economy, which has seen it join the Schengen Treaty and the Eurozone in the smallest possible time. Malta believes in selling itself and this can be seen in the tourist offices and advertising agencies. It is very clear that the EU will transform the economy of Malta like it did that of the Irish Republic. The Maltese economy and population are probably smaller than that of a large American, British or Australian university.

The outward appearance of Valetta is different from anywhere else in the world. It is all walls and fortification. They have been repelling potential invaders for 2,000 years. Everything is built of the same cream-coloured limestone; there is nothing else to use. In some senses it seems like a cheap and nasty economy, and in others demonstrates a real promise.

Valetta is the world's first planned city, built on an impregnable rock by the Knights about 400 years ago, with long 'parallel' streets which have enough curve in them so that you cannot see 'further than the flight of an arrow'. Try to imagine a British city superimposed on the street grid of Athens. The buildings are close together and with small residences, but it is all clean. The phone boxes are red with the British crown on the outside. Postboxes are red. The Maltese drive on the left with cars which have steering wheels on the right. They leave their garbage on the footpath overnight. It all resembles London in that regard. All advertising is in English. In fact, everything is in English except that the street signs are in two languages. The local quality morning paper is *The Times*, in English. You can buy the *London Daily Mail* or *The Sun*. Yet they speak Maltese, which is part-English, part-Arabic, part-Italian and anything that they choose. But never French!

The difference between staying in hotels and travelling by overnight train is not only a question of comfort, but of time. The hotel traveller will have a pleasant, late breakfast, spend a couple of hours sightseeing, return to the hotel for lunch, have a quick nap, spend a couple more hours on his feet and retire for dinner. If he is lucky, he might go out after dinner for an hour or so. On the following day he packs, heads for the airport or station, travels by day to his next destination and, having arrived weary, books in and remains at the hotel to prepare for the next day's sightseeing. Net result is about six hours of seeing anything, in one location, every two days. Not so the overnight rail traveller, who arrives at the station at daybreak, has no base until the evening train and therefore is on the hoof for around 14 hours and then departs for the second location. The day's accommodation cost is then that of a station locker. The net result here is 28 hours' sightseeing in two different locations in two days. Somehow an occasional bath has to be inserted in the itinerary. My method of travelling was once the latter and this took me to huge numbers of places in very short times. After about 15 years of this, and retirement, there is no need for the rush, so a compromise has evolved, using day trains as part of the sightseeing. It still results in more productive hours than for the hotel traveller. This difference became obvious at the hotel in Valetta. The temptation to start late, see a bit and come back for a nap was huge. One unexpected bonus arose. Breakfast included white bread and use of the toaster. British supremacy is alive in Malta. Alas, for the Australian, there was no Vegemite!

Valetta by day is as expected, hot, swarming with people, and everything is a new experience. The tourist office lady, at the end of my morning's excursion, confirmed that everything that should have been done in one day had indeed been on my itinerary.

It was interesting to watch the tourists from the cruise ship docked in the harbour and how their guides were herding them around. At a given signal, all would climb onto an air-conditioned coach and be moved to the next spot. Finally they were all taken back to the ship. It also sounds a little like the sub-servient Eloi people in H. G. Wells' *The Time Machine*; only the subjects here were being fed to generate more money for the ship, not to be food for others.

The ferry returned us to Catania, again depositing us under the shadow of Mt Etna. The lights around Mt Etna by night show where the fertile soils lie. The surrounds of the mountain demonstrate the value of living in those areas.

Many years ago I was travelling back to Messina by train and a storm ahead of us brought down the wires. My engineering colleague, Wayne, and I followed the locals to the bus stop and the local bus, when it finally arrived, was jam-packed. This did not stop the crowd who simply climbed on to the bus and pushed. We were the last on and the bus was now full. But no, after several more stops the compression grew and we found ourselves part-way down the bus. Perhaps our feet were not on the ground. Then at a time when surely nothing more could move, an inspector forced his way on and began checking tickets. I had cash (lira) in my hand, but no ticket. A young lady seated near me spotted this and it took her only a few seconds to realise that we had no ticket. She took her strip ticket, passed it to the person in front of her with a few words and so the ticket went to the front of the bus, was can-celled and returned to her. When the inspector arrived, she showed the can-celled ticket for three of us and he was satisfied. Once we were off the bus we thanked her profusely, but she would accept no money.

Our next destination is Palermo, Pearl of the Mediterranean. C.S. Forester had Hornblower call here to repair his battered ship.

This city does indeed match its name and is a delightful place in which to spend a day. Its history is extensive, but it is no Firenze or Venezia.

My last visit was matched by that of a rainstorm and I had to be content with sitting on the bottom deck of a double decker, red, open-topped tourist bus. It was dry, but not as rewarding.

From Palermo a night train once more can take us back across the Straits to be in Roma early next morning.

30. MORE ITALY

In the previous chapters on Italy, I have selected all of the great 'must see' locations in Italy and it might appear that these will fulfil your visit. This, of course, is not true and here are a few more locations which can be fitted in to your round trip.

Sardinia and Corsica (France)

These two very mountainous islands are readily accessible from the Italian or French coasts. Thomas Cook lists the various ferries available.

At most times of the year it is possible to travel from one of Napoli/Roma/Palermo to Cagliari at the southernmost point of Sardinia, at a time to suit. Sardinia is, of course, an integral part of Italy.

From Cagliari, a local train can take you north over some delightful mountainous country.

It is easy to see why lawlessness is synonymous with these islands. Vast areas are very difficult to reach and, even though the train has little trouble, it undoubtedly has chosen the easy route.

The train will ultimately bring you to Olbia and Golfo Aranci at the north of the island. From there a bus is available to Santa Theresa where there is a very frequent ferry service to Bonifacio in Corsica.

Corsica, an integral part of France, is the birthplace of Napoleon and some interesting monuments can be found commemorating their great hero. From Bonifacio you must find a bus to the railhead further up the island at Ajaccio, whence a train goes to Bastia for a ferry on to France, either Nice or Toulon.

The most interesting part of both islands is that they do not cater for casual tourists. Locals know the connections and, if you are not quick, the trains or buses will go without you; not with malice, but because you were not there.

Very little is available to provide for the traveller who is accustomed to finding facilities offered wherever the journey goes. The journey is worth paying the fares, by bus, train or ferry. My journey was interrupted by forest fires and the inevitable buses had to be used to shuttle passengers around the parts of the rail considered unsafe.

Brindisi

When coming from Greece, one may choose to use an alternate ferry and finish up in Brindisi or Bari, rather than Ancona,. This is yet another part of Italy, but most related to the Calabria region.

San Marino

In San Marino we have another micro-state embedded in Italy in a manner resembling the Vatican, but very different politically. San Marino is another vestige left over from the Middle Ages in the same manner as Liechtenstein, Monaco and Andorra. Since it is Italy-locked, with no airport or external border, San Marino automatically becomes another *de facto* member of the Schengen Treaty and is recognised as a part of the EU by default. These are not the official terms, but they make the point. San Marino has the right to check your passport and baggage on entry or exit, but it never does.

Take the train to Rimini, south of Padua and Venezia, and find a bus to San Marino, 40 or 50 minutes away. Thomas Cook even mentions this bus in the table including Rimini, so you can be sure that it will be there, some time.

As you approach San Marino, you understand readily why it is still there. It resides on an almost impregnable hilltop and has no resources about it to speak of. In other words, it was left alone because it was not worth bothering about and when it was finally remembered, the days had gone when neighbouring countries were able simply to walk in and take over. Of course, its greatest source of income is the tourist, but it must be admitted that the visit is worth the bus trip and the climb from the bus terminus.

Vatican

The independent state of the Vatican has been discussed elsewhere. The Vatican has its own laws, is ruled by the Pope and is guarded by the classically-uniformed Swiss Guards. This is definitely an anomaly, but Italy and the EU have been able to rationalise the situation so that the oddity is minimised. After all, it does exist and cannot be ignored with the hope that it might go away. As an absolute dictatorship and being church-based, the Vatican would have about as much chance of joining the EU as the camel trying to pass through the eye of a needle, to use one of the Church's own similes.

Livigno

All of the rivers in Italy's north flow southward toward the Mediterranean, together with some from Switzerland, and find their way there mostly via the River Po. There is, however, one exception. Beyond the head of one of these south-flowing valleys is a small enclave containing the village of Livigno, which is on the other side of the Alps. From here the water flows northwards into the River Inn, thence into the Danube and ultimately to the Black Sea. Since this village has no direct access to Italy, you must enter from Switzerland. The locals do not pay Italian VAT and it is strictly not in the EU. If anyone tried to use this fact for personal gain, they would probably be in trouble from both the Swiss and Italian authorities. Because of this village, Italy is on the watershed of the Danube and features in the agreement which governs its waters.

A similar isolation applies to the village of Campione d'Italia, which lies on the Lake of Lugarno but is entirely surrounded by the Canton of Ticino, Switzerland, and a few kilometres away from the nearest point in Italy.

How is that for two pieces of information of absolutely no use?

Milano

The City of Milano, Lake Como and Lake Maggiore regions and Tirano, are discussed in the chapters on Switzerland.

Turin, Torino

This very pleasant city is the home to the church containing the *Turin Shroud*. This city is the northern extremity of the Italian high speed network and is part of Italy's industrial north. Be aware that there are two railway stations in Torino linking with Milano.

Those on the watch for scenic railways might note the railway from Torino to Cuneo, and then on to Ventimiglia or to San Remo. Thomas Cook rates this line as one of the ten best scenic railway journeys in Europe.

Here I will digress to tell what I think of the east-west axis of the railway between Venezia, Milano, Torino and Nice. There are no through trains today but there once were and, in particular, there was a convenient night train. My first experience was with a colleague who declined to clear out his wallet before leaving home and consequently had a very fat wallet in his rear pocket. Philip and I had commandeered a compartment on this train and were comfortable for the night. I only recall in retrospect that Phil was sleeping with his rear in the air, and with it facing the door at that. In the morning another passenger came in with Phil's wallet, containing his photo, in his hand and asked if it were his. Minor panic, the wallet is not here, yes it is mine, where was it, thank you. The other passenger had found it in the loo. The cash was all gone, but all of his papers including the last two year's receipts and dry cleaning slips had been left. The thief, and good luck to him with a target offered like that, had taken the cash and left everything else, so that there was nothing to be gained in reporting the incident, only embarrassment.

On the same train several years later, my wife and I and the two boys had yet again commandeered a compartment on the overnight train. I slept near the door and Heather near the windows with the kids between us. Like any woman would, she put her handbag between the seat and the window and slept over the top of it. In the morning, it had gone. The thief must have crawled under the seats to where he knows a woman will put her handbag and helped himself. Much hysteria, and I suggested checking in the loo. Sure enough there it was, without money but otherwise intact.

Strike three was in Nice recently and my back was troubling me to the extent that I had to hold both handrails to go up and down stairs in a crowded bus. I reached the bottom without wallet. Once more the wallet contained nothing of great value, but I was not able to track it down. My wallet now is clipped to my belt with a chain. Perhaps it makes me look like a 1980s punk but, unless a thief has a pair of bolt cutters, he is not getting my wallet. On my last visit to Rome, I found my wallet swinging from its chain in a crowded train. Bad luck for the woman (I saw who she was) who had managed to unbutton my pocket and remove the wallet. Such wallets are easy to obtain in scout shops or camping stores and are well worth the outlay.

Thanks go to my brother for the suggestion.

Having left Italy by train going west, we will jump the remainder of France temporarily and move into Spain.

31. SPAIN

The historic rail gauge in Spain and Portugal is broad compared with the rest of Europe (1668mm cf 1435mm), so there are only very few specialised trains which can cross the border from France. The towns of Irun and Hendaye on the Atlantic coast are like Albury and Wodonga once were in Australia. The French trains deign to go to Irun in Spain and beat a quick retreat into home territory, while the Spanish trains venture out to Hendaye and do the same. Thanks to the Schengen Treaty, there are no passport controls but customs personnel and police are evident.

While Germany and France are building high speed lines across their country (and Britain only talks about it, or rather talks about how nice it would be), none of these countries have gauge change problems. The Spaniards, however, are building standard gauge (1435mm) high speed lines across the nation and managing to keep the services running as usual; no small feat. You don't build hundreds of kilometres of expensive rail track and leave it to lie idle while others catch up. Spain's railways are nearly all radial; all lines lead to Madrid, with only a few tangential (circumferential) lines, some of which are very important.

As of 2011 most of the initial phase of the high speed line, AVE, was in operation, which included direct services by fast standard gauge trains from Madrid to Barcelona in the north east, from Madrid to Cordoba, Sevilla and Malaga in the south, and from Madrid to Valencia and Albacete in the east. Through services operate from Barcelona to Sevilla and to Malaga, skirting Madrid. Spain also uses multiple gauge trains to run from these lines over secondary or non-completed links to other major cities. By this method, a shorter standard line from Madrid to Valladolid is used to reach other cities in the north west.

One very important section under construction is the standard gauge extension from Barcelona north to Figures, a mere 145km, where it will link with the standard gauge French system and, through it, the rest of Europe. Most of the new infrastructure visible from the old track is completed (2011), which would indicate that the development is beyond the point of no return. When this is opened, one can expect through services by high-speed trains from Paris, Nice and Switzerland to Barcelona and Madrid. Continuous 1435mm track will exist from Cadiz and Sevilla to Narvik or to Istanbul.

One negative aspect of this high speed race is that the overnight train within Spain is a thing of the past. Overnight radial services appear now to be limited to those from Madrid to Lisbon, Madrid to A Coruna/Vigo/Pontevedra in the north west, and Madrid to Pt Bou connecting to France. These remaining services will possibly disappear when later standard gauge phases, already near completion, are brought into use.

The question must now be asked, for how long will this building continue? Greece, Ireland and Portugal have had their credit questioned since the 2009 bust, and Spain appears to be waiting on the edge of the precipice for an unwanted trigger. Should this happen, Spain's ability to continue with this programme will surely be reconsidered and one can only hope that those projects now in progress will be allowed to reach completion.

Spain is a collection of different provinces, many of which believe that they should not be part of Spain. The languages of the provinces differ slightly or, in some cases, markedly. An outsider calls them all 'Spanish' but he will make no friends if he does this in an area which values its own individuality. Shades of Quebec float into view here. This must be compared with Switzerland, which handles four disparate languages, each of which is overlaid by an almost perfect knowledge of English.

Parts of Spain were controlled by the Moors from the south until 1490, when they finally surrendered to the Catholic monarchs, Ferdinand and Isabella. History here is rather complex and reaches out to various popes and even to England, where Catherine of Aragon was the first wife of Henry VIII. When the pendulum did swing, the Spanish nation became one of the most rabid Roman Catholic centres in Europe and the persecution is well known. The Spanish Inquisition is the aspect usually quoted.

Spain is still one of the strongest Roman Catholic nations in Europe, but it must be seen that for many people this must be a religion of convenience. Spain, along with Italy, has one of the lowest natural birth rates in Europe; a fact which would not be in accordance with a nation of strong believers. Like the history, this is a matter which the reader can take up elsewhere.

Coming from Switzerland (2011 timetable), one can use the hotel train *Pau Casals,* of which there is one unit which operates alternate nights from Zurich to Barcelona. Which nights, you ask? Why, of course, the night on which you don't want it. By day, one can leave Zürich early in the morning and, with a combination of IC, TGV, TGV and Alvia (in Spain), reach Barcelona before the day is out. One can easily reach Montpelier from Paris by TGV, and two services per day extend to Figures to connect with dedicated Alvia Spanish trains connecting to Barcelona. The gauge change should be a thing of the past in a few months at Figures, but it will exist inside Spain for many years to come.

From here I will pick on some places of note for a brief introduction, bearing in mind that the transport to and between these centres is no longer as it was when I was there. Further, there are many more locations of note in Spain, for which space does not permit inclusion.

Madrid

It is always easier to describe the provincial regions of a nation than the capital. Madrid is no exception; it is a beautiful but crowded city and has structures and collections to be admired.

Madrid is the hub of Spain's railways, out from which they radiate like spokes of a wheel.

Toledo

Here is the one-time capital of Spain where the religious history is most apparent. This is an easy standard gauge, high speed train ride from Madrid.

Barcelona

This is a beautiful big city, worthy of several days' visit. Its most notable structure (to some) is the cathedral designed by Gaudi. This was abandoned at the architect's death, but has been carried on by public wish. The cathedral has a design of its own and has to be seen to be appreciated, or otherwise. As a physicist and believer in straight lines, I will reserve my case. It could be another century before it is completed, but this is in keeping with the architect's comment that God is not in a hurry.

Pyrenees

From one of the outer stations of Barcelona, a line proceeds northward through the Pyrenees. Thomas Cook tells you that the times are valid from March 28 to September 12, so it is very likely a 'no winter service' line. While the direct line from Barcelona to Perpignan in France is able to skirt the mountains at slightly above sea level and through tunnel, this line tackles the mountains head on. For over four hours this second class only train climbs quietly into the mountains heading for La Tour de Carol. Each stage feels like it should be the last as the track comes to a partly flat plain, travels on for a while and then begins to climb again. Ultimately La Tour de Carol is reached and it is necessary to change to the French standard gauge train for the onward journey to Toulouse. The last train of the day actually has a couchette car and continues from Toulouse to Paris.

The first station down the French side is Andorra L'Hospitalet. From here you can take a bus, always at the wrong time of day, to Andorra La Velle. Other services exist but, without a detailed map, it is difficult to work out the relative locations. 'Subject to cancellation when mountain passes are closed by snow'.

An alternative way down on the French side is to Ville-France and Perpignan via *Le Petit Train Jaune*, the Little Yellow Train, a second class only, narrow-gauge train, which once again only appears to operate outside of the winter months. Thomas Cook lists all three trains as scenic rail routes but gives the coveted star to the Little Yellow Train.

Andorra

Here we have another European microstate, this one a Principality set up by treaty in 1278. The head of state is shared jointly by two Co-Princes, one of whom is the Bishop of Urgell, in Spain, and the other the Head of State of the French Republic. M. Sarkozy is thus an elected Prince, in an office once held by de Gaulle, Napoleon and Louis XIV. After chuckling at this, it is easy for one to see how microstates like Andorra could be dismantled at the whim of one person, and ultimately they will be when their presence proves other than useful.

Andorra is specifically NOT a member of the EU and NOT party to the Schengen Treaty. If you enter Andorra, you leave the EU and, without a re-entry visa, you cannot return. This is not done with any malice, it is purely the way it has always been. My entry to Andorra was in the days when there was a good connection from the train from Spain. The route today is all bus from Spain.

Andorra depends on the ski slopes for its income and obviously knows how to do this and how to do it well.

Ferrol

Lieutenant Hornblower was captured and imprisoned by the Spaniards for around two years in the north western Spanish harbour town of Ferrol. This was enough to set me going there. Despite the fact that a direct train was advertised from Barcelona, there was not, and so the only way to reach there without involving endless poor connections on local trains was a fast train to Madrid and a night train to A Corunna, followed by a bus. Here I found Ferrol to be a pleasant port and I spent the day travelling by bus around the local coastline. As found previously, Mr Forester had condensed many of the features into a small area, but this obviously made for a much better story.

Ferrol is the western terminus of one of two privately-owned, narrow gauge railways in Northern Spain, which run from Ferrol to Bilbao and Bilbao to San Sebastian closer to the French border. This does not have any stations with three different gauges as there had once been in Australia, but does give thought to the possibility.

Valencia

A lovely city, much enhanced by the decision of the city fathers some years ago to reclaim a waterway through the city and to use the land for civic buildings. The aquarium, for instance, has few equals across the world.

Palma, Majorca *Mallorca*, Balearic Isles

Palma is easily reached by overnight ferry from either Valencia or Barcelona. The island is mainly dependent on tourists and it has an air resembling Capri.

To me the most exciting feature of the island was the private railway from Palma to Soller, on the other side of the island. For 55 minutes one is taken through and over the mountain range which makes up the island, to be deposited at sea level on the far side. From here one can take a tram to the port of the same name which is an intriguing small tourist town, undisturbed by the ravages of the cruise ships.

Granada

This city sat at the top of my wish list for many years, until finally I was able to include it in an itinerary. Here you will find the world famous Alhambra Palace, one of the greatest gifts of the Moorish empire to our present heritage. The hotel desk clerk warned me that I must be at the front of the queue at something like 0730 if I did not hold a reservation, because the line grew very quickly. His advice was well taken because, by the time the gates opened at 0900, the line may have been two hours long. I usually skim through such places and am out in minimum time, but not so here. The history in this building was immense and well worth the trip to Southern Spain to see.

Algeciras, Tangier

There is nothing notable about this southern coastal city of Algeciras, except its access. From here the fast ferry leaves for Tangier, about once every hour, and takes about 45 minutes. No additional visas are necessary. So you are in Africa, in Morocco to be precise. At the ferry dock are all the guides attempting to solicit your business. My guy was not very impressed because I did not offer him a very large fee, but he did show me all I needed to see. He called frequently on his mates who were anxious to give me a cup of coffee and to sell me a carpet, or some other local products. He eventually turned me loose to find my own way back to the ferry. All I can say is that this is not my scene and, while I am glad to have been there, it is well near the bottom of my list of places to return.

Many friends of mine have stayed longer and indeed taken the train to Rabat and other locations. I have no wish to copy them.

Gibraltar

How the Brits came to have possession of Gibraltar is another matter, but needless to say it has been an important base for the Royal Navy for centuries. Hornblower failed to complete his examination for lieutenant here and later set out on his journey to the Turkish Levant.

Spain has never been keen on the idea and closed off land access to Gibraltar for many years following WWII. This hurt mainly Spaniards, as many were wont to find employment at the base and walk to work each day, as they currently do. To join the EU Spain was forced to abandon such antics and the border was re-opened. Even today, there is no form of public transport by land into Gibraltar. One must come to the frontier at La Linea by bus from Algeciras and then walk across the airstrip to the transport on the Gibraltar side.

In the days before the Schengen Treaty, Spain would only allow single entry to certain foreign nationals in the life of one passport. This sounds reasonably fair, but indeed meant that the person who travelled overland through Spain to visit Gibraltar or Morocco could not come back into Spain to return home. How these folk fared being stuck in Gibraltar is not in my ken. Even today, if you cross into Gibraltar without a multiple entry Schengen visa you will not be allowed to return.

Gibraltar is a 'Crown dependency of Great Britain', which means that you are in Great Britain if it suits them and not if it does not. As a Crown dependency, Gibraltar is inside the EU but not part of the Schengen Treaty. The currency is a Gibraltar pound, which is exactly equivalent to a British pound. Similar conditions apply in Jersey, Guernsey and the Isle of Man.

After the trip from Algeciras and the walk across the border, one finds Gibraltar an interesting place. You can walk anywhere, around the port, on to the rock and through the town. On the rock you find the famous Barbary Apes whose demise would signal the end of British ownership. They are well cared for and protected, and they know it. The water catchment for the territory is on the side of the rock, clearly visible.

There is no relief from the heat anywhere and, having done my quota of sightseeing, I retired to my lodgings for an afternoon nap. This was a mistake as when I ventured out once more in the cool of the evening, there was nothing open anywhere; not even for a hamburger. The workforce had gone home to Spain, the Navy to their respective messes or married quarters, and the town was deserted. No young people lived in Gibraltar. My stomach had to wait until next morning. Admittedly this was 1998 and things have surely changed since then. McDonalds would have seen to that. After a feed next morning, a walk across the airstrip and a bus back to Algeciras, I was ready for the night trip back to Madrid.

Cadiz

It was from Cadiz that the Italian, Christopher Columbus, set sail for India, going westward, in the *Pinta*, *Nina* and *Santa Maria* and under the patronage of the king and queen of Spain. Rarely in history has a better deal been struck, because this effectively gave sovereignty to Spain of the whole of South and Central America for nearly 300 years. North of the Rio Grande came into this, so Texas and neighbouring states were part of Mexico, part of Spain, for a long time. I recall seeing a replica of the *Santa Maria* in the harbour of Cadiz back in 1978, but on subsequent trips have been unable to find it. They were tiny ships, 300 tons; no wonder the crew members were discontented.

Philip and I arrived on the train in Cadiz, only to be told that the Spanish railways were on strike and there was no train back. Not only that but all offices were closed for the afternoon siesta, so there was no room for negotiation. Further, the railways were the agent for Avis, so that avenue was closed. We were on a three-week continuous Eurail pass and we did not need to stay in Cadiz indefinitely. Finally, we fished out Señor Hertz, after siesta, loaded our bags in the boot and were off. We were headed for the French border if necessary, via what seemed most sensible, the circumferential route. Little did we know that these roads, although marked as national highways, passed through every village on their way and most of these villages had a one way system of streets which were often narrow for our little car. We drove under the walls of the Alhambra, we camped overnight in camping grounds, and we stopped at small cafes to partake of a genuine Spanish meal. One place was so genuinely Spanish that they were showing *Macbeth*, in Spanish, on the bar-room TV.

Ultimately we reached Valencia to find that the strike was over, returned the car and continued our journey to the border by Spanish railways.

On to Portugal

The train out of Madrid for Lisbon, the *Lusitania*, is what the Spanish call a hotel train, a collection of mini hotel rooms, pulled along behind a locomotive and of fixed capacity. One imagines that the definition used for a 'hotel room' has been much modified. In deference to the un-moneyed, there is a fairly pleasant sitting car at the rear. There is only one such train per day, overnight, which requires even seating reservation well in advance.

32. PORTUGAL

On my most recent arrival in Lisbon on the hotel train from Madrid, the first thing which confronted us was a large number of people, mainly backpackers, who were irate at finding that they could not obtain a seat on the night train to Madrid. They had arrived on our train, or perhaps from Paris, only to find that the onward train to Madrid was fully booked and for days hence. We were OK; we had onward reservations back to France.

If you have a copy of Thomas Cook in your back pocket, you will find that the only other possible way of reaching Madrid directly is through a combination of three daytime local trains, some second class only, taking 14 hours rather than nine hours by the direct train. It may be challenging but it does not sound inviting.

Thomas Cook also shows a diverse collection of bus connections from (Lagos to) Faro in the south of Portugal to Huelva (to Sevilla) in Spain. Perhaps in my younger days I might have tried these, but no longer.

Lisbon is one hour behind Spanish time and, therefore, on London time. All other countries of Western and Central Europe, not including Finland, Estonia, Latvia and Lithuania, nor Romania, Bulgaria and Greece, are on Frankfurt time. On the same day every year, each one of these countries, around 30 of them, moves to daylight saving time. Australia can't even be uniform within one country. It has three time zones and some, and occasionally parts of some, move to daylight saving, others do not and some move at different dates. This last anomaly was only corrected in Australia as late as 2009. It has been reported that Russia will remain on what is now daylight saving time (GMT + 4) all year round from 2011.

Lisbon celebrates its past as a seafaring nation and the port of Lisbon is the best place to see this. A large monument details the greatest of these, including Henry the Navigator and our old friend, Vasco da Gama. Henry was a younger son of the king in the early 1400s (Columbus was 1492) and he set up in Lisbon what could be most easily be called a navigational academy. To here he brought the best talent and knowledge of sailing that was possible. Up until this time sailors had remained close to the coast and their navigation was done using the coast. Remember that Galileo did not come on to the scene until around 1600, so that before Columbus the edge of the world was a 'known fact'. Henry wanted to go south, around Africa. There was the renowned Cape Badaujoz, around which no-one had ever sailed; the weather kept bringing them back. There had been 15 known attempts made to pass this point. This then must have been the end of the world. Someone, by accident, had discovered the Cape Verde Islands further out, which indicated that the end of the world might be a little further afield. Finally Henry persuaded his captains to have a crack at sailing out to sea, turning south, sailing by dead reckoning and then coming ashore. Of course, this worked, and in 1474 Henry's ships were on the way to India.

Diaz arrived at the Cape of Good Hope in 1496, only four years after Columbus went in the other direction, and old Vasco reached India not long after.

To avoid any misunderstandings, the Spaniards and the Portuguese drew up a treaty, the Treaty of Tordesillas, ratified by the Pope, which drew a line down the Atlantic at about 35 degrees east of Greenwich so that the Spaniards went west and the Portuguese went east. This suited both parties. There were two clauses omitted from the treaty, in retrospect. The first should have noticed that there was a piece of South America on the Portuguese side of the line, which later became Portuguese Brazil. The second should have foreseen that the world was indeed round and that there was a 'back way'. By 1512 the Portuguese had reached East Timor which, according to their reckoning, was the end of their territory as being about 145 degrees east. They were only the little guys in this agreement so they did not want to offend the Spaniards. It is worthy of note that East Timor is not much over 200km from Australia, as is Cuba from the American mainland. If Columbus is given the credit for discovering America when his closest point of approach was 200km, then the Portuguese surely are the unquestioned discoverers of Australia. It is inconceivable that the Portuguese, after having come halfway around the world, would not have packed a picnic lunch one day and gone to see what Australia had to offer. They would have hurried back, of course. Being of a God-fearing Anglican nation in those late 1700s, the British knew that it MUST have been Cook who discovered Australia.

Well, the Portuguese did venture further and knew well the area across northern Australia through to Torres Strait. In 1524 one of their captains passed through and explored the east coast of Australia around as far as Warrnambool in Victoria, where he met with some misfortune and lost two of his three ships, one of which, *the mahogany ship*, is buried inside the sand-hills but has not been seen since 1890. The only possible cause of losing your ship INSIDE the sand-hills is a tsunami. What rotten luck! Otherwise they may have discovered Adelaide or even circumnavigated Australia. Well this tsunami was enough evidence for the crew that they were nearing the end of the world, so they returned the way they came.

All of Henry's navigators were frisked by customs on their arrival home (not then in the EU), and any maps that they had in their possession were confiscated and lodged in the royal library, just in case the Spaniards might see them. This library was lost, irretrievably, in 1755, so there is no way of checking the authenticity of these explorations. There are four known copies of maps that escaped and these are held with great reverence by their host libraries in various European cities. They show, without doubt, the outline of Australia as it would have been 'known' at the time. Obviously the Englishman Alexander Dalrymple did not have one of these, as he advocated finding the great southern continent.

There were undoubtedly other renegade maps and James Cook clearly had one of them.

Cook was perhaps the greatest navigator of all times, but he had three real advantages over those who might claim otherwise. The first was that there was a space out there to be mapped, the last real unknown accessible space on the globe. The second was that he had a copy of John Harrison's clock, which meant that he could accurately determine longitude. He would have had two such clocks in fact. The third was that he had the Portuguese map. Why did Cook arrive precisely at the south eastern 'corner' of Australia? Any further south and he would have missed. How did Cook 'anticipate' in his log some of the bays that he found? Why did Cook, when wrecked off the Barrier Reef, proceed *north* to the only estuary along that coast when the most logical thing would have been to go directly to shore, or at the very least retrace his steps southward? Why did Cook stop at Cape York and proclaim all to be NSW, when he should have had no idea of what lay ahead? There was no signpost there. Most important, why did Cook claim all land to the west of what he had found as far as longitude 145 east, the edge of the Portuguese domain? In other words he only claimed what could have been seen as Spanish rather than Portuguese, and in 1770 the Brits were no great chums with the Spaniards.

Incidentally, why do we call him Captain Cook? Everyone else lacked honorifics. We talk of Columbus, Drake, Magellan, Nelson, Banks, Phillip, Flinders, Bass, Macquarie, Sturt, Burke and Wills, Dampier, etc. but always of *Captain* Cook. Cook was only a Lieutenant when he came to Australia anyway.

***

We come to the second great reason for visiting Lisbon, and this is to see the outcome of the great earthquake of 1755. Having seen the monuments to Henry at the port, now continue by exploring the cathedral and local buildings. The next stopping place is the middle of the city.

On a Friday morning (I'm not checking) in 1755, a piece of Lisbon about three kilometres long and about one kilometre wide dropped towards the centre of the earth, apparently by a distance of the order of 100 metres. It must have been some show. The resultant tsunami and the fires which followed were not in the interests of the citizenry of Lisbon, even of those who did manage not to follow the plight of the main streets and try to pay their respects to Pluto. Why do people build cities on earthquake fault lines?

The Lisboans were not to be put off and replaced the mess with a set of wide parallel streets which remain today. The central street is for pedestrians only and provides a wonderful city centre for locals and for visitors.

One must mention the food. Along the central boulevard are food shops selling all types of Portuguese food, eat in or take away, which are a delight to the palate.

Then there are the trams. These things have four wheels and buck about like something possessed. Join the tram, the driver hops on, pulls a handle and off it races. It goes up and down hills, squeezes between cars and slides through one-way streets to reach your destination. Don't miss riding the tram when you are in Lisbon.

The next part of a visit to Lisbon must be to the old city; the part the earthquake left behind. The centre of the old site is the castle which the tram has a good try at reaching, but does not quite succeed. The remarkable thing about this castle is that it looks like a castle is supposed to look, according to the books. If you drew a castle with entrance, walls, main courtyard, accommodation, storerooms, ramparts, stairs to the top of the walls, etc., in the same way as the best novels do, then you would draw this castle.

The *Surex/Sud Expresso*, a *Trenhotel*, from Lisbon (1668mm gauge) will take you out in the late afternoon arriving at Hendaye in France in the early morning. By comparison with French trains, this is poor comfort. It is well ahead of Bulgarian trains in quality, but one would not have expected this low standard so close to Frankfurt. Bulgarian trains go 'ka thump', elderly western trains go 'clicketty clack', but this one does both at once and with vigour. The connecting TGV will debouche you early in the morning in Bordeaux, ready to enjoy the sights of France.

33. FRANCE

The history of France can fill volumes and its basis is roughly known to most people. Names like Joan of Arc and Louis XIV are bantered about in most primary schools. Those who have not chosen to learn of it are probably not likely to be interested.

France was occupied by Hitler in World War II, with General de Gaulle in London encouraging the French to dissent. When the Germans went home the French went through a tiresome period of instability and conflict over Algeria, in which de Gaulle played a major role. Not to be forgotten is their fighting in Indo-China from which they withdrew, leaving a situation which allowed the US to become embroiled in the Vietnam War.

France was a founding member in 1957 of what was to become the EU, and adopted the Euro at the outset.

France is a little tiresome for the Eurail pass traveller, for reasons which can be extracted from the discussion below, hence many pass holders are deterred from travelling widely in France.

Unlike Germany and Switzerland, rail transport in France is very radial, similar to Spain, and based, as you can be sure, on Paris. All trains are owned and operated by the SNCF (the French Railways, the *Société Nationale des Chemins de Fer Français*),

About 40 years ago the French embarked on a programme of upgrading their railways to have them based on a high speed network. Contrary to the method of other countries, they began by building a series of long distance high speed lines, *Ligne à Grand Vitesse*, LGV, capable of running appropriate trains at speeds (then) of 200 kph and in later years of up to 350 kph.

For these they constructed fast trains, *Train à Grand Vitesse*, TGV, which could also run on conventional lines. The first such service was from Paris to

Lyon in 1981.

Today's radial network includes:

TGV Nord	Paris, Gare du Nord	Lille
TGV Est	Paris, Gare de l'Est	toward Strasbourg, Nancy
TGV Sud	Paris Gare de Lyon	Lyon
TGV Sud, Mediterranée	Paris Gare de Lyon	Marseille (Nice, Montpelier)
TGV Atlantique	Paris Montparnasse	Le Mans, Tours (Bordeaux)

International services using these LGV and TGV include:

Lyria	Paris Gare de Lyon to Geneva and Lausanne
	Paris, Gare de l'Est to Zurich and Basle via Strasbourg
Thalys	Paris, Gare du Nord to Netherlands, Belgium via Lille
Eurostar	Paris, Gare du Nord to London via Lille (purpose built trains)
TGV Est	Paris, Gare de l'Est to Frankfurt and Stuttgart, alternating with ICE trains
TGV *Artesia*	Paris, Gare de Lyon to Milano

One of the features of the present day LGV network is that there are only very few intermediate stations on the network and these are dedicated to TGV services. The onward service to provincial areas is provided either by connecting trains at these stations, or by allowing the TGV to run through on conventional lines.

The few inter-provincial TGV services which do not terminate in Paris usually run around the outskirts of Paris without entering the city, generally calling at Charles de Gaulle airport station.

TGVs are specially-designed sets of around ten cars and capable even then of being operated in tandem. Their original design was the height of comfort and fashion, but much of this has been overtaken by trains in other countries coming later in the spectrum, such as the latest ICE trains in Germany.

At a test run on the completed but unopened LGV Est on 3 April, 2007, a world record top speed for train, on rails, of 574 kph was registered, a fact which is emblazoned on the exterior of the successful train. It is alleged that this was achieved on the first test run and no higher speed was sought. Some promotional motive exists here which I fail to understand. A higher speed has been recorded with a *maglev* train in Japan.

It is necessary to obtain a reservation to travel on a TGV and this is where the pass holder has difficulty, because one of the virtues of the pass is the ability to walk onto a train at any time. Rather than this, the Eurail pass holder must stand in the line at the Parisian station behind all those folk who have difficult itineraries to work out, while Monsieur et Madame General Public buy their tickets and reservations at the machines. There are machines which will create a reservation only, but these are hard to find. Occasionally, for a busy train, the SNCF officials will check all intending passengers as they enter the Paris platform to ensure a reservation is held. As an unintentional '*quid pro quo*' on some trains, such as Montpelier-Geneva, the reservation requirement can be ignored.

Psychology plays an important part here, even if negatively. There are still perfectly good conventional trains operating in parallel with these lines, which take the same time as they took before the TGV began operation, and the pass holder can use these without reservation. The fact that the faster train is there with a slightly more difficult method of entry is annoying.

There are two more difficulties.

It is not always possible to make a TGV reservation in another country, thus making planning of a through trip to a third country very difficult. This tends to coerce one into travelling to Britain on the Eurostar via Brussels rather than Paris, and to make similar adjustments. Going from Switzerland to Spain via Paris, for instance, is very hard to plan ahead. For the Eurail traveller without a fixed itinerary, it poses no problem.

Despite all this mumbo jumbo, it is possible generally to board a TGV without a reservation, identify a vacant seat and pay the reservation fee to the conductor. This does involve a certain risk that the conductor might try to charge you the full fare, but I have never encountered this. It is to be hoped that the SNCF will not read this and decide to take action. The other is that there might indeed not be a seat and one might have to sit on the floor with others in the same situation, for the full length of the journey.

The TGV has, as has happened with fast trains in many countries, even in Britain, reduced the availability of overnight services which cuts back the 'join-the-train-and-wake-up-in-the morning-in-X' syndrome. There are now very few night trains operating within France and these at best carry only couchettes and second class seats. Trains into Germany are operated by CNL and those to Italy by Euronacht, via Switzerland.

Almost alone in continental Europe, the French wish only to speak their own language, and despise people who don't. This they are entitled to do, in the same way as folk from all English-speaking countries do. Throughout the colonial era, the policy of the British was always, 'Make the buggers learn English', so English speakers must be careful before criticising the French. A few years ago the Australian Federal Minister of Education would include in some of his speeches:

'A person who speaks three languages is trilingual.
A person who speaks two languages is bilingual.
A person who speaks only one language is Australian.'

If you don't speak French, a Frenchman does not want to speak to you. This must be modified to some extent by the need of the French party to the transaction. An option for you is to use your schoolroom French. He may be so horrified at your hideous approach to the language that he will respond in English, which he speaks well. More than likely though, he will then respond in fast and complex French which you will not be able to understand. I have found that the best approach, as with speakers in all languages, is to be civil and polite and assume that the speaker is better versed in language than I am. This generally brings out the best in people. A humble, 'I'm sorry, I cannot speak French', carries with it the implication 'but you are more clever than I am and speak two languages' and often works. The time dishonoured, 'Hey, Buddy, do you speak English?' will almost invariably receive a 'non!'

'In France it doesn't matter what you do, as long as
you pronounce it correctly!'
Alan Jay Lerner – *My Fair Lady*

34. PROVINCIAL FRANCE

We will commence our journey around France in the south west.

Bordeaux

The railway station at Bordeaux is a considerable distance from the town and there is not a lot of information to be found at the station. There is very little alternative but to head in the direction of the town centre via the old town. This route leads through all the backstreets and past old churches and squares, which really contribute to the feel of the city. At the information office they will give stacks of brochures on places to go and many that you will already have covered. In the end there will not be enough time in the day to see everything which they recommend. A pleasant day was spent by me in Bordeaux, probably my first ever in a provincial French city of this size. The food was indeed delightful.

The trams in Bordeaux are impressive! They come in from the outer parts of the city under conventional wires which suddenly come to an end, but the tram keeps on going. All that can be seen is a third rail in the centre of the track, which can be walked on without any ill effects. The secret is in modern technology. As the tram moves over this centre rail, it activates that part of the rail beneath the centre of the tram where there is a collecting shoe. This provides the power for the tram. As the tram moves on, the rail behind it becomes inactive. This is a splendid way of ridding the streets of overhead wires and is being tried, apparently, in several other cities around the world.

Brest

Lieutenant Hornblower spent several years on the blockade of Brest in the early years of the Napoleonic Wars, so I headed for Brest, once again to confirm Mr Forester's geography. Brest sits at the terminus of the TGV line from Paris and in its day has been an important naval base. It is located at the head of the Rade de Brest, a long enclosed fjord-like feature making it extremely easy to defend in the days before aircraft. Conversely it is extremely easy to blockade, which Britain successfully achieved in its attempt to quell Bonaparte.

On an attempted walk to the outer reaches of the Rade, I once found that distances were much greater than I had been led to believe, either by modern day maps or by Mr Forester.

Nantes

It was to this port that Hornblower in *Flying Colours* made his way after escaping from Napoleon's gaolers in the Loire Valley and recaptured 'The Witch of Endor'. This port is at the mouth of the Loire and was a major entry to France when shipping was the prime method of transport. Today it is on a spur of the TGV Atlantique,

Le Havre

Le Havre is at the mouth of the Seine and strategically very important to shipping. Hornblower also came here in the latter days of his career. With Cherbourg, Le Havre (correctly *Le Havre de Grâce*) was the calling point for the trans-Atlantic liners once they had left Southampton on their way to New York. In the days of Glory of these ships, *Queen Mary*, *Queen Elizabeth*, *Normandie* and even the *Titanic*, they constituted the only way of crossing the Atlantic. Frighteningly, today, the cruise liner market is generating bigger and more luxurious vessels which make those Blue Riband greats appear tiny. Recently launched was the Royal Caribbean '*Oasis of the Seas*' which, like its twin sister, '*Allure of the Seas*', has a shipping weight of 225,252 tonnes and can carry 8,000 people. Neither of these ships can pass through the Panama Canal but should be able to do so after proposed extensions expected in about 2014. May I please not be asked to insure one of those?

It was in this estuary that Hornblower recovered HMS Flame from the mutineers and subsequently began the re-establishment of the French Monarchy.

Rouen

Rouen is the city of Joan of Arc. Her cathedral stands today amongst the more beautiful in France, along with the location of the stake where she came to her end.

Dieppe

This quiet little port is the southern terminal of the ferry from Newhaven in Sussex, England. This ferry constitutes an exceptionally cheap way of reaching England for a Eurail pass holder. Furthermore, it is almost on a direct north-south line from Paris to London. Unfortunately the ferry times are chosen to meet the schedules of the truck drivers who are their main source of business. If you are prepared for an arrival in France at 0330, then this could be for you. The first train to Paris is after 0530.

Dunkirk

Dunkerque was the site of one of the great rescues of World War II, but had the potential to be a huge disaster. From here Allied troops were evacuated to Britain in the face of Hitler's oncoming forces. A quiet walk around the harbour will show some of the memorials which have been erected and give a good idea why this port provided a good location for such an evacuation. It was on the beaches of this area that the Allies returned to repel Hitler's forces.

The Battlefields

Fast trains run from Paris Nord to Arras and Amiens, from where you can venture forth to see the battlefields and graves from World War I. Only by seeing these can you appreciate the appalling casualty rate and futility of this pointless war. Similarly, many historic towns along the Rhine made famous, or infamous, in both World Wars are on the railway map.

Historians tell us that, from a population of 4,875,000 in 1914, 313,000 Australian troops served overseas. The final total of casualties reached 215,000, an astonishing 68%, which included 59,000 dead. There were a lot of widows in Australia.

Nice and Monte Carlo

To the south, Nice is, of course, the location of the rich, when it suits them. It is a pleasant city with two outstanding attributes. The first is its beaches; a quality it shares with neighbouring towns and cities. A visit in the winter when the beaches are little used will show the value of these. The second is the opulence of the shipping in the harbour. Anyone who is anyone leaves a craft in Nice, and good luck to them. Similar havens are also to be seen in neighbouring cities.

One of my memories of Nice came following the introduction of the all-singing, all-dancing TGV trains from Paris to Nice. I dutifully booked my trip both ways in Paris with a good turn-around time in Nice and enjoyed the trip south, except that it was delayed quite considerably. It was delayed so much that I missed my return train to Paris. There were no seats available on the only remaining TGV to Paris that night, so I joined regardless. They were right, there were no seats and I was not the only standing passenger. Then followed one of the longest six-hour train trips I can remember. Seated passengers around me were good to me and 'loaned' me their seats as they went for a meal, and ultimately even as they went to the loo. My feelings for the new TGV Méditerranée were not very positive at the time.

Monaco is another of the micro-states existing within the boundaries of the EU. Once more Monaco has been left behind by time and is, in effect, a feudal monarchy or, more correctly, a principality. The Prince of Monaco is an absolute monarch, but the days of behaving like this are a thing of the past. Most notoriety was gained a half century ago when the Prince married the film star commoner, Grace Kelly. She was tragically killed in a car accident. Her children have achieved much notoriety in their own time by behaving in public in a manner unseeming for royalty.

All that being said, Monaco is by default part of the EU and in the Schengen Treaty area. Its foreign affairs and immigration/customs are managed by France. Monaco uses the Euro.

The main railway line between Nice and Marseilles runs through Monaco, mostly in a tunnel, so one does not see much of Monaco that way. Even a short stop-over will not show much, as the entry to the station is well away from the notable locations.

Once again, as for Nice, Monaco is the home of the filthy rich, but with the difference that the laws here are local and good use can be made of the tax laws. France and the EU have watched over this over the past years and Monaco is not in the same league as Leichtenstein or even Switzerland, but many have obviously chosen to use its tax laws. It has been said that France could 'repossess' Monaco without any effort and that this could happen when the current Prince dies.

The biggest drawcard in Monaco is the Casino, once almost the only one of its kind in the world. Other countries have discovered how to make money from such an activity and it has been copied worldwide. It is, however, *the thing* to be seen at the Casino in Monte Carlo.

At the other end of the tourist spectrum is the palace and surroundings, with the quaint ceremony of changing of the guard.

A picturesque, narrow-gauge, non-SNCF train runs through the mountains from Nice to Digne and is well worth a trip. A bus will take you the short distance from Digne to the main line at St Auban. Thomas Cook rates this train on the list of scenic railways, but it does not rate the 'highly recommended' star.

This has been a small thumbnail picture of only a few of the many attractive locations in provincial France. The best description is always the same. Go there yourself.

Let us now venture into Paris!

35. PARIS

Paris is, like London, Moscow and Vienna, bedevilled by a large number of terminal stations around the periphery of the city, permitted to come no further by the obstinate city fathers of the day who had the same objection to progress then as those who object to nuclear power stations today.

Paris has taken action in this regard, 50 years ahead of London. In this time the SNCF and the RATP, the travel authority of Paris, have linked, under the streets of this mature city, the suburban railways previously terminating at the outskirts and provided through services on these lines, the RER. The long distance termini remain as they were, but now with far less congestion. From these termini, it is possible to use the RER to reach most other termini directly.

Five of these lines now operate and the map shows that there is scope to build two more of these to incorporate almost the entire suburban system into the RER system, to provide a very swift service into and around the whole of Paris. Whether the resources exist is another question.

The terminal stations have not improved over the years and are still like something you would expect in an Agatha Christie novel. With a few exceptions it is all push and shove, with no refinements such as baggage porters, or somewhere to sit. At all termini you will see members of the military walking about carrying what appear to be loaded and primed automatic weapons.

The Paris Metro, also under the auspices of the RATP, is the underground network running throughout the area of the central city of Paris. Its lines crisscross Paris in an even more complex manner than the Underground does in London. New lines are still being built and the latest, line 15, provides a fast service along a corridor which had otherwise been wanting. The format of the trains varies from line to line, compared with only two types in London,

189

and includes trains on rubber tyres which was another favourite topic of my teacher in Grade Six. One simple ticket, for a little over €1, will admit you to the underground system and to the RER lines inside the city limits, and remains valid until you leave the system.

The citizens of Paris must take great delight in trying to cheat the system, as there is a complex arrangement of barrier gates which stops all but the most athletic from entering the network without payment. This compares with the opposite numbers in Germany, Austria and many other countries where free access to the network is provided at all stations. In the latter, however, the penalty for being found travelling without a ticket is quite high.

In theory, the RER lines of Paris under the control of the SNCF, as distinct from the RATP, are free to the Eurail pass holder, but those under the control of the RATP are not. To use the former it is necessary to present the pass at the ticket office and receive a 'no charge' ticket.

Paris has an intricate network of buses and even boasts three tram routes constructed in recent years.

One of the notable attributes, shared with only a few other major cities, is that building height restrictions exist in the city centre and surrounding areas so that, with a few exceptions, it is possible to see unobstructed across the whole city.

The next piece of grisly news it that there are very few left luggage facilities in Paris. These exist at some, but not all, of the terminal stations where you must first run your baggage through an airport-style scanner before being able to lodge it in a locker.

The second difficulty, but not so much for the young and healthy, is that Paris has not proceeded very far with an equal access policy, and to move around anywhere involves interminable numbers of steps. The latest RER lines are equipped with escalators, but even access to the main termini from street level requires steps. Paris is a city for backpacks rather than wheelie suitcases.

One could spend a week in Paris and still not be satisfied. Here, on the other hand, is a description of how to see a selection of the principal sights of Paris on a summer day, arriving and departing by night train.

Assume you arrive at Est or Nord and are leaving from one of them. Collect a free map from one of the information bureaux. If you are at Est, walk across to Nord; about ten minutes. Deposit your bag as described above, remembering to retain a water bottle and a hat. Buy a 'carnet' of Metro tickets, ten for the price of nine, and stick all but the first in your wallet for later. Take the blue RER line 'B', south to St Michel. Alternatively a walk down the Rue St Denis to St Michel at 0600 will be quite revealing, as the ladies of the night have not yet gone off duty. Your imagination will tell you what section of the market is still present.

If you arrive at Paris Lyon (Austerlitz, Bercy), follow the same procedure but this time move north to St Michel on the green line 'D'.

Cross the river and walk to Notre Dame (five minutes) and have a quiet peaceful wander around the square before the crowds arrive, postponing your entry into the cathedral until later.

From St Michel go west on the yellow line 'C' toward Versailles, leaving the train at Champ de Mars. Now you are at the Eiffel Tower. You should try to arrive here by about 0930, before the queue becomes too long. It costs about €30 to go to the top; well worth the effort. Allow 2 to 2½ hours to see the tower. If you arrive any later, you could stand in line for a couple of hours.

Now give your feet something to do. Walk to the river and head a short distance upstream. Cross the River Seine and make your way north to the Arc de Triomphe, find your way under the tunnel to the arch and go to the top. After a few minutes there, head back along the Champs Elysées, stopping at McDonalds to go to the loo.

Finally you come to the Tuileries Gardens and the Louvre. If it is Sunday, entry to all museums is at half price. If it is Tuesday, all museums are closed. See the Mona Lisa and everything you can in the Louvre, but remember not to spend time doing that which you would not do if it was put in front of you at home. Go a little further up the river and you come to the Île de France and St Michel once more. From here you should now go inside the Cathedral of Notre Dame. The windows are stupendous at sunset. Climb the towers and see where the Hunchback lived. Cross the river again to the area of Rue St Michel and the university. The street is the university and vice versa.

Tucked away in the streets between Rue St Michel and Notre Dame is a great array of eating houses, all offering three course meals at a fixed price. You receive what you pay for, but the meals from about €15 will more than satisfy you. The restaurants make their money by selling you drinks.

From the Notre Dame area, continue up the Rue Sebastopol and you are back at Est. If you want to see the ladies of the night, go a block west to the Rue St Denis. Alternatively go back to St Michel, and take the RER to Nord. For Lyon take the green RER line 'D' from St Michel. You can collect any of these RER services from Chatelet Les Halles where you can, as needed, change trains.

The above will take all day and have you back in time for a night train. If you have more time, go to Montmartre, the small church with the great view of Paris.

The night trains from Paris Est are assembled and left in the platform, without lights, early in the evening but they are not shown on the boards until 20 minutes before departure. All departures (Hamburg, Berlin and München) are part of the same train departing at 2020 (2011 timetable). When you arrive at the station, go for a wander until you find your train, and specifically the coaches to your destination, and set yourself up nice and early.

***

If you are staying longer in Paris, or returning for a second visit, you will now be equipped with enough information to choose the sights you wish to see next. Alternatively you might have checked on the internet to see what you wanted next. There is, of course, an endless list of things to see in Paris: museums, Napoleon's tomb, churches, La Defense, the nightlife, the Pompidou Centre, Rue Pigale, the Bastille, Les Halles, the Follies Bergère, Disneyland and the Moulin Rouge. The list goes on.

One place you might like to visit is the Palace of Versailles, which is around half an hour out of Paris on the yellow line 'C'. Now you will learn a little of French history. Versailles Palace is the epitome of pre-Revolutionary France. This does not mean that Napoleon was not too proud to use it. The most notable thing is that the queues are very long and the walk-in tourist has little option but to stand in line for over an hour before reaching the door. Make it your first port of call for the day. The tourist bus passengers have their tickets in hand. The similarity with the Schönbrunn Palace in Vienna will not go unnoticed.

A day in Paris can be finished with a nice meal of French mussels, with chips, at a footpath table of a restaurant opposite the Paris Nord station.

36. BELGIUM AND LUXEMBOURG

One short description of Belgium begins with the notion that it straddles the boundary between Germanic and Latin Europe.

There are two main linguistic groups: the Flemish, who speak Dutch and occupy the north part of the country, and the Walloons who speak French in Wallonia in the south. The capital, Brussels, is mostly bilingual and is an enclave in the Flemish region. A small German-speaking region exists in the west. Everyone can, of course, speak English and will do so if you are polite and civil.

Belgium has been pushed around by wars over the centuries and was occupied by the Germans in both world wars. In the period since WWII, tensions between the two halves have been building up and, like the Scots and English, they are never happy together. Of course, with a common enemy they would stand shoulder to shoulder. In the last few years partition has become a word which is often used.

The King of the Belgians occupies a titular role, similar to the sovereigns in The Netherlands, Norway, Sweden and Denmark. It was King Farouk of Egypt who is alleged to have said, on being forced to abdicate, that in time there would only be five kings in Europe: Diamonds, Spades, Hearts, Clubs and Britain. These additional five sovereigns have proved him wrong.

Voting is compulsory in national elections in Belgium and, along with Italy, Austria, Malta, Luxembourg and Chile, Belgium has a voter turnout of over 90%, according to a source in Wikipedia. This is only exceeded by Australia at 95% and compares with 76% in Britain and 54% in the US.

Belgium was a founder member in 1957 of what was to become the European Union, the EU.

Brussels is the home of the European Commision, the administrative arm of the EU. There is a standard line:

> 'How many people work for the EU in Brussels?'
> 'About one-third of them.'

Just as a Brit lays the blame for anything on Whitehall and an American on Washington, so Europeans pass the buck to Brussels.

***

We might pause here for a moment to discuss the EU.

After WWII the surviving nations of Europe, that is, those who survived from being given to Russia to look after, came together to form a loose federation. This progressively grew and expanded its operation until it became a much stronger federation in the form of the European Union.

Only three present day nations have tried this experiment: the US, in its haste to free itself from Britain; Canada to ensure it was not swallowed up by its neighbour; and Australia, which did it through sheer common sense. These three nations are among the five geographically largest nations of the world, Russia and Brazil being the others, and certainly among the richest on a per capita basis.

There are 37 European nations on the western side of the border of Russia-Belarus-Ukraine-Moldova. Of these, 27 have chosen to join the EU and have all benefitted; some to a greater degree than others. Of the remaining ten, three (Norway, Iceland, Switzerland) have chosen to stay out and the remaining seven have not the government to meet the entry requirements (Croatia, Bosnia, Serbia, Kosovo, Macedonia, Albania, Montenegro). In addition, there is a collection of micro-states (Liechtenstein, Andorra, Vatican, San Marino and Monaco) and a set of British 'Crown dependencies' (Guernsey, Jersey, Isle of Man, Gibraltar) inside the borders of Europe. Turkey remains an enigma.

Entry of members to the EU took place as follows:

1957	Italy, Belgium, Netherlands, Luxembourg, Germany, France
1973	Britain, Denmark, Ireland
1981	Greece
1986	Portugal, Spain
1995	Austria, Finland, Sweden
2004	Estonia, Latvia, Lithuania, Poland, Czech, Slovakia, Hungary, Cyprus, Malta, Slovenia
2007	Romania, Bulgaria

Among the roles assumed by the EU are customs and external immigration. Before entering the EU for the first time, you meet the immigration service of the EU, administered, of course, by the government of the country of arrival.

The EU, in its wisdom, listed a large number of external countries which were its friends, its 'mates' in Australian; countries with which it could build bilateral passport arrangements. If you come from one of these countries, it is merely a matter of handing over your passport, answering a few civil questions, receiving a rubber stamp and you are inside the EU for three months. What you don't see is the quick electronic scan of your passport and the full details concerning who you are thrown onto the screen. This is the price you pay to be in the mate-ship of nations. Big Brother can find you anywhere.

The proponents of the EU once described a European heaven where the police were English, the cars made by the Germans, the chefs were French, the lovers Italian and it was all managed by the Swiss. This sounds great! To this the antagonists replied, but what if it turns out that the police are German, the cars are made by the French, the cooks are English, the lovers are Swiss and it is all managed by the Italians?

***

Brussels Midi station is one of two, Paris Nord is the other, departure points for the Eurostar to St Pancras, London. Eurostar is not included in the global Eurail pass, but has a special price for pass holders, a price which is otherwise not hard to reach otherwise by early booking, etc. A fairly simple regime exists in Brussels for buying a ticket, passing through security, passing through EU and British immigration and joining the train, which can be done in around 15 minutes. *Advice: leave more time than this, at least 30 minutes.* Most people associate the Eurostar with Paris but the real advantage of Brussels is that direct connections are available within a few tens of metres of your departure platform from Paris, Amsterdam and Köln by Thalys and from Köln and Frankfurt by DB ICE3. Some of the latter originate even further than from Frankfurt. While Eurostar does not guarantee these connections, there is an hourly service on most routes. Thus, unless the journey is complex, Brussels is the way to go. In Paris, on the other hand, it is necessary to change stations from Paris Nord to go anywhere, with the consequent lumping of baggage up and down stairs and into taxis, Metro or RER, and then negotiating stairs at the other end. Most travel agents ask for 90 minutes connection time in Paris.

Nothing is less impressive than nothing, and nothing is best expressed by blackness. There cannot be a bigger anti-climax than taking a train through a tunnel, and in particular through the Channel Tunnel. An announcement is made, in English and in French, that the train will shortly be entering the tunnel and will be in the tunnel for approximately 20 minutes. Then the view from the window changes from an English (French) railway yard to blackness, and stays like that until the railway yard is resumed on the French (English) side. Everyone continues reading, chatting, sleeping, or whatever they were doing before the sights disappeared. You don't even feel the urge to say 'Ooo' as it happens or 'Ah' when you come out. Over this stretch you have been travelling at around 300kph.

All this has not described Belgium or Brussels.

After leaving the station, follow the signs for the *Grand Place*. This square is surrounded by an amazing collection of buildings, generally of uniform height, which I have heard described as the most beautiful collection of buildings in the world. One can spend hours walking about, taking in the various sights of the square. The ubiquitous vendors are all present in the square, selling you food and drink and the inevitable souvenir which you would never buy if you thought a little about it.

From the sublime to the ridiculous, about half a block from the square is the *Mannequin Pis*, a small statue dedicated to a little boy who, in one version of the legend, discovered a fire and put it out by the only method at his disposal. The statue is only a few centimetres high, disappointing to most, but is fully operational. Taking far more space and time than the statue are the souvenir vendors who will sell you anything which might depict the statue as two metres high. Go and see it, but don't expect to be enthralled.

The lace from Brussels is world-renowned. The street vendors or the professional shops will make anything you want available to you and you might well find an article or two which would be a useful souvenir. Granny might welcome that more than a statue of a small boy.

The rest of Brussels is for you to explore. The tourist offices will provide you with the literature.

From Brussels an IC train takes less than two hours to Ieper (Ypres) and Poperinge, where an even more dramatic picture of the horrors of World War I can be seen.

Luxembourg

The nation of Luxembourg is a Grand Duchy, which means its head of state is a Grand Duke rather than a king. Luxembourg is the world's only remaining sovereign Grand Duchy from a much larger collection in past centuries.

Luxembourg, like Belgium, was a founder member in 1957 of what was to become the EU. Luxembourg provides the 'lux' in 'Benelux', the name given to a collection of the three 'low countries'.

This small nation is a fascinating country to visit. While its area is small, it is certainly large enough to be a country in its own right with a population of over half a million. Probably its greatest claim to fame is that it minds its own business. It is an investment centre, legally, for persons from other countries. Luxembourg can claim to have the highest GDP per capita in the world.

The three official languages are French, German and Luxembourgish, the last being the language used in conversation. Official written business is done in French and the media use German. Children are taught all three languages, as well as English, at school. You can expect a local to speak English.

Train services are up-to-date, the traveller seeing more of the services which pass through the country rather than being centred on the country.

Once again a useful period, certainly a day, can be spent wandering about the capital, Luxembourg City.

37. THE NETHERLANDS

God created the world but the Dutch created the Netherlands.

***

The name of this country in most languages means the low countries. In French it is Pays-Bas and in German, Nederlande.

The name *Holland* is not correct and is rightfully the name for two local districts adjacent to the west coast. The word *Dutch* is equally incorrect, but it is the only word used in English to describe their language. There is no such thing as a *Dutchman,* although English uses the name all the time to describe a Nederlander.

The Netherlands is a parliamentary democracy with a sovereign who has largely only titular authority. The seat of government of The Netherlands is The Hague, *den Haag*, while most of the commerce centres about Amsterdam and the trade about Rotterdam. The three cities of Rotterdam, Amsterdam and The Hague make up what the locals call the *Randstadt*.

Nearly all Nederlanders speak Dutch, English, French and German, recognising that their own language is not useful in communicating with outsiders. They can pick up local TV from all of those countries, meaning that experience in all languages is open to them. If you encounter a man who speaks excellent English, such good English that you are convinced that he must be a native speaker, and you try to place him by his accent and are unable to do so because his English is so good and you consider he has 'no accent', then be sure he is a Dutchman. Of course there is no such thing as 'no accent', but for some reason a Dutchman speaks English so well that his becomes the base definition of the language. I was speaking to one such person in Firenze of all places and, after recognising me as an Australian, he challenged me to tell him where he came from:

'My native language is not English.'
'Then, of course, you are a Dutchman.'
'Quite correct.'

The Netherlands is divided roughly into three portions:

1. The sand dunes which front the western, or North Sea, coast and continue as the Friesian Islands to the German coast.
2. The higher ground in the west and the south against Germany.
3. The low lying area in between the above, which is mainly below sea level, but now part of reclaimed land or the remaining areas of water, once the Zuider Zee and now the Ijssel Meer.

These low-lying areas have been drained over the centuries and continuously pumped or kept dry, so that a large proportion of the Netherlands population, and certainly of their agriculture, is below sea level. A glance at a map where the 'below sea level' regions are marked in a different colour, will make this apparent.

In the not-so-deep parts, the water can be drained using locks and the tide, but more often windmills were used to pump water when the wind blew. Hence the primary school picture shown of the Dutch children in clogs standing near a windmill. These mills have been mostly replaced by electrical pumping, but one can see the day when the mill might be returned to use, in a more modern form of course. When all you have to do is to pump water, you can afford to wait until the wind blows.

Since WWII, grand schemes for draining the whole of the Ijssel Meer have been devised, and it has been closed off from the sea by an extensive dam. This has had the effect of turning it into a freshwater lake. More recently it has been seen that no more land is needed and only those polders which have been drained are to remain; the rest remains as lake. Apparently the land clears itself of salt very quickly once reclaimed from the sea. The city of Lelystad is in the most recently drained (for several decades now) polder, Flevoland,

and there is a project nearing completion to take the railway via Lelystad from Amsterdam to other large cities like Groningen and Leeuwarden in the north east.

One of the more notable, and often overlooked, engineering feats in the Netherlands, completed in 1876, is the *Noordzeekanaal,* the North Sea Canal, linking Amsterdam on the inland waterways with the North Sea, through the sand-dunes. Most of the world's biggest ships can use this canal, taking around an hour to traverse. The remarkable part is that the ship is riding well above the surrounding countryside which is, of course, below sea level. The locks at the outer end to the ocean do not have much fall, but keep the water fresh.

It has been pointed out that if sea-level was to rise by five metres, then most of The Netherlands would be under water. This may be true, but since levels are only likely to rise by the order of centimetres per decade, it is fairly obvious that the Dutch could keep up with the rise. It is the low-lying countries like the east coast of Britain, where there is no protection, which would suffer from such a rise; a rise which has been going on in some areas for centuries.

As might be imagined in a country of over ten million people and only about 200km across in any direction, the density of population is high and the country is criss-crossed by railways and cycle tracks. Take a train from anywhere and it could have any number of destinations, with the train dividing and re-joining on the way.

Amsterdam *Centraal Station* is built on wooden piles in the water and forms the centre point of the city and of the nation. Not all trains leave from here, as you may need to take a train originating from Schipol, the international airport, which does not pass through *Centraal*. Schipol was added to the network at a time when the value of such a connection was not confirmed. It now sets an example to most other cities in the world to have a rail hub at the airport. Netherlands' trains are modern, clean and electric, although there are diesel lines in the provinces, if one could describe the less urban areas as such.

Walking forward from *Centraal Station* will take you along the Damrak and give a good indication of the pace of life of the city. Surrounding *Centraal Station* is a series of semicircular canals which are bridged as the streets cross them. The central square includes the cathedral, the Dam. The city can then best be viewed by taking to the smaller streets, which give an even better idea of a prosperous and bustling city. In the Dam Square, the diamond sellers are very happy to show diamonds being cut in the hope that you will buy one. Now, there is a souvenir of consequence with a very good value-for-volume ratio for your baggage. Granny might like that.

As a visitor to The Netherlands, you will need to remember that the country is not purely Amsterdam and to move further afield. The surprising part then is that none of these cities is any great distance away and can be visited almost in a half day. Den Haag, Rotterdam, Utrecht, Delft, Alkmaar, Dordrecht, Amersfoort, Leiden and Gouda, are only a few of the cities worth visiting.

Cycles make up much of the transport in The Netherlands for many reasons, perhaps the most persuasive being that the country is flat. Using a bicycle and supplementing it with the train is undoubtedly the most sensible way of moving about The Netherlands. Many families have no car and do not see the need for one. Some years ago the government issued all students with a national rail pass, and decreased their grant accordingly, to ensure that the students stayed out of cars and on their cycles and on the trains rather than the roads.

Netherlands Rail is a partner in Thalys, which operates high speed, TGV-style trains between Amsterdam and Antwerp, Brussels, Paris and Köln. Germany, France, Belgium and The Netherlands have built high speed lines along these routes to give very fast journeys. The journey from Amsterdam to Paris currently takes 3h20 and there is more reduction to come yet as the track is further upgraded. Thalys and *Deutsche Bahn* ICE3 operate frequent services from Amsterdam to Köln, with the latter continuing to Frankfurt. No trains have yet been proposed to go directly to London, but ultimately such a project will be taken up. Another conventional intercity service links to Berlin, though from Schipol, not from *Centraal*.

City Night Lines, CNL, runs sleeper trains from Amsterdam each night to Berlin, Prague, Copenhagen, München and Zürich, while the *Jan Kiepura* runs to Warsaw with a through car to Moscow. All of these services depart on one of two trains leaving Amsterdam each evening.

The Netherlands has fairly liberal laws on drug use which do not, in general, concern the locals but do draw large numbers of the world's losers to Amsterdam, where they believe that the world will be theirs. It is not, of course, and for many years the area around Amsterdam Centraal was a place to avoid, with all of the unwanteds of the world hanging about. The city fathers have taken steps to remove these to locations further out in the city where they bother only themselves. *Centraal Station* is now becoming respectable once more, but the increase in traffic will never restore it to its original glory.

38. GERMANY, THE NATION

Here is definitely not the place to be expressing views of what occurred in World War I or World War II, but merely to pick up the description as the latter ended.

After Germany collapsed in 1945, the Allies and the Soviets advanced across Europe and ultimately met at what roughly became the demarcation line between eastern and western Germany, the Soviets having occupied Berlin. After the Yalta conference, the western area was placed under the occupation of the US, Britain and latterly France. The eastern section was occupied by the Soviets, but not before the western part of Berlin was granted to the Allies and a portion of the previous western part, around Jena, was assigned to the Soviets. As well as all this, a large corridor of the eastern part of Germany, that beyond the Oder and Neisse rivers together with the southern half of East Prussia, was transferred to Polish sovereignty.

So the division between eastern and western Germany came about.

The sections controlled by the Allies went on to become West Germany, the *Bundesrepublik Deutschland*, the BRD; and the section controlled by the Soviets as East Germany, the *Deutsche Demokratikische Republik*, the DDR. The capital of the BRD was set up in Bonn.

By 1948 the flow of persons to the west from the DDR had become so great, and these were often people valuable to the nation, that tough emigration regulations were set up by the DDR and ultimately 'The Berlin Wall' was built; a wall surrounding the whole of the enclave of West Berlin. The people of the East were told it was to keep the capitalist Westerners out, but it was clearly to keep the beleaguered East Germans in. This brought the world very close to another war, but in any case inaugurated 'The Cold War' which was to last until 1989.

The Allies left West Germany and the BRD subsequently became, in 1957, a founder member of what was to become the EU.

This was the situation which continued throughout the 1970s and 1980s.

In 1989 the economy in the communist world was such that the status quo could not be maintained and, under pressure from every direction, the Wall fell and free movement was restored.

The BRD was very anxious for re-unification to take place and this was finally achieved by bringing the elements of the DDR into the BRD in 1990. One of the first moves of the expanded government was to transfer the capital from Bonn to Berlin, and details of this are included in the chapter on Berlin.

The reason for presenting this brief history is not only for general interest, but also to give a preamble for the development of the rail system as given in the next chapter.

39. GERMANY, THE RAIL SYSTEM

After being given its 'independence' from the WWII allies, West Germany, the BRD, set about in the 1970s rebuilding its railway system.

The BRD now had no central capital city in the same form as London, Paris or Madrid. The commercial centre was Frankfurt, the administrative capital Bonn, the industrial area Köln (Cologne)-Dortmund, the port Hamburg and in the south München (Munich). This was therefore no 'out-and-back' railway system as in the case of other European cities, but a new 'linking everywhere-to-everywhere-else' model had to be developed.

The BRD adopted a policy of new fast lines and new fast trains and commenced by building a high speed line from Hannover south to Würzburg, thereby linking Hamburg and Hannover with Frankfurt, Nürnberg and München. For this they designed and purchased 60 new Inter City Express trains, ICE-1, of ten or so cars, with an integral locomotive on each end. These were introduced in 1991 and normally are timetabled at 250 kph maximum, although they can achieve 280 kph. This became the core of the DB system.

The second leap came with unification of the two Germanys after 1989 and the re-instatement of Berlin as the capital city. A new fast line between Berlin and Hannover was built and the ICE-2 brought into service in 1997 linking Bonn, Köln, Dortmund with Berlin. The ICE-2 was a 'half train' of the same form as ICE-1, but which could be coupled or uncoupled to serve multiple destinations or travel alone. ICE-2 is timetabled at 280 kph maximum.

In parallel with this there was a scurry to rebuild most of the trunk routes in the old East, in particular between Hamburg and Berlin and München and Berlin.

To complete the network to first order, a new high speed line was built from Köln to Frankfurt, for which the first set of ICE-3 trains was delivered in 1999; this time a fully motored set with no free-standing locomotives and capable of 300 kph. These trains extend now in all directions to Dortmund, Amsterdam and Brussels in the north and to Basle, Stuttgart, Nürnberg and München in the south. ICE-3 is timetabled for 300 kph maximum, but they can run at 320 kph. The highest recorded speed is 368 kph.

The final set of trains to attract attention was the ICE-T, a similar set to the ICE-3 but not as large or fast, and capable of 250 kph on non-purpose-built lines such as the old, upgraded, lines in the east. Further versions of the ICE are being continuously added to the fleet and journeys of the ICE extend now to Zürich, Interlaken Ost, Vienna and Paris. Some ICEs have been adapted to run on voltages of neighbouring countries.

In May 2011, DB concluded a framework agreement with Siemens Mobility for up to 300 trainsets, known as the ICx. The ICx will be the backbone of the future long-distance network of the *Deutsche Bahn*. In the initial phase, 130 ICx-type trains have been ordered and, beginning in 2016, they will replace the Intercity and Eurocity fleets put into operation between 1971 and 1991. At a later time, it is planned to replace ICE 1 and ICE 2 vehicles. The ICx will then be responsible for roughly 70 per cent interurban transport revenue of DB.

The following is an overall view of the ICE fleet, but without an attempt at technical specification:

Title	Number Date	Cars	Speed kph	Voltage	Built for:	Used also:	Recognition
ICE 1 401	41 1991	12 + 2 power	280	15 kV AC	Hannover to Würzburg	Germany to Zürich	2 power cars.
	19 1991	12 + 2 power	280	15 kV AC			2 power cars.
ICE 2 402	44 1993	7 + 1 power	280	15 kV AC	Berlin to Köln/Bonn	München to Hamburg	Single power car. Usually double units.
ICE 3 403	50 1997	8 EMU	330	15 kV AC	Frankfurt to Köln		Red stripe turns down at front.
ICE 3M 406	7 2000	8 EMU	330	1.5 kV DC	Amsterdam, Brussels, Paris	Basel	Pantograph on the second car.
ICE 3MF 406F	6 Modified	8 EMU	330	3.0 kV DC	France		
ICE 3M 406	4	8 EMU	330	15 kV AC	Amsterdam Frankfurt	Owned by 'NS Hispeed'	
ICE 3M 407	15 2011	8 EMU	320	25 kV AC	France London	Upgraded body styling	
ICE T 411	60 1997	8 EMU	230	15 kV AC	Classic lines, Leipzig, Vienna	Small number owned by ÖBB	Horizontal red stripe at front. Pantograph on the end car.
ICE T 415	11 1997	5 EMU	230	Tilting		Mainly used as supplement	
ICE TD 605	20 1997	4 DMU	200	Diesel Tilting	Non-electric lines	No longer used by DB. Some in DSB	Horizontal red stripe at front.

Source: *Modern Railways*, November 2010. Exact dates and details are not guaranteed. Total, 257 electric ICE.

DB's greatest achievement is the ICE-T, a tilt train, built after other countries had experimented with, and beaten, the problems of tilt. As you go around a corner fast, you feel that you are being flung outwards; this is straightforward physics. Roads and railways are banked to compensate for this and cause you to lean slightly inwards, hence feeling nothing. Railways are banked for their standard customers, local passengers and freight, which don't go at high speeds. When DB took over the railways in eastern Germany, some tracks were both in the mountains and very winding. Banking the track was not an option, so the alternative was to tilt the train. So a ride on the ICE-T means that you are continuously being tilted to and fro to imitate the correct banking for that speed. The initial tilt trains caused passengers to become seasick, but this has been cured by making the tilt 'not quite perfect'. It is these ICE-T trains which provide the service between München, Leipzig, Berlin and Hamburg Altona, and it is on these trains that the scenery is fabulous, the ride is great, the comfort is next to the best, and so the list goes on.

Because of its position, trains from Germany are now timetabled to run across borders into most other surrounding countries. ICEs can be seen operating into The Netherlands, Belgium, Denmark, Austria, Switzerland and most recently into France. These services are generally balanced by a reciprocal set of trains, such as TGVs from Paris and Thalys trains from Brussels and Amsterdam. Alternatively, as with services to Copenhagen, Vienna, Zürich and Interlaken Ost, a joint form of operation is used.

One blot on DB history is the disastrous crash at Eschede in 1998.

Anyone who rides a bicycle knows that balance of wheels is critical to good operation, and one attaches small nodules of lead to the rim of the wheel to achieve this. In this way the wheel can be balanced so that it will spin for many minutes without coming to rest. The same is necessary for train wheels, and before Eschede this balance had been achieved by drilling a hole in the wheel at the appropriate place. Now train wheels are under tension and even the most elementary engineering or physics will tell you that if you cut a hole in something under tension, then stresses develop which could lead to collapse. Well, this is what happened at Eschede on 3 June, 1998 with one of the wheels on the front carriage of an ICE-1 collapsing and throwing the car across the aperture of a bridge. with a whole fast moving train behind it trying to go under the bridge. The death and injury toll was enormous, over 100 dead, with the consequence that the fleet was grounded for most of the summer while all other trains in the fleet had the fault rectified. Only with a smile can you see how one part of the engineering maintenance had not consulted the other. Of course, the problem has now been eliminated throughout the world, making all trains that little bit safer. You can see some terrible photographs on Wikipedia by visiting 'Eschede'. There are only 59 ICE-1 in service today.

Most of the original German lines follow river valleys and are therefore very scenic tourist routes. The recent purpose-built high speed lines tend to follow more direct routes using tunnels and cuttings and are therefore visually less attractive.

The number of overnight trains in Europe has decreased drastically in the past 20 years, referring back to the 1970s when almost every city had a direct overnight train to Calais to connect with the boat to England, or perhaps to continue by boat to England. Day trains in Germany now take probably half the time that they took then, and you can travel as far now between dinner and bedtime as you previously could overnight. The night trains which originate in Germany are now generally run by a specialised company, City Night Lines, CNL, which operates internally in Germany and to Paris, Copenhagen, Amsterdam, Prague, Zürich, Venezia and Roma. A 'sister' company, which operates under the name of Euronacht, EN, operates services mainly based out of Vienna. In many other countries night trains are marketed by their national railway company.

There is, however, in Germany, one, and one only, pair of conventional IC trains made up of daytime coaches (train numbers IC2020 and IC2021), going north and south respectively, which travel overnight and do so between Hamburg and Frankfurt, stopping at most of the stations which enjoy a regular IC day service. There must be some hidden reason why these trains operate, but they have a good loading in second class. IC trains such as these have first class cars, but it is to be expected that revenue-paying night passengers would use the otherwise extra cost to pay for a couchette, so there are very few first class passengers on trains IC2020/21. Hence an empty first or second class compartment can be expected. Pull the curtains, douse the lights, pull out the seats into full length 'beds', spread out the baggage and the compartment is yours for the night. This is far more comfortable than a couchette, which involves sharing with others and paying money.

As can be seen from these few comments, Germany is both a train watcher's paradise and a train rider's paradise. It is possible to go from anywhere to anywhere and in a ridiculously short time at a one hour frequency or better. Nowhere in the world other than Switzerland can provide such a good service.

40. GERMANY, THE SOUTH, THE WEST AND THE RHINE

Basle

Let us begin our virtual tour of Germany from the south-eastern corner at Basle. Basle is actually in Switzerland and the Basle SBB (Swiss Railways) station is a major junction for Swiss, German and French services. For the SBB and DB, Basle is a terminal station, requiring trains to reverse to continue their journey. The SNCF lines enter Basle from the western side and, in the days before Switzerland entered the Schengen Treaty, SNCF also operated Basle as a terminal station. Currently many of the French trains venture into Switzerland and a two-hourly or better service by TGV from Paris to Zürich results.

The German station, Basle Bad Bahnhof, is inside Switzerland and is a legacy of when all passports had to be checked in either direction. DB trains pass through here heading for the Swiss station from where access is gained to the Swiss trains.

The line north from Basle virtually follows the right bank of the Rhine as far as Mannheim, the Rhine being the border between France and Germany for most of the trip. Some of this route has already been supplemented with a pair of high speed tracks, and more of the high speed route is under construction.

Mannheim is a very old city on the River Neckar, quite close to its confluence with the Rhine, but is an important rail junction as the line from Stuttgart meets us here. A new high speed line to Frankfurt from Mannheim is promised.

Further up the Neckar is Heidelberg, the famous old university city which is a *must* on any traveller's itinerary.

Frankfurt

Frankfurt am Main is the most important rail and air hub in Europe and a world financial centre. Of course, many other cities will dispute this. Berlin would claim to be the German capital, London would claim that The City was more important, Paris would claim supremacy, the Swiss would tell you that the gold was in Zürich and the Swedes would tell you that it does not matter.

When the capital of the BRD was settled on Bonn, the financial capital of the BRD developed in Frankfurt. From there it simply grew.

Today, Frankfurt Airport is gigantic. Once you set aside the monolith that is Heathrow, Frankfurt is certainly the biggest airport in Europe and has allowed development to match. The airport facilities are streamlined, clean, polite and need no apology for carrying out the task of moving millions of people. Frankfurt benefitted from the foresight of the DB in building a railway station beneath the airport. What started as a small station on the suburban network, quickly outgrew its capabilities. Mainline trains were routed through that way. Eventually a mainline station had to be built under the airport and this promises to become the biggest rail interchange point in Germany, outstripping even Frankfurt Hauptbahnhof (main or central station, Hbf).

While financial centres generally do not provide for tourist activities, there is enough history to be found by proceding into the city from from the Frankfurt Hauptbahnhof to satisfy anyone but the complaining. Frankfurt is, of course, a port on the River Main, only a little distance from the Rhine.

As in München, the S-Bahn system of Frankfurt is relatively new and is based on a tunnel continuing under the Hauptbahnhof at the western end of the city, and connecting with services at the eastern end. As is the case with many of these systems, the trains first used the main lines which were progressively supplemented by purpose built S-Bahn tracks. The U-Bahn network is quite large but not as extensive as that of München.

The Rhine

The Eurail pass holder can enjoy the privilege of a cruise by KD (Köln-Düsseldorfer Deutsche Rheinschiffart) on the River Rhine, at no charge. To see more of the river, a downstream cruise is recommended. Take a slower train from Frankfurt Hauptbahnhof in the direction of Koblenz and leave the train at Bingen. A short walk will bring you to the wharf where several departures occur each morning in the summer months. It takes a good proportion of the day to reach Boppard on the boat, from where you find a return train. Boppard is worth a visit as an old river town with an interesting church. If you have started early enough, your boat may continue to Koblenz or even Köln, but the best of the scenery is before Boppard. Beware that sailing conditions are never satisfying to everyone. A well prepared sailor will need a good hat, sunscreen, a warm coat and a raincoat. Any of these could be needed at any time. Another such journey is the KD service down the Mosel from Cochem to Koblenz

The new high speed line from Frankfurt to Köln made a big difference to the journey north from Frankfurt. Previously the line followed the left bank of the Rhine and was both winding and slow. The new route goes directly and, as common sense would indicate, parallels the motorway for much of the distance, cutting the rail journey from 2¼ hours to 1¼ hours. The journey could be made in one hour, but it was prudent to include Frankfurt Airport for greater connection flexibility, so the publicity for the new line merely talked about 'cutting one hour'. There is little to see from the train window as the line is mostly in tunnels, in cuttings or behind sound baffles. The use of the line is restricted to the ICE-3 which had been designed with this line in mind so only fast trains pass this way.

Köln (Cologne)

Köln, still on the Rhine, has a pair of unusual bedfellows in the centre of the city; the Cathedral and the Hauptbahnhof, one of the largest rail hubs in the region. The Cathedral in Köln is a massive Gothic building which glowers down over the Hauptbahnhof. Certainly you would go a long way to see such a huge Gothic building. The inside gives the impression of an infinite space, reaching upward and outward. My wife and I were first there during an organ recital, possibly during a rehearsal, and the effect, coupled with the grandeur of the building, was memorable. During WWII Churchill made an all-out attempt to destroy the railway yards of Köln as they were a key to the transport of the area. His instructions were to spare the Cathedral, and they were followed. This is very different from those of another nation we know where the instructions were, 'Blast the hell out of everything!'

Koblenz, Dortmund, Essen and Düsseldorf are only a few of the other major cities worthy of a visit along this western alignment

41. GERMANY, HAMBURG AND THE NORTH

Big bustling commercial cities appear to have very little soul, but this is not true of Hamburg, even though one must go looking for the soul. Hamburg has that soul, but it is widely distributed.

Hamburg Hauptbahnhof is not a railway station you would like to visit, as it is a through station with around 12 platforms, many commuter trains, too many diesel trains as well as a full complement of IC and ICE trains. The precinct is thus very noisy but, as comes with large numbers of people, the fast food service around the concourses is very good. The streets outside the Hauptbahnhof are populated with persons you have no desire to meet, even though a police station has been installed on the site.

Hamburg has the fortune to have, in addition to the Hauptbahnhof, a secondary station, huge in its own right, at Altona, a few kilometres further north. This means that most trains to and from the south will pass through the Hauptbahnhof and originate or terminate at Altona. Starting your journey from Altona will give you the seat or compartment you desire before the masses swarm on at the Hauptbahnhof.

The Hamburg S-Bahn system is centred on the two routes from the Hauptbahnhof to Altona, and stretches further along most main line routes to the boundary of the city and often beyond. These trains are third-rail powered and thus not compatible with the main lines. The U-Bahn, as in most German cities, is more modern. One quirk of the system is found at the station at Landüngsbrucke where the U-Bahn crosses above the S-Bahn.

Let us start with the port. While not being on the open sea, Hamburg has all the facilities normally found there, thanks to the estuary of the Elbe. One only has to go to Landüngsbrucke on the S-Bahn to be able to see major shipping, containers, cruise ships, dry docks and fishing; it is all there. Remember Hamburg is one of Germany's very few deep sea ports.

Associated with ports is always the world's oldest profession, to be found at the Reeperbahn, one S-Bahn station further on. If not the largest such area in the world, this is certainly one of the best known. The ladies are not alone as there is a huge area occupied by those other people whose activities are related and not considered in such good taste.

The city is built around several stretches of water which can be seen on any map. Around these are the numerous public buildings of Hamburg, ancient and modern.

Bremen is famous outside Germany for the legend of *The Musicians of Bremen*. This centres around a group of animals which sets out to frighten an individual. A statue of the animals is in the town centre.

Hameln has a reputation based also on legend, as it was from here that the *Pied Piper of Hamelin* led the children when the city fathers would not pay him for removing the rats. A monument also exists here.

Hannover is an important city at the point where the major east-west and north-south routes of the pre-unification DB crossed.

42. HELGOLAND

It is unlikely you have ever been to Helgoland and no more likely that you have even heard of it. It is an island which is part of Germany, sitting in the North Sea, facing England. Why are we going to discuss it? Because it is there, that's why.

When I was a child, even during WWII, we had acquired some postage stamps from Helgoland. Father called it Heligoland. According to him, and it is likely to be true, Churchill bombed the place out of the water because it would have made an ideal base for fighter planes and U-boats intent on causing mischief for England.

Helgoland is two islands, sitting like Pluto and its satellite Charon, 70km out in the North Sea; the only offshore islands in Germany. It is far enough out to enjoy the benefits of the Gulf Stream, like the Scilly Islands in Britain again. According to the locals, Helgoland has more hours of sunshine than anywhere else in Germany and purer air than anywhere in Germany, including the top of the Zugspitze. The latter is not difficult to understand.

The main island consists of the up-lands, a red sandstone peak about 50 metres high and about 500 metres long, visible as you come toward the island. Surrounding this is an area of about the same size, but only slightly above sea level. About 500 metres across the 'bay' is the Dunes, the second island, about the same size, none of which would be more than five metres above the high water mark. Everything is surrounded by deep water and part has been formed artificially into safe anchorage. On the Dunes there are extensive, safe, white sand beaches. There is a helipad on the main island and an airstrip on the Dunes, but not big enough for anything substantial.

Helgoland is yet another 'opt-out' from the EU regulations. Everything on the island is duty-free with no VAT. As you return to Germany, you must go

217

through customs to ensure that you have not exceeded your EU allowance. Hence it is a haven for sales of liquor, cigarettes, perfume, etc. and other miscellaneous, but otherwise dutiable, junk.

There is no air service to the island and the main transportation is a catamaran, daily from Hamburg or Cuxhaven, which takes a little under four hours. This carries of the order of 700 souls. Thomas Cook gives very little detail as the services vary with the season. The tourist drawcard of the island comes from its novelty in location and from its tax status, until you arrive that is. Once on the island, you find that there is far more of interest than the four-hour turnaround will allow.

The arrangement of the buildings is quite something. One is reminded of great swathes of council houses, all the same, but all not looking at all like houses, rather like overgrown bathing boxes. These *Hummerbuden* were once cabins of the fisherfolk. The various hotels blend in with the buildings and there is a youth hostel at the far end of the island.

An unbelievable ferryboat will take you across to the Dunes, taking about five minutes. This is a true commuter service, with a few benches and lots of standing and baggage space. By the time you have found that there is really nowhere to sit, you have arrived.

Once on the Dunes, you realise what flat means. A couple of metres rise in the sea level and Charon's analogy will have disappeared. There is a set of buildings of classy accommodation, all identical, another of cheap accommodation and a camping site. That's it. The beaches, though, are out of this world. They are several hundred metres long, protected by groynes and are kept clean by tides. The colour of the sand is white, like Adelaide's beaches once were.

The food of Helgoland is remarkable. Of course there are the inevitable pizza and burger places, but in the main you have seafood. Fish of all varieties abound, together with scampi, North Sea lobster, crabs and other bottom dwellers. The main delicacy is crab claws which you buy by the kilogram, break by whacking with a spoon and pick. One thinks of all the clawless crabs which might be crawling about in the bay. You can buy the fish off a trestle table, in a pub or in a classy restaurant and you can eat it out of a paper bag, from a cardboard plate, or from best porcelain.

Shopping, of course, is the key. Trade is quietly and pleasantly done, not with the vulgarity of places like Venice but there all the same. Discretion seems to come in the form of suitcases, as there are huge numbers of these winched on and off the catamaran before and after the journey.

There even seems to be a local language, as many words on signs are in German and in 'something else'. Who knows?

Should you go to Helgoland? Probably not, as the cost is high. Any number of Baltic Sea locations will provide most of what you are after. It is hard to imagine that you would cover the fare with the saving on duty-free goods. There are a few other duty-free havens inside the boundaries of the EU which might give you the same goods as cheaply.

Perhaps I have wasted my time giving such a long description of Helgoland when all I could muster was a shared sentence for Dortmund. But the island was fun.

43. GERMANY, LEIPZIG AND THE EAST

Travelling through eastern Germany and watching the transition from the old Soviet-style existence to modern day Germany has been a great experience over the last 20 years, and the changes still continue. At first everything was grey and drab with junk everywhere. Cities resembled penitentiaries rather than homes. Slowly, but much faster than once considered possible, all this has changed.

The railways demonstrate the change more than anything else. The legacy of Honecker, the last boss of the DDR, was a run-down rail system, the *Deutsche Reichsbahn*, DR, mostly diesel, with antiquated trains taking an eternity to reach anywhere. The advent of the BRD brought on a major change. The DB laid new tracks, installed overhead power and introduced ICE trains. Every one of my successive trips along the Nürnberg-Leipzig-Berlin-Hamburg axis has revealed new development and faster, cleaner services. This will shortly be overtaken by a completely new high speed line linking Nürnberg with Halle and Leipzig.

Leipzig

Leipzig is one of the more amazing places in eastern Germany. It escaped the bombing given to Dresden and is thus a little more intact. The city has an impressive skyline of metal and glass buildings and at ground level is a bustling metropolis, with advertising being the predominant theme. What a change this is from the Leipzig of 1990, which was dull and dingy with a drag-one-foot-after-the-other appearance. The streets are now clean and modern, the trams and buses new and the people enjoying their life. Then there is the old city. You enter there and feel that you might walk into old Johann Sebastian, dressed in his Cappell-Meister garb. In the streets, however, are restaurants and beer houses, and probably brothels, indicating that the average Leipziger enjoys life.

Nowhere is a better example of the renewal than the Leipzig railway station, which must now rank amongst the greatest in the world. In 1990 it was filthy, dank and smelly, and suited to cater for the steam train era, untouched throughout the Soviet days. This has all gone and the station has been given back the glory it deserves. The huge station building covers 25 platforms; enormous when you compare this with 11 at London Kings Cross or 10 at London Paddington. The head of the platforms leads to an area bigger than the forecourt at London Euston, but under a roof about four storeys high. Below this are two floors of shops, enough to cater for a city. Beyond this is the main station hall, again about four storeys high and big enough to include Sydney Central Station and more. Everything is beautifully clean, with marble floors and perfectly painted roofs. All of this has been achieved in much less than 15 years.

The station would have been built for steam trains and is a dead-end for mainline trains, like Frankfurt, Zürich, Stuttgart and München. The trains would have come in, uncoupled the loco, added a loco on the outer end and headed off again with a new crew some 30 minutes later. Not so now. The ICE-T comes in, there is a new driver waiting at the outer end and new on-train crew at the inner end. The timetable allows four minutes between the arrival and departure of the trains.

This is not all. A completely new underground suburban station is being constructed beneath the mainline station, which will allow through trains to run beyond Leipzig. More changes, therefore, are about to occur.

Dresden

Dresden was bombed, flattened,by Churchill in the dying days of WWII so not a lot was left for Stalin to take. The city has the same bustle about it as Leipzig. The rebuilding of Hauptbahnhof, which links with nothing more exciting than the railway to Prague, has been left until last and is now having its facelift. The trainshed, every bit as amazing as Leipzig, is being rebuilt in a more modern rather than traditional style and the platforms are being progressively renovated. Most other former East German stations had this happen ten years ago. Dresden station still has the unpleasant 'tunnels', which are the locations of the merchants in the station building, mostly in takeaway-sized holdings.

Once your train heads north from Dresden Hauptbahnhof, the truth of the development unfolds. Those works which were not necessary for progress have been sidelined as the money became tight. The cleaning up of the railway yards has been postponed. There are old track layouts, signal boxes, round houses, turntables, sheds and more sheds, etc., all dating from the Soviet or even pre-WWII days. Everything seems abandoned, with the exception of the new concrete sleepered tracks. Here you can see the East Germany of the Ulbricht and Honnecker days and this is likely to remain, as it must be low on the money priority list. The untidiness makes you want to go out there with a shovel and a bin, but preferably with a front-end loader and a truck.

Dresden is very different from Leipzig. The core of the city is toward the river and a good way from the Hauptbahnhof. A walk to the river shows the commercial development that is happening. There is no walled enclosure as in Leipzig, so the city monuments are spread more widely and are harder to identify. They are, however, all there.

The journey from Nürnberg through the eastern part of the old East Germany, close to the Czech border, then through Dresden, to Berlin provides an excellent example of the rail development. This line was brought to Western track standards quickly after re-unification, but it winds around the mountains and is therefore very slow. The overhead power extends only about one-third of the way south from Dresden and then stops. Other projects must have had higher priority. Hence the train from Nürnberg is a very slow, conventional, loco-hauled, diesel IC. At least it trades the diesel for an electric loco when it reaches the wires. The countryside here is not very heavily populated, in fact it is mostly wooded, but appearance from the train can be deceptive as only a few hundred metres are visible on either side. The total picture is green and the houses well painted, so there is evidence of no shortage in quality of life. There is very little evidence of the Soviet days either, except in the ubiquitous untidy railway yards.

There is a legend that in 1945 one of these cities watched with apprehension the approaching Russian armies, with their reputation of rape, loot and pillage, and remembered that it had a huge bronze statue of Stalin in a basement somewhere. All of us have one of those, surely? So the city fathers fished it out, cleaned it up and hoisted it into the city square. When the Russians arrived, they were overwhelmed and treated the citizens like long-lost brothers. The statue is in the historical museum in Berlin.

Many smaller cities exist in this area which would show even more of the contrast between then and now. Leipzig and Dresden do it well.

44. MÜNCHEN, MUNICH AND BAYERN

München is the capital of Bayern, Bavaria, the biggest province of the BRD. The population of München is about one million, about the same as Adelaide, and the distance to the outskirts would be of the order of ten kilometres. Compare this with the spread of an Australian or North American city. The name Bayern shows in the München football team.

München is a natural crossing point of the River Isar, which originates in the Bavarian Alps. Apparently back in years past when robber barons regularly set up house on such crossings to exact tolls from the travellers, a company of monks set up at this particular crossing and, not only did they not extract a toll but they gave aid to those in need. Hence the crossing became known as 'München', meaning 'little monks'. The city badge is a small monk.

As with Hamburg in the north, rail lines heading south in Germany reconverge on München from Nürnberg and Stuttgart, then diverge to locations in Austria. An hourly service exists over both lines from Frankfurt. Arrival in München is at the Hauptbahnhof, one of the largest terminal stations in Germany, with over 24 platforms. Frankfurt claims to have as many platforms under its roof, but comparisons are confusing.

The S-Bahn and U-Bahn system in München is probably the most efficient and up-to-date in Germany, or perhaps in all of Europe. The S-Bahn was formed by joining, by a tunnel, the Hauptbahnhof and the Ostbahnhof, on opposite sides of the city, and running the suburban trains through and on to the main lines. Over the years dedicated lines have been built for the local network and the service has grown independently of the long distance services. The S-Bahn goes, of course, to the airport, and by two different routes. A second S-Bahn tunnel is being built under the city, roughly parallel to the first, to take account of the growth in S-Bahn traffic and possibly to allow regional express services to cross the city. This is not expected to be opened until 2025. I doubt that I shall be interested.

The first U-Bahn line was built to the Olympic Stadium, also worth a visit, for the Olympics in 1972 and has been growing ever since.

To see the city, walk straight ahead from the front of the Hauptbahnhof, via Karlsplatz to the Marienplatz. This is the spiritual centre of München. There you can see the Old City Hall, which dates back hundreds of years, and its replacement the New City Hall (Rathaus), which is only about 100 years old. In the tower is the *Glockenspiel*, a name given to a group of figurines which perform a symbolic mediaeval dance. Actually the word *glockenspiel* applies to the chiming from behind. The figurines are a bonus. Crowds come from everywhere to see it but very few stay to watch the whole sequence.

There is so much to do and see in München that it is difficult to know where to start. Extensive areas of the centre of München around the Marienplatz have been placed under flagstones, so that the density of foot traffic far exceeds that which cars would have provided. During the day these streets are filled with people going about their business. By night and weekend, the restaurants and beer traders spill out onto the entire area. Buskers, ranging from magicians to the inevitable instrumental rendition of *Ave Maria,* are everywhere. Wandering around München is a delight.

There are churches everywhere in this Roman Catholic city but five, all close to the Marienplatz, deserve a special mention.

1. The Frauenkirche, the Church of Our Lady, has its towers forming the dominating outline of München. Inside the front door is a footprint in the concrete. Apparently when the church was built, the Devil had a quick look and pointed out that there were no windows visible and, to prove it, he stood in the one place in the church where there were indeed no visible windows. His footprint remains.
2. St Michael and All Angels in the main street is easily passed by without notice, except for the statue above the door showing Michael ousting the Devil, all covered in bird wire to keep the pigeons off. This is a beautiful but austere church.

3. St Peter, which stands in the traditional style near the old town hall and will allow you to climb his tower for a fee; something you should do.

4. The Theaterinkirche, where the crypt holds the bodies of the Wittelsbach family, from which came Ludwig II, the last king of Bayern.

5. The Assamkirche in the Sendlingerstrasse, which is of a smaller sect of Christians and shows what beauty can come from a small church.

Nearly all of these churches were damaged or destroyed by bombing in WWII, but the nation received recompense from the Marshall Plan to rebuild them. You will find many more churches in München, maybe even more beautiful, but your feet will not forgive you.

Back in the 1880s the King of Bayern was Ludwig II. Ludwig was convinced that he ruled a nation of Philistines and was determined to do something to improve the culture of the land. Ludwig was, for instance, the patron of Richard Wagner, whose theatre is situated at Bayreuth in the north of Bayern. One of Ludwig's ideas was to build castles and several of these are in easy reach of München. Neuschwanstein, for instance, is about two hours by rail to the west. If you are going there, and you must, take a train from the Hauptbahnhof before 0900 or the wave of tourists will overtake you. Neuschwanstein is the castle from which Disney copied his castle for *The Sleeping Beauty*. Inside is absolutely magnificent and designed with the motif of the Swan. This all matches the story of Wagner's *Parsifal*, which is of the same vintage. If Disney used this for his *Sleeping Beauty*, which story Tchaikovski used for his ballet of the same name, then Peter Ilyich must have revelled in the idea of this castle for *Swan Lake*.

Old Ludwig had no idea of finances and his ideas were rapidly sending the country broke. One night he was found floating face down in the lake. The Bavarians have never forgiven themselves for their evil deed. Ludwig's replacement was never again termed 'king', but always Prince Regent. In the midst of all the Wittelsbach tombs in the crypt of the *Theaterinkirche*, Ludwig's tomb always has fresh flowers laid on it.

To the right of St Peter's is the *Victualen Markt*, the food and vegetable market for München. Not only can you buy local produce, meats and cheeses, etc., but there are good servings of typical Bavarian hot foods as well as the NordSee fish market. Of course all of the traditional drinking holes are also located here.

If you continue through the arch of the old city hall, go as far as McDonalds and turn left, then walk two blocks, you come to the Hofbrauhaus. This is probably the most famous drinking house in the world. Hofbrau is a brand name and this was once its brewery site. Watch the Bavarian gents, often in traditional costume, drinking their 'mass', one litre. Tradition has it that you drink slowly in München, a very sensible approach. After every few tunes the band, all in lederhosen etc., plays a drink-it-down theme to assist patrons to pass their money to the proprietor. Apparently they are paid by the quantity consumed. Enjoy the Hofbrauhaus, but don't attempt to keep up with the locals.

The greatest amount of drinking occurs at the Oktoberfest, starting on the last weekend in September. This festival was first held in 1810 to celebrate the marriage of Crown Prince Ludwig (later Ludwig I) and has been held each year since. Oktoberfest brings visitors from all over the world. Unfortunately it brings in some irresponsible types, including Australians, but the locals know how to deal with them.

The English use of the name *Bavaria* comes from the name of the lady who watches over them. *Bavaria* is a very Brünhilde-type lady whose statue has looked down over the Thereseienwiese since 1850. She shows herself at infrequent occasions on coins, stamps and medals, but not as much now as in the past. She has at least two cousins: *Helvetia*, who looks at us from the Swiss one franc coin; and *Britannia,* who was once on the British penny and has a passing resemblance to Queen Victoria. She also has a great aunt, *Germania*, an even more Wagnerian lady, who is not used much any more by the BRD, but was once on stamps of the *Deutsches Reich*. One suspects that she probably had Nazi sympathies and was sidelined. It is Germania who gives us the name *Germany* which is the English word for *Deutscheland.*

Continue away from the Marienplatz for a few more blocks, or take the S-Bahn to Isator, and you find the *Deutsches Museum*. This remarkable museum is dedicated to science and the history of science as it relates to Germany. One could easily spend a full day in there without running out of patience.

The cultural museums and galleries available in München are countless. Choose according to your own interest.

Walk behind the New City Hall and, after a few blocks, walk into the Hofgarten and follow the paths to the Englische Garten. Here the city fathers allow unclad sunbathing and swimming which is always seen as a novel, albeit rather unattractive, aspect of München. Beyond this is the Chinese Tower, yet another beer garden which serves a rather good Schweinhaxe, a baked pig's knuckle.

One of the best ways of seeing München is by taking a two-hour bicycle tour. These guys (Mike's Bikes) have the tour business down to a fine art and take you to almost everywhere in München that you would want to go, without leaving your bicycle. I decided to have a try a couple of years ago and, although I had not ridden a bike for about 40 years, I survived. Most pleasing was to find that they showed me nothing that I had not seen previously or even shown others in my walking tours of München.

Many other cities and surroundings in Bayern will justify a visit and are all easily reached by train.

The old mediaeval walled city of **Nürnberg** still exists in its original form but with all the comforts of home added, mainly on the outside of the walls.

Passau is located at the confluence of Rivers Danube (from the Black Forest in Germany), Inn (from Switzerland and Innsbruck) and Ilz (from the north), and where the Danube consequently almost doubles its size. A very pleasant pedestrian plaza leads from the railway station to the old city with eating houses abounding. The old city, dating back over a thousand years, centres about the cathedral of St Steven on the promontory between the Danube and the Inn. St Steven's houses the world's largest cathedral organ, the largest organ outside the US and the fourth largest organ in the world. Sydney Opera House and Sydney Town Hall come 14th and 24th respectively. Across the Danube is the fortress *Veste Oberhaus* (built 1219) from where the earlier princes would control commerce across the rivers, which simply means extract tolls from the passing trade. Today it is a museum and a youth hostel.

From Passau it is possible to take a cruise downstream on the Danube to Linz. For the hardy there is an established cycle track to the mouth of the Danube, over 2,000km.

The *Passion Play* is performed by the citizens of **Oberammergau** each ten years, fulfilling a promise made centuries ago to the Almighty for freeing them from plague. Virtually everyone in this small town becomes an actor or a support person when the time comes. One can visit the wardrobe where the costumes are maintained.

Zugspitze is the highest point in Germany and accessible by a series of funiculars and cable cars. These are not my favourite conveyances so one visit there has been enough.

Berchtesgarten is where Hitler had his retreat and where the von Trapp family would have reached, had they climbed their mountain from Salzburg. The longest single train journey within Germany begins here each morning and ends in Hamburg some 12 hours later.

Ulm claims to have the tallest cathedral spire in Germany. This can be climbed, but by a stairway which projects you into the open air at every turn. This is OK for those who realise that they could not be forced through the aperture, let alone fall through it, but it is not for the faint-hearted.

Bayreuth is home of the Festspielhouse of Richard Wagner, where a series of his operas is performed each year. The Festspielhouse is a timber structure which would not conceivably pass any fire regulations of today. The building has such historic value and unique acoustics that it remains in full use. It is reputed that the local fire department is ready on site for each production. My experience is limited to standing outside the theatre and looking on.

Lindau is a small city on an island in the Bodensee, the Lake of Constance, and connected by a road and rail causeway. Trains from München to Zürich pass through here and a pleasant break can be spent walking about the town or taking a boat cruise to Bregenz in neighbouring Austria or to Switzerland.

45. BERLIN

Berlin cannot be described; it would be too complicated. Divided for over 40 years, it was one of the principal sufferers of the Cold War until unification in 1989. Once the German Parliament in Bonn decided in 1990 that the capital of the re-united country was moving to Berlin, the money began to flow. The skyline was a mass of cranes throughout the 1990s and after. Areas around the line of the Wall were razed and a modern city has appeared. The western side, around the Zoo station, is very little different from the pre-unification days and feels a fairly hateful, over-capitalistic place. The eastern side, around Alexanderplatz, is now a living, shouting city. Costs are still not high in this area, which makes it a boon for tourists. It is the area in between these two, around the line of the Wall, where the building is most notable. Words cannot do it justice. And yet, if you had not seen the divided city, it would mean nothing.

For as long as can be remembered, Berlin has had a raised east-west railway through its midst, the Stadtbahn. During the years of occupation, trains from West Germany were allowed to cross the DDR and enter Berlin on the Stadtbahn. Passengers for West Berlin alighted at the Zoo station and the train generally continued across the line of the Wall to Friedrichstrasse station in the East. Here it was possible for tourists with appropriate passports to enter East Berlin on a one-day visa and enjoy the 'sights' of the DDR. Trains proceeding further, through Alexanderplatz, to Berlin Lichtenberg, the main station of the DR, were run by the DR with diesel trains. These services are now all operated by the DB using ICE or very efficient electric regional trains.

The main railway station, the Berlin Hauptbahnhof, is a wonderful example of the change. Since the inception of railways, Berlin had suffered from not having a north-south railway, purely the east-west one. Many attempts had been made over 150 years but the money was never found. There is/was a part of the S-Bahn on the north-south axis running under the Wall in places. This was suddenly flooded in about 1944 and it took until after unification of Germany for anyone to summon enough courage to find out what was actually down there. In June 2006, in time for the World Cup, the new Berlin Hauptbahnhof was opened. The station goes down three levels and takes all of Berlin's mainline and regional trains, north-south and east-west. The whole structure has been built from nothing. It is surrounded by new buildings as part of the development. This will give the visitor an idea of what has been done in Berlin in the last few years.

For many years my student tours to Berlin were led with an air of some authority. It was only when an 18-year-old student in 1999 said, 'Which wall?' that it became obvious that there was more past history to be added. The subsequent revised tours were a success but they have not been used for some years.

The time had thus come for me to see the 'professionals' running the tour, so the walking tour of Berlin, run by local English-speaking expatriates, was tracked down. The morning tour of three hours took the group around the city, showing the various aspects of the city of the two World Wars and before, right up to the location of Hitler's bunker. Of course, it showed the contrasting appearance of the eastern city centre, Alexanderplatz, and the western city centre, Tiergarten, but it left the wall for later. The afternoon tour, this time only two hours long, starting only long enough afterwards for a Coke and a bite to eat, took us along the line of the Wall, and showed the horrors of the Soviet days and the sequels of unification. Don't miss these tours if you have time in Berlin. Can you walk for five hours? Five hours on the hoof was a little daunting, but it left me only a little weary and certainly not incommoded. It was pleasing to find that the facts on the tour matched those of my tour fairly well.

With little trouble, you can do it all on your own. From the Hauptbahnhof walk toward the Reichstag, the parliament building burned by Hitler in 1933, and later rebuilt, now with a transparent beehive on top, visible from the Hauptbahnhof. All of the surrounding buildings are new. Then head across the park to the Brandenberg Gate which was the feature point of the Wall. It was here that US President Reagan said, 'Mr. Gorbachev, open up this gate!'

It was probably here that US President Kennedy said, 'Ich bin ein Berliner!' which made him a kind of bun. Note the *Quadriga*, a chariot drawn by four horses, on the top of the Gate. This was cast in 1793. Napoleon took a fancy to it and 'borrowed' it in 1806, but it was returned in 1814.

On the eastern side of the gate is the Parisier Platz which contains many buildings of influential countries, including the US Embassy. It has been suggested that the US Embassy was allocated a prime site near the Gate, but delayed building. Their plans submitted, which included all types of defence mechanisms, were rejected by the city fathers but they were told to 'build, with an accepted plan, or lose the site'. The US Embassy in Berlin is thus one of its more open in the world, but no doubt it you came too close something would jump out and grab you.

Continue down the Unter den Linden, seeing all of the commerce of Berlin.

Ultimately you arrive at the Museum Island which is the centre of the ancient showplace of Berlin, with the cathedral, the museums, the castle, the Humboldt University, the opera house, the memorial and the Lustgarten, to name a few. The last was a parade ground-like area in the 1930s and it was here that Herr Hitler persuaded the German public of his intentions. It has a very frightening place in history. Find the description on one of the boards in the street and stand in the garden, while imagining Hitler on the podium.

Continuing further, you come to Alexanderplatz with the high communication tower, no doubt built to demonstrate the superiority of the DDR but enabling them to see clearly anywhere in the West.

Berlin eating houses abound, but a good, non-expensive selection can be found in the vicinity of Hackeschermarkt S-Bahn station.

Further away from the axis of Berlin are even more sights, but with as many things to see as just given it will be some time before the short-time visitor has them on the list.

The Berlin S-Bahn system was maintained by the DDR during the days of the divided city and was quite a mess on unification. Most of the efforts of the DDR went into preventing the East Berliners from using it to go to the West. After about 15 years from unification it was restored to a very workable system, with its small but extremely efficient third-rail trains running very frequently in all directions. A large proportion of the S-Bahn routes parallel the main lines along the Stadtbahn. The ring line, similar to the old Circle Line in London, takes slightly over an hour to complete. Next come the regional services of Berlin and Brandenburg, which pass both east-west and north-south through the Hauptbahnhof. Intercity services, mostly ICE, use mainly the north-south 'in tunnel' axis but some still work east-west 'above ground'.

The Berlin U-Bahn system was maintained by the BRD and only needed a small patch-up and relinking to become quite serviceable. Work is presently continuing on the balance of the U5, which will link the U5 and the east of the city to the interim U55 and to the new Hauptbahnhof.

Almost as an afterthought, it must be remembered that the trains for Warsaw and beyond mainly begin in Berlin. Warsaw day trains are a dedicated set designed to cross the border. The big Russian sleeper cars with their darkened windows, which must change wheel gauge at the Russian frontier, are singularly out of place in this modern station.

46. AUSTRIA

Churchill is alleged to have said that Vienna in Austria is like having an elephant in your back yard. Vienna is extremely large compared with its host country. This may be true politically, but there is much more of Austria to see than Vienna.

Back in the early 1800s, Vienna was the third largest city in the world. Even 100 years ago it was third in Europe, after London and Paris. Today at 1.8 million it is being overtaken by many of the rapidly growing cities such as Moscow and Madrid.

After the wars with Napoleon, Austria was granted a huge empire which included most of the present Croatia, Slovenia, Czech Republic, Slovakia, Hungary and more. This was ruled from Vienna in various forms by the Habsburg Emperors. Franz Josef I, who came to power in 1848, was apparently a fairly benevolent emperor where he chose to be, judging by the number of projects attributed to him around Austria. But then the same could be said of the Tsars.

FJ married the beautiful Elisabeth (Sisi), who is still adored by the Austrian people. Sisi lived a very tortured life, being obsessed by her beauty and her waistline. She was murdered in 1898. Prince Rudolf, the son and heir of FJ, died in 1889, allegedly by suicide. The next heir of FJ was his nephew, Archduke Ferdinand, who was assassinated in Sarajevo in 1914. This caused old FJ to sign a declaration of war and so WWI began.

FJ did not survive the war and died in 1916 having reigned for 67 years and 355 days, longer than any monarch of recent years, comparable only with Britain's George III (59 years; 1760-1820) and Victoria (63 years and 7 months; 1837-1901). Elizabeth II in Britain has a sporting chance of beating all of them; in 2012 she reaches her Diamond Jubilee (60 years). The heir to Franz Josef I, his nephew Karl, was Emperor from 1916 until 1918 after which he was forced into exile and the Habsburgs banned from any future place in Austrian politics. Otto von Habsburg, eldest son of Karl I and in his time Crown Prince of Austria, died in 4 July 2011 at the age of 98. His coffin was laid to rest, midst much ceremony and reverence, in the crypt of his ancestors in central Vienna, where it ocupies the last available corner.

After WWI the old Austro-Hungarian Empire was carved up and Austria was left as a small republic, centred, as Churchill implies, on a major city, Vienna. After all, they did start WWI

Since Austria was German-speaking, it provided Hitler with his first target in WWII, and Austria was annexed to the Third Reich by the *Anschluss* in 1938, without a peep from anyone. No, this is not quite correct. Mexico apparently raised the matter internationally but received no support. Mexicoplatz, in central Vienna, is said to be named in honour of this action.

After WWII Austria was divided amongst the four powers for occupation, but this was terminated in 1955 when Austria became the Republic of Österreich with a neutralist constitution. Most significant events in Austria today have an origin post-1955.

When Soviet General Secretary Mikhail Gorbachev stated that he had no objection to Finland joining NATO and the EU, Austria amended its constitution, as did Sweden, and all three countries were fast-tracked into the EU in 1995. The Schengen Treaty took effect in Austria shortly after and Austria was one of the founder members of the Eurozone.

So, from this potted history you derive a very proud little nation whose achievements outweigh its apparent insignificance.

***

Austria extends from where the Rhine comes through the Alps in the west to where the Danube rounds the eastern end of the Alps at Vienna. In between are the Austrian Alps and Tyrol, which contain some of the more beautiful mountains in Europe.

Since it is logical to finish in Vienna, let's start our Austrian rail journey from Switzerland.

ÖBB, Austrian Railways, has introduced the *Railjet* to operate initially along the München/Zürich-Salzburg-Vienna-Budapest axis. These are fixed configuration loco-hauled units and have all the excellent components of a modern day railway. Currently they operate up to 200km/hr but are capable of 230km/hr. Their *premium* class is a step ahead of traditional first, in both comfort and price, and is fairly clearly intended for the businessman who wants to do a few hours undisturbed work as he travels.

The train from Switzerland must reverse in Buchs before crossing the Rhine and, in the case of conventional trains, change locos. From here the line continues to Feldkirch, with trains having gone non-stop through the Principality of Liechtenstein. In Feldkirch the service is joined by services from Bregenz, near Lindau on the Bodensee, also as far north and west as the rail in Switzerland extends. It is said that through services between Switzerland to Austria cannot occur, despite them having the same voltage, because the pantograph setting is different. *Railjets* have therefore have been equipped with a third pantograph to handle this.

From Feldkirch, both services head into the Vorarlberg, an unbelievable mountain area, and run through the Arlberg tunnel before beginning their descent through the Tyrol to Innsbruck, some two hours from Feldkirch.

Innsbruck is, of course, known for its ski resort and the competitions held here. To the railway, Innsbruck is the northern access to the Brenner Pass, carrying freight from Italy north to München and vice versa. Currently a Brenner base tunnel is being built and much of the line in Austria is being replaced with high speed track to provide this essential international link for the EU.

The main line turns north here, following the valley of the River Inn, and runs into Germany toward Rosenheim, which it skirts, and heads east to Salzburg. The line continuing through Austria toward Salzburg has another mountain range to traverse, so through Austrian trains do not go that way but use the German route.

The German railway ends at the border in Salzburg, so this was once a major customs point. It is no longer and the station is being completely reconstructed to allow through running without hindrance.

Salzburg originally depended for its existence on the salt exports coming from the mines along the River Salzach. In keeping with the customs of the day, Salzburg was a toll-point and a very lucrative one at that. Its owner happened to be the local archbishop.

The city thus abounds with churches, each built by successive wealthy archbishops to show their superiority over their predecessor.

The station in Salzburg is some distance from the old city, so to see it take a trolley bus from in front of the station and leave the bus immediately after you cross the river. Go through the first small street and see the main old city shopping street parallel to the river. Apart from the variety of souvenir shops and the inevitable Mozart museum, each shop carries a form of heraldic emblem. This is all very well until you notice that one of them includes Colonel Sanders and another carries the Golden Arches. Moving on from here, you can see the old town and its churches by heading generally in the direction of the castle. You will pass the cathedral, built in 774 AD and rebuilt in 1628, and gain some idea of the age, the importance and the wealth of the city.

A castle is a castle, but this one holds a somewhat important place in the image of the city and besides, there is a funicular railway waiting to take you up. Apart from the view across the hills, the vista of the city with its apparently unending collection of churches cannot be bettered. The hills are indeed 'alive' and there are walking trails from the castle.

Undoubtedly you will have noticed that this is the city of the musical, *The Sound of Music*, and the merchants and tour operators make the most of this. The locals probably have not even seen the movie. *Sound of Music* tours will take you to see the locations of the film shots, which they see as more important than the city, which is undoubtedly a reflection on their clients. You can see the cemetery of the last scene in the film, next to the bottom of the funicular.

Salzburg, of course, abounds with music and opera. Each summer for six weeks the *Salzburger Festspiele* brings together music, concerts, theatre and opera of world renown. One interesting extra is the Salzburg Marionette theatre, which does some very good productions of operas and operettas, an order of magnitude superior to the others mentioned elsewhere. Heather and I saw a production of *die Fledermaus,* using voices and music from the Vienna Staatsoper and the Vienna Philharmonic, and it was very hard not to keep thinking that it was the real thing.

In the surrounding countryside, the *Salzkammergut*, are many unique attractions to visit.

The town of St Wolfgang, on the Wolfgangsee, can be reached by taking a bus from Salzburg Hauptbahnhof to St Gilgen and then a launch to the town. Allegedly, over a thousand years ago St Wolfgang had an argument here with the Devil and as part of the solution built a church on the shore of the lake. The church is only small, but of amazing decoration, and would feature in my 'top 10' in Europe. Each time the altarpiece is opened, and a beautiful object it is, the bell of the church must toll. But that is not all. St Wolfgang is the home of the *Weisses Rössl*, or the *White Horse Inn,* which features in the musical of the same name by Bernatski and Stolz. Their dining room is as good as you can find. Still further, a few hundred metres out of the town, is a steam cog railway to the summit of the Schafbergspitze, a railway buff's absolute heaven, with a magnificent view of this lake and others round about. Don't miss St Wolfgang.

Further on is Bad Ischl, where the rich came to take the waters. The summer palace of the Habsburgs is where the Kaiser Franz Josef I spent his holidays.

The train will take you further up the valley to Hallein, where you can visit one of the salt mines and see the intricacies of the mining operation using water, not impressed labour. Entry and egress is by train. How else?

Back to our journey. While there has been upgrading of the line as far as we have come in Austria, this does not match the work done between Salzburg and Vienna. For most of the distance from Salzburg to St Polten, the existing double track has simply had a second pair of tracks built nearby, avoiding all the bends and towns, going through tunnels instead of around or over hills and so on. The time between Salzburg and Vienna (308km) has been reduced to 2h45 (2011), down from about five hours or so of not-so-distant years, and there is a lot more reduction to follow, perhaps to 2h20. This route basically follows the Danube but the new tracks do not meander as much.

One spectacle which has now been by-passed is the dominating monastery at Melk, sitting above the village of the same name on the old railway. The fast railway now uses a tunnel and the view of Melk is lost for ever for the through trains. A train-plus-ship tour through the Wachau, the local name for the valley of the Danube, brings you from Vienna as far as Melk and you have a chance to see the art works and the library, which are priceless and should be on any itinerary.

After St Pölten, 40 minutes from Vienna, a complete new line is being built venturing slightly further north and avoiding the mountains. To bring the line to the new Hauptbahnhof in Vienna, it will take two tunnels under the Vienna Woods (11.6km) and under Lainz (12.3km). Judging by the amount of work and expenditure involved, this must result in a good time-saving on the route from Salzburg.

Another route is available from Salzburg to Vienna, much longer, but covering a different section of the country. From Salzburg, this line goes south over the ranges and through the Tauern tunnel, coming eventually to Villach from where lines run southward to Italy and to Slovenia. The route then passes the shores of the Wörthersee and on to Klagenfurt. As it returns to Vienna, the line passes through St Veit an der Glan, after which is visible a castle, Burg Hochosterwitz, built around a hill with a very novel spiral access which is much like a miniature of San Marino in Italy.

The turn-off to Graz, Austria's second city, is at Bruck an der Mur, after which the line steadily climbs up over the Semmering Pass, a line which carries the star in the Thomas Cook list of scenic railways, before descending to the Danube plain and Vienna.

47. WIEN, VIENNA

Vienna, City of my Dreams

My close association with Vienna began in the 1980s, when the Australian team for the International Physics Olympiad was given the privilege of doing its final week's preparation for competitions in Europe in the physics laboratories of the University of Vienna. Once I had retired I was fortunate enough to be given an attachment at the University, which resulted in my living there for an academic year. Since then I have come back and stayed there for three months each year, in the same apartment, because I love the city so much.

In my first year there, we consulted the list of the 'most liveable cities of the world' to confirm that Vienna was first on the list. The top ten generally includes a selection from Geneva, Zürich, Vancouver, Sydney, Melbourne, Brisbane, Oslo, Stockholm, Copenhagen and Auckland. The order depends on the definitions of the day but those cities are always near the top. While I was working in Vienna, the new version of the list gave Vancouver at the top and I had fortuitously selected Vancouver as my next post-retirement position. Unfortunately Vancouver later slipped back a little, due probably to a combination of an awful winter, drug-war shootings and the problems of the homeless on the streets. Coming back to Vienna, therefore, fitted well.

In the years preceding 1683 Vienna was besieged by the Turks, camped on the opposite bank of the Danube. Promises of aid to Vienna from other kings persuaded them to go home, but the scars of those days remain in Vienna. The city developed inside the walls as a very high-density living area, with narrow streets and multipurpose residential and commercial accommodation. The city later spilled over the walls and followed the same pattern of development, with all of the streets in addition carrying a drain leading to the nearest brook or river. Nobody therefore has driveways or sheds, or even front fences. The front door of your building opens onto the street and outside the back door is a place to stack the bins, and once upon a time to empty the potty, and that is all. In my apartment building on each floor is a tap and basin, like a fountain, called a *Bassena*. This is where the original occupants would come to collect their water. You can use your imagination as to what went out of the windows into the street. *Gardez l'eau!*

In the later 1800s, Kaiser Franz Josef I ordered the city walls to be torn down and replaced by a ring of parks and municipal buildings. It is this ring which makes Vienna so workable. Very little development took place on the other side of the river which, one of my colleagues tells me, is referred to by those who live on the city side of the river as *Trans-Danubia.*

Another of FJ's projects was to build a water supply for Vienna, coming from the mountains in the south. The aqueducts can be seen south of the city. Today Vienna enjoys a stable and clean water supply, envied by most cities.

Streets of suburban Vienna are very narrow and, in contrast to the logic of many cities, the traffic is forced to follow the buses and trams rather than obstruct them. Parking is a question of pot-luck and there are more cars with permits than parking spots. Every space is always occupied and the moment you see someone moving out, there is another waiting to come in. Spaces are only marginally longer than the cars, but this does not deter the Viennese drivers. The old dears manage to manoeuvre their cars into the spots as easily as if the space were twice as long, and the younger ones zip in and out while talking on their cell phones.

The *Anschluss* with Germany resulted in the city being knocked about very little during the early phase of WWII, but the destruction in the last throes, with the Allies and the Soviets on opposite sides of the Danube, was enormous. Specifically the *Staatsoper* (the State Opera House) and St Stefan's Cathedral were both badly damaged. In 1945 the area outside the ring was allocated to the several occupying nations, but inside the ring was joint occupation. This meant four people for every action and four people for every decision. Not a lot could have been done.

The occupation from 1945 to 1955 by the four powers did little to help the damaged city, but at least the Allies and the Soviets helped to repair the buildings mentioned that the other destroyed.

The British film, *The Third Man,* based on the novel by Graeme Greene, is still widely acclaimed as one of the better films of the era ever made and depicts some of the problems of those days. The movie is still shown twice weekly at one of the smaller theatres. Featured in the movie is the Prater, the giant Ferris wheel which is always seen as part of the Vienna skyline. This is the core feature of an amusement park which certainly extracts more money from tourists than from the locals.

After 1955, after the Russians left, the Austrians set about rebuilding their country with an unprecedented enthusiasm. Everything was cleaned up, buildings restored, housing went ahead, education was improved and the country became important again. It is said that most of the cleaning up was done by women, as the men had either been killed or had to go outside to find work. These women, the 'mommas' of my definition, were referred to as the *Trümmerfrauen*, or 'rubble women'.

Since 1955 every school student has been required to learn English, which means that every Austrian who finished school from about 1960 speaks English, and generally very well. This, therefore, includes everyone under the age of 60, but many people who are older can also speak it very well. The 'old dears' of the city, who move about freely (there are no 'mommas' today), all chat away in German but can usually respond to clearly-spoken and well mannered English.

Building regulations in the centre of the city have preserved the original flavour of the city, but behind those facades are more modern facilities than the front door would indicate.

The Russians left behind a typical huge monument to their war effort and one of the conditions for them going home was that nothing be built in front of the monument. The cunning Austrian avoided this by arranging the huge fountain in front to throw up an obscuring sheet of water. If required, it can be shown that there is nothing obstructing the view. When the USSR collapsed, the city fathers were happy to let the monument be seen once more, commemorating a part of the city's history.

For those wanting a more detailed but mythical description of life in Vienna, there is a section in *The Fist of God* by Frederick Forsyth, which purports to show something of the city.

Vienna is yet another city in which the mainline railway stations were built on the periphery of the city centre and generally unconnected. Since the railways recovered after the end of the occupation, the ÖBB has been working to build up the S-Bahn network and cut down the number of mainline stations. This will come to fruition, perhaps in 2013, when the new Hauptbahnhof, presently under construction, will take all long distance trains and the other stations will be relegated to that of an S-Bahn station or, at most, catering for a few regional services. The building of this station is said to occupy the largest construction site in Europe.

At a time when money for construction is scarce, Vienna is still building up its U-Bahn network with a new stretch of line opening every year. More modern trains on all U-Bahn services and more modern trams on the streets are coming into service. Nearly all stations are equipped with lifts, or at least escalators, making the network generally step-free, the old obsolescent vehicles excepted. One of the jokes of Vienna is the whereabouts of line U5 in the set from U1 to U6. Money was obviously not as plentiful as I am suggesting, and the U5 gap is clearly visible on the map, like a missing tooth.

Over the past few years the city has been expanding, not necessarily in population but in area. This is probably due to an increase in general prosperity and a demand for greater living space. The UN built a huge complex on the other side of the river and this has brought in people who want driveways and garages, all now found on the UN side of the river, *Trans-Danubia*. It also brought improved public transport to the other side. This is the third largest UN office complex in the world, after New York and Geneva.

There are four Danubes in Vienna, none of them blue. The river was straightened about a century ago leaving the old course as a recreation area, a veritable billabong. Then the main course was duplicated as part of flood prevention. This has given to the city the *Donauinsel*, an island recreation area 20km long with beaches, cycle tracks, walking tracks and above all, no cars. This is also the location for the *Domauinselfest* held each summer, yet another major musical attraction for Vienna. Finally there is the Danube Canal, a form of anabranch which comes up to the city edges.

Moored in the river to the north of the city can be seen two ships. These make up a fully equipped high school, using our terminology, making use of the facilities of the *Donauinsel*.

On the western and southern sides of the city are the Vienna Woods. This is a large area of the surrounding countryside, above the city level, which has been left mainly untouched and provides recreation areas for all who choose to go there.

Vienna is 48 degrees north of the equator, compared with Australia's most southerly point near Hobart being 45 degrees south, and in North America where the 48 degree line passes north of St John's Newfoundland, Thunder Bay Ontario, and between Seattle and Vancouver. As Austria is at the extreme east of the time zone of Paris and Frankfurt, the sun comes up much earlier than it does in the west of Europe. Unfortunately, it also means the sun sets earlier and in December even at 1500 it is quite dark.

My apartment is only two tram stops from the City Hall, the Rathaus. As well as this, trams or buses pass within 300 metres of my apartment going to all railway stations and the city centre. I could not be better served. Combine this residence with a three-month Eurail pass and you can see how and why I travel so much.

Any tour of Vienna begins at the Opera House, the magnificent building which dominates the Ring. One walks up the Kärntnerstrasse past the various shops and comes to St Stefan, a cathedral which cannot be bettered. The roof is made with coloured tiles giving patterns telling of its history. Along the Graben and by the Kohlmarkt are the named-brand stores of Vienna, leading to Michaelerplatz and facing the old palace buildings. The Treasury Museum and the Sisi Museum are here but so also are the stables for the Spanish Riding School, which performs about once weekly. This returns you to the Opera House and the circuit can take about a day for the new tourist. It is possible to walk around the centre of Vienna for days and still be seeing new and exciting things.

Then there are the museums and galleries which abound. There are certainly enough of these, at your choice, to keep you busy for weeks.

Slightly away from the city centre, still on the U-Bahn, is the Schönbrunn Palace, the palace of the Habsburgs. Looking very much like the Palace of Versailles, it is now a very detailed museum of the era, with very extensive grounds. These include the Tiergarten, which claims to be the oldest zoo in the world. One of my colleagues asked why I give the Schönbrunn, one of the most beautiful and important Viennese monuments, only two lines, while other much less important locations receive half a page. The answer is that my powers of description are eclipsed by those of almost any other source. I will confine myself to more mundane and unloved topics like railway stations.

Vienna has a fair amount of snow over the winter period, but the snow never manages to disrupt the work of the city. In Britain the nation would come to a standstill with a tenth of the snow that falls in Vienna, but in Vienna it is always business as usual. In Britain, everyone would have spent too long cleaning the snow off their car and so be late, hence they would hurry, have a prang and the roads would all be blocked very quickly. Schools would close, trains and buses would not run and there would be general mayhem. Business runs as usual in Vienna.

It is the music, however, which makes Vienna live. One estimate was given which suggests that on any night there would be 20 orchestras playing in Vienna. Even if there are only 10, this is a lot for a city of 1.8 million people. The Vienna Philharmonic, the largest orchestra and the one with the highest reputation, has 150 musicians and, as well as providing the orchestra for the *Staatsoper*, performs frequently in the Musikverein. It is also the featured orchestra for the *Salzburger Festspiele*

Here it is not a question of what is on anywhere tonight, but which one to select. With five major opera/ballet/operetta theatres and several top-level drama theatres, all with different performances every night, who could ask for anything more? Sydney, with four million people, has one venue of comparable quality which does not show regularly and then often shows pop concerts.

The Opera House, *Staatsoper*, was built in 1869 and was partly rebuilt after bomb damage in WWII. Currently performances are given every night from September to July, generally with different performances each night of any week. Stage properties arrive and depart in a huge truck each morning and are stored well away from the venue, after their experience with a disastrous fire. Similarly the immense wardrobe is stored in yet another location. The auditorium can hold an audience of about 2,100 persons and prices range from the order of €200 per seat down to €5 for a standing space, of which there are 567. Standing spaces are available from the afternoon of the performance. The stage is bigger than the auditorium and has to be seen to be appreciated. This can be done most afternoons in a guided tour.

For Christmas the Staatsoper performs the ballet, *The Nutcracker* by Tchaikovski and on New Year's Eve *die Fledermaus* by Johann Strauss. The latter is the only event at the Staatsoper which is neither opera nor ballet.

Then there is the Opera Ball. For one day of the year, the Thursday before Ash Wednesday, the Opera House is converted to a ballroom and possibly the most spectacular and exclusive Ball in the world takes place. This was first held in 1936, but may still be a legacy from the Congress, which was held in Vienna in 1814-1815 to carve up the world after the defeat of Napoleon.

For the less serious is the *Volksoper*, a much more modest theatre with an equally great tradition. The *Volksoper* presents opera, operetta, ballet, musicals in the best style. Seat prices here are only as high as about €80 and standing spaces as low as €2. There is usually a performance of *die Fledermaus* or *die Lustige Witwe* (Merry Widow) on the bill, as well as something from the English repertoire. *My Fair Lady*, and to learn how to speak proper English in German, was a hoot. *Hello Dolly* was as much fun and nearly as good as with Barbara Streisand. The title song was, of course, sung in English. Then there was *The Sound of Music;* Richard Rodgers at his absolute best. It showed how much better the theatre version was than the film. As with the *Staatsoper*, the repertoire for any year can be viewed on the web.

Vienna and Austria subsidise the *Staatsoper* (and *Volksoper*) to the sum of €50 million per year from Government funds. It is impossible to imagine the Australian Government spending a cent on opera. But Australia must spend that amount per year on the Australian Institute of Sport and I know of no other country which does. Little wonder that Australia does well in the Olympics and its classical musical culture leaves quite a lot to be desired. Australia is the ONLY country, other than Greece, to have participated in all summer Olympic Games.

Vienna is the location of many great concert halls, the best known is the *Musikverein*. This is the traditional home of the Vienna Philharmonic. I was once lucky enough to obtain a seat on the back of the stage for a concert of the Philharmonic, with Zubin Mehta conducting. While I could not see much of the soloist, the great man was conducting me, along with the harps immediately in front of me. Each year the fabled 'New Year's Day Concert' is held in the *Musikverein*, for which seats are ballotted. Now, if you have not watched that New Year Concert, write a note on the wall to do so this year.

The following is a diary extract from a Sunday morning a couple of years ago, when a friend was visiting. I don't do this on many Sundays but the opportunity is there.

At 0915 we went to the Hofburgkapelle where they were celebrating mass with Josef Haydn's 'Paukenmesse' with the Vienna Boys' Choir (Wiener Sängerknaben) and members of the Staatsoper Orchestra and men's choir. There were not just a few of the latter either. There were the boys from the choir in their sailor-type uniforms (as in 'Sound of Music') and all in a beautiful church in which Mozart probably played. If you have ever been to a top level performance of 'The Messiah' (Händel) then this would rate alongside it (or possibly put it to shame), and there is a different mass every Sunday morning.

At 1100 we went to the Augustinerkapelle, nearly next door, and heard 'Deutsche Messe' from Mendelssohn with their choir and organ.

After lunch we did the tour of the Opera House, very standard, with lots of tourists but very educational.

We finished the afternoon with 'The Magic Flute' at the Marionnette Theatre at the Schönbrunn, with recorded music from the Opera House cast and orchestra. Mind blowing!

Then there are the tourist concerts. There are four or five of these at various top quality locations around the city, including the venue at which Johann Strauss performed. A good concert might consist of a 15-piece orchestra, including grand piano, with the conductor at the violin. Some play all Strauss, some all Mozart, but most are a composite. Usually there are soloists and dancers. The Mozart orchestra is in period costume. People dressed in period costume sell these tickets on the streets of the city at about €45, so no booking is necessary.

Out front of the Rathaus in December is the *Christkindl Markt. Christkindl* is 'Christ Child', a much more appropriate name. Celebration goes on until 6 January, which Anglicans call Epiphany or Twelfth Night, but here is called *Heilige Drei Könige*, three kings: the night the wise men came to Christ. Of course, this is all convenience to cover up the fact that for centuries the calendar was confused after the switch from the Julian calendar to the Gregorian calendar, and some faiths even today still celebrate Christmas 12 days later. *Christkindl Markt* is in the huge square in front of the city hall where all the vendors have set up stalls selling all sorts of food, plus Christmas junk with coloured lights, tinsel and trees. Well, add all the snow to that and it is an amazing sight. And there is much more.

Is it any wonder that I have chosen to live in Vienna for three months of every year?

48. SWITZERLAND, THE NATION

Switzerland has been left until last because, unless you want ocean, Switzerland has everything you want in Europe and more. Maybe I am biased, because I choose to make Switzerland my base for three months of the summer every year, but is that not cause and effect?

The population of Switzerland of about 9 million is, in very round figures, 60% German-speaking, 30% French, 5% Italian, 2% Romansch, and the rest as you find them. The Romansch speakers live in the mountains in the bottom right corner in Graubunden, the most south-easterly canton in Switzerland. They lived there largely un-noticed by the rest of the world until Napoleon's time.

My adopted village of Brienz is very firmly in the German-speaking region but, like nearly all spots in Switzerland, has a dialect of its own.

The history of Switzerland begins around the *Vierwaldstättersee*, the lake of the four wooded cantons, known to the rest of the world as the Lake of Luzern. It was these four cantons which made up the original Swiss Confederation a century or so before William defeated Harold at Hastings.

The citizens of the area were being oppressed by the nasty local representative of the wicked king of Austria and, led by a chap called William Tell, they rose up and sent him packing. In doing so, Tell was made to shoot an apple resting on his son's head, which of course he did. This is claimed to be the origin of the Swiss nation. Whether there was a William Tell is debatable, although his image is on the back of the five Swiss Franc (CHF) coin and he has events in his name all over the country.

Nowhere is this seen better than in Interlaken, where each year Schiller's play of the same name is performed in a specially dedicated theatre, showing the story of these events. The background is the side of a local mountain and the local citizenry take part. Everything is, of course, in German but the performance is so gripping that it matters not.

Like several other nations of Europe, the Swiss claim to have the oldest constitution in Europe, and in Switzerland's case, the world. The original date of the constitution was in the tenth century. The last revision of any note was in 1802. Both the Isle of Man and Iceland claim to have legislatures with a longer history than anyone else, but Iceland was broken by a period of colonial rule, while The Isle of Man cannot claim to have complete sovereignty, as it has allegiance to the British Crown as a Crown dependency. Unlike Australia, who recognises the same sovereign, The Isle of Man is not a member of the UN and has the UK handle all of its external affairs.

David Smith, once secretary to five Australian Governors General and the man who stood in front of John Kerr in 1972 and read the infamous proclamation dissolving the Government, was once heard to say that Australia had the eighth oldest constitution in the world. Only seven preceded Australia in 1901 and are still *in situ*. The first few are obvious. UK returned to the monarchy after Cromwell in 1660. The US talks about 1776. The British North America Act established Canada around 1867 and New Zealand has the Treaty of Waitangi of 1840. Only Switzerland and Sweden, of all European nations, were not taken over by Hitler, or Napoleon for that matter. The seventh is apparently Thailand (Siam of those days) which was never colonised and the monarchy continues.

Switzerland grew, very slowly, over the centuries, by adding cantons (provinces, states, etc., in other forms of politics) but the size has not changed a lot since the days of Napoleon.

The Swiss Federal Government is a good example of a federation of independent entities. The cantons are responsible for nearly every action within the nation, with the exception of foreign affairs, the military, the Swiss franc and the railways. The last then becomes of special interest to us here.

While the Swiss elect a federal parliament, it is very rarely discussed by the general public. The President is hardly even known. The unique part of Swiss law is that at any time the citizenry can call for a referendum on any issue by presenting a petition of 50,000 signatures. This is done not infrequently. The Swiss Government is in favour of joining the EU, but the populace is not. This was demonstrated when a referendum was called to oppose the government's wishes on the EU and soundly defeated the issue. In 2005 the Government chose to join the Schengen Treaty. A vociferous citizenry opposed this but did not gain sufficient votes to stop it. A recent referendum (2010) bans the building of minarets in Switzerland. The world is waiting to see the ongoing effect.

The Swiss, then, have a policy of strict neutrality. On this, the electorate is more definite than the government. The Swiss managed, like the Swedes, to keep Napoleon away. History knows, but does not often tell, of the *'quid pro quo'* that the Swiss used to keep him at bay. During two World Wars the Swiss had no visitors, but the same comments apply. In World War II the Swiss took their precautions and one can still see concrete works designed to keep the tanks from entering the valleys. After WWII the Swiss built atom bomb shelters for their citizens. The extent of these is not easily determined but in times of crisis, like the floods in Brienz, these can be called upon.

So, no, the Swiss are not members of the EU but they do follow many of the legal changes to conform with EU provisions, where it suits them.

One area where it does not suit them has been in the confidentiality of banking legislation. Until very recently the records of a Swiss bank have been impregnable and Switzerland became a tax haven for many. Pressure from the EU and the US is breaking this down slowly, and the world's financial renegades are having to place their money elsewhere in future.

Switzerland joined the Schengen Treaty after the referendum in 2005, perhaps because it suited them. Any person, once inside the EU, can now move in and out of Switzerland without showing passport or visa, although each party reserves the right to check identity of those entering if needed.

The Swiss franc, CHF, is, of course, a rock in the foundation of international finance and occupies one of the three wallets (Euros, British pounds and CHF) that the European train traveller must carry. One can, of course, pay with Euros in Switzerland if the merchants agree. Typical of this is the sign in the supermarket explaining that Euros will be accepted, but the change will be given in CHF. The sign is, naturally, in English and only in English.

Why CH you ask? The Swiss have four language groups which they appease as far as possible, often by finding a word which reads the same in all languages, much as the Canadians do are very good at doing. The adjective Swiss, Suisse, Schweitz, etc., does not have a common abbreviation so they have done the obvious, chosen a language known to all but used by none; Latin. So Switzerland is 'Confederatio Helvetica', or simply CH, and these words are used wherever a common name is needed, in particular on the coins and notes and as an email address '.ch'. This is a little like 'SPQR' in Rome.

One can wonder whether the day will ever come when the CHF remains the currency of the nation, but all public trading is done in Euros. If it suited the Swiss, they would do it. Another scenario is that we might all finish up trading in Swiss francs.

With such a small nation to describe with so many facets, this discussion is divided into the French-speaking sector, the north, the central lakes, Graubunden, the Italian-speaking area and, of course, the railways. The last we consider first.

49. SWITZERLAND, ITS RAILWAYS

When the Swiss saw the need to build railways, they very fortunately did so as a federal matter, undoubtedly after a referendum, and called upon the British for advice. This was duly given and a railway network, based on a spine from Geneva through the non-mountainous areas of the north to St Gallen, was devised. This has suited the Swiss well, but two legacies remain. The first is that Swiss trains drive on the left. This bothers very few people unless you are confused by the platform in a two-platform through station. The other is the architecture. If you are in a major Swiss station such as Zürich, Luzern, Bern or Geneva, you can be forgiven for thinking you are in Paddington or St Pancras in London.

Legend has it that in the early 1900s when the Swiss were building power stations (the Swiss are still net exporters of electricity), they discovered that they had capacity in excess of their needs, so to use it they electrified the railways. Whatever the reason, the Swiss network is completely electrified with the only non-electric regular train service being the coal-burning service on the Rothornbahn in Brienz. Diesel traction is rarely, if ever, seen in Switzerland. Compare this with Britain, the founder of railways, where they were still proud of their steam trains even after World War II and today trains are still, in the majority, diesel-operated.

The Swiss railway, the SBB/CFF/FFS *Schweitzerische Bundesbahnen/ Chemins de fer Fédéraux/Ferrovie Federal Svizzere,* is absolutely time punctual. You can set your clock by it, and if there should occur a perturbation, it somehow dissolves rather than multiplies as it would in Britain.

In the late 1900s the Swiss pioneered the clockface timetable, which is now, years later, finally covering all mainlines in Britain and is becoming widespread in Australia. Trains in Switzerland leave the stations at the same minutes past the hour, every hour, and every day of the year. Further than that they have staged their hub stations so that trains leave these stations immediately after the hour and, where appropriate, the half hour, that is at xx00 and xx30 or as soon after this as the logic allows, and arrive at their destination at a few minutes before the hour or half hour. This has meant upgrading some of the longer stretches of line and not concentrating on others.

If you are travelling in Switzerland, arrive at your hub station a few minutes before the hour or half hour and your train will be there for you. You find that at this time there is a train for everywhere in Switzerland, some directly and some by changing further along the line, either at xx00 or xx30, and mostly by cross platform interchange. Accordingly, you could travel around Switzerland all day and cover most of the country, without ever having time to leave the platform. This would make an Englishman cry! Think of Birmingham New St.

Still there is more. At almost every substantial station there will be a station buffet or shop where you can buy provisions, and probably in enough time to make the connection.

As the ultimate gesture, the toilets on the SBB trains and in the stations are clean, free and have both soap and paper.

There is a small fleet of Panorama cars (floor to ceiling windows, etc.) which the Swiss originally had built for their EC services into Germany and Austria but are no longer used outside Switzerland, taking into account also the fact that both Germany and Austria have purpose-built trains for these international services. So these wonderful cars are confined to internal routes, such as Zürich to Chur, or Basle to Locarno.

In Britain there is a 'Public Performance Measure', which tells how many of the trains in a given company were on time over the last four week period. Over the nation, the average (2010) is about 91% and they are pleased about it. This means that one train in 10 is at least five minutes late and no-one mentions connections. Some companies have figures as low as 80%, which means that one in five trains are over five minutes late. What a way to run a railway.

Compare this with Switzerland. Here you have a network of fast, comfortable, spacious trains which can take you the extent of the country, east-west from Geneva to Sargans or north-south from Basle to Chiasso, in about four hours. Punctuality is close to 100%. One only needs to see the SBB system in operation to realise why it works. This means that in Switzerland there is a seamless railway system across the national network and if there is no direct train from where you are to where you want to go, then there will be an onward connection somewhere of two or three minutes.

What is not so often talked about is the network of narrow gauge railways which links the main networks with the smaller towns, particularly those in the mountain valleys and often on peaks. These are generally narrow gauge, all electrified, and most often with rack and pinion to pull them up the inclines.

One can pause here to think of Australia. There is one train per day between Brisbane and Sydney, two per day between Sydney and Melbourne, three per week between Melbourne and Adelaide and two per week between Sydney, Adelaide and Perth. By contrast there is a direct train every two hours travelling the 750km from Vienna (Austria) to Frankfurt (Germany), 7 per day. Australians prefer to fly!

50. SWITZERLAND: PARLEZ-VOUS SCHWEITZ?

Let us start our tour of Switzerland from Basle. This is extremely logical, because trains from Germany and France come this way.

We are not the only ones to do this because there is a statue of *Helvetia*, the lady on the Swiss coins, sitting on the bridge in Basle with her suitcase ready, alongside her spear and shield.

Shortly before each hour, two ICEs arrive from Germany and one TGV from Paris, the last not yet operating each hour. Shortly after the hour, in accordance with the clockface timetable, the Swiss IC leaves for Geneva and Lausanne. This takes passengers through the French-speaking Jura, through the cities of Neuchatel (Neuburg) and Biel (Bienne) toward Lausanne and Geneva (Genève, Genf, Ginivra).

Lausanne is the first intersection with Lac Leman, the Lake of Geneva. Once I described Lac Leman as large and flat. Sure, all lakes are flat, but my meaning was that this is unlike most glacial lakes of Switzerland which have high and steep sides. In that sense, parts of Lac Leman are rather boring. Lausanne, however, sits well above the water and can be accessed from the station by a funicular railway. Views from the level of the station are superb.

Geneva is not the most interesting part of Switzerland. The city is best described as antiseptic. Nothing is out of place, everything is correct. The canton of Geneva, and the city, is about 20 kilometres square and on three sides you find France. The fourth side is shared by the lake and a small land border with the adjoining French-speaking Swiss canton. Is it never surprising then that the people are French-speaking, French-thinking and French-eating? The food in Geneva is out of this world. Regrettably, so is the cost.

The pastries and takeaways, though, are really top, despite the price. A trip to Geneva is therefore in order and the food to be much enjoyed.

The locals have made good use of their lake and the River Rhône into which it flows through the town. The city uses the water feature, which includes a vertical water jet which is apparently a few metres short of the one in Canberra which was latterly eclipsed by one in the US.

Virtually all fast trains coming into Geneva continue on to Geneva Airport, which gives the airport a connection to almost every centre in Switzerland. Frequent TGV services link Geneva with Paris, but by an entirely different route to that from Basle. From the second station of Geneva, across the town, Eaux Vives, runs a service heading towards Chamonix and Mont Blanc via France. This is where the high mountains really can be seen but perhaps not so easily ascended. The last stretch on narrow gauge train continues from Chamonix back into Switzerland at Martigny, a line which carries a star from Thomas Cook.

Returning around the north of the lake, the line continues up the Rhône Valley toward Brig.

The last major city on the lake is Montreux, from where the *Golden Pass Panoramic*, a strangely composite train service, departs for Interlaken and Luzern. The narrow gauge train leaves Montreux and begins to zig-zag its way up the side of the mountain. The lake is not 'flat' here. This gives ever increasing panoramas of the lake until suddenly the line goes into a tunnel and comes out in a new world: the upper valleys of Central Switzerland. Names like Les Avants, Chateau d'Oex, Montbuvon, Gstad are passed within a two-hour vista of real Switzerland, mountains, valleys, cows, etc. Even Monsieur Nestlé has a factory up here. The train is of a class generally superior to the regular first and it is possible to sit at the front panoramic windows of the train, the driver being above and slightly behind you.

Ultimately you reach Zweisimmen, where the standard gauge *Golden Pass Panoramic* waits to take you on to Spiez and Interlaken Ost. A dual gauge train is planned for this line which will take passengers without change from Montreux to Interlaken Ost.

On the journey up the Rhône Valley from Montreux, more towns are passed with narrow gauge cog railways up to the various ski resorts. After a couple of hours of interesting travel through towns such as Martigny, Sion, Sierre/

Siders and Leuk, the train comes to Visp and then Brig, where the Swiss train ends its internal journey but may continue to Milano.

At Visp the *Matterhorn Gotthard Bahn*, MGB, heads up the valley to Zermatt at the very foot of the Matterhorn. The fare on this route is very high as its primary customers are the well-heeled ski set. Locals automatically qualify for a 50% discount. The last section into Zermatt is a monopoly, as the road is closed to private vehicles. I once bought a ticket to go up and discovered the cost. To my delight I met a local lady on the train who had a 50% discount coupon to spare, which she passed on to me to use on the return trip.

From Zermatt there is a further train to Gornergrat, on a ridge overlooking the aspect of the Matterhorn and from where the skiers begin their jollies. On a clear day the view of the mountain from here is priceless.

SBB has invested in a set of high quality international trains, classified as 'Eurostar, ETR' in Italy, but merely EC in Switzerland. These are used by SBB (which from Geneva start as CFF and finish as FFS) on services between Geneva and Milano, between Basle and Milano via the Lötschberg tunnel and between Zürich and Milano via Gotthard. The first two services run by the Simplon tunnel into Northern Italy, changing to Italian control at Domodossala. These are exceptionally comfortable and quiet trains and run well under the auspices of the SBB. Milano is discussed under the section on Northern Italy.

51. SWITZERLAND, NORTH

From Basle there are several trains each hour to Zürich but at least one, the first one after the hour, will be an ICE or a TGV having come from Germany or France.

Zürich Hauptbahnhof is a huge station and it keeps growing. Slightly over 20 years ago the entire Zürich suburban system was remodelled, based on four underground through platforms. Shortly after that an additional set of surface suburban platforms had to be built to cater for those services which would not fit in the tunnel. Now a second set of underground platforms is under construction to incorporate these services and more. In the meantime, the long distance services take up all the surface platforms and become busier. The long distance traffic has doubled in those 20 years.

The destination board lists nearly all major centres in Switzerland and all mainline trains but one (to Stuttgart) depart within a few minutes of the hour. Then there is a break and a second flight leaves after the half hour. The number of trains keeps increasing with the years and the trains are always bigger.

A colleague once took me to the entry of the station and pointed along the main street. 'Under that street,' he said, 'lies most of the world's gold.' His statement may not be literally true but he is probably right in assuming that those along the street control most of it. There are no '*gnomes*' to be seen, but this is where they reside.

The city is at the northern end of the Lake of Zürich, a substantial north-south lake which drains northward into the Aare and thus into the Rhine. The city's development has been governed by the valleys running north-south. An efficient ferry service brings passengers from along the lake shore and an auto ferry carries vehicles across near the halfway point. Then there are the trams. No matter where you are, there is a tram which will take you almost anywhere you choose.

To the north of Zürich runs a German train for Stuttgart; once an ICE, but relegated to an IC as the demand for stock grew elsewhere in Germany. The crossing point is the town of Schaffhausen, an enclave of Switzerland north of the Rhine, here flowing west toward Basle. One village on the Rhine worthy of note, and accessible by rail, is Stein am Rhein where the buildings all carry illustrations of life in the area. Near also is the Rheinfallen, a small but significant set of waterfalls on the Rhine, which prohibit any through navigation. A ferry service can take you east from Schaffhausen into the Bodensee, the Lake of Constance, and along the lake to Bregenz in Austria and Lindau in Germany beyond. The rail line through the Black Forest of Germany, the Schwarzwald, reaches the lake at Konstanz and crosses to Kreuzlingen. The Bodensee can be crossed by ferry at numerous points further east, with a train coming in to each side.

Some years ago the Swiss railways experimented by running one of the Zürich suburban lines under the airport. This 'experiment' resulted in a major mainline station at Zürich Airport, similar to that at Frankfurt, through which many services to all over north and central Switzerland pass, including to Geneva Airport. The railway continues eastwards, relatively free of mountains, to reach Sargans on the River Rhine, flowing south to north, which makes up the Swiss border with Austria.

52. LIECHTENSTEIN

Across the Rhine from Sargans lies the Principality of Liechtenstein, *Fürstentum Liechtenstein*, FL, population about 35,000; a feudal state of mediaeval standing. The ruler is an absolute monarch, although somewhat more benevolent than might be expected. He might well be, as there is money to spare.

Briefly, and with a large amount of writers' licence, the story begins with the family of the House of Liechtenstein in bygone days, which had accumulated great wealth and an enormous art collection, comparable with that of the sovereigns of Britain. The head of the family, who styled himself as the Prince of Liechtenstein, lived mainly in Vienna.

In the early 1900s when the taxmen of various countries became more efficient, the family found it discreet to move on. So they checked their assets and found they owned a little province, quite small, between Austria and Switzerland. They moved the family there and took up residence in the castle as classical feudal monarchs.

Liechtenstein is not in the EU and, with its present form of government, has little chance of becoming a member. Its 'feudal monarchy' hardly fits EU rules of democracy.

When Switzerland joined the Schengen Treaty, Liechtenstein became an embarrassment as it had an open border with both Switzerland and Austria, but was not in the EU, nor party to the Schengen agreement. The problem was sidestepped by leaving the borders opened and monitoring any flights from Liechtenstein's single heliport. This places Liechtenstein in a position similar to that of Monaco, San Marino and The Vatican.

Liechtenstein uses Swiss francs and all external affairs are conducted by Switzerland. Only the railway is run by Austria.

To maintain an acceptable position in Europe, without being completely fenced off from its neighbours, Liechtenstein has been forced to change some of its ways, in particular by amending its laws to take away the tax haven status which it has had in the past. It might be suggested that the reason for its existence at all is for its 'owners' to be able to live under their own tax laws.

The Liechtenstein art collection is maintained at the Liechtenstein Museum in Vienna. This, or what you are allowed to see of it, is a superb collection and well worth the visit.

The railway from Buchs in Switzerland to Feldkirch in Austria runs through Liechtenstein but does not stop. Local trains, however, run between these cities and stop at Schaan-Vaduz and several other Liechtenstein towns.

The capital city is Vaduz, a small town a few kilometres south of Schaan-Vaduz. Above the city is the castle, visible from the Swiss side of the Rhine and hence from the Swiss trains. There is an excellent bus service in Liechtenstein, incorporating Feldkirch, Buchs and Sargans, run by the Swiss. You may, for a fee, have your passport stamped in the capital with a Liechtenstein visa.

The principal income of Liechtenstein up to about 50 years ago was selling postage stamps, which they had printed in such a way that all collectors had to have them. Other countries eventually cottoned on to this, doing the same thing, reducing the value of the business, so Liechtenstein moved into the technological world and is doing quite well, thank you.

Vaduz can best be described as a 'quaint' out-of-the-way town with unusual ideas of decor. In 2010 there were plaques along the street giving images of the commemorative stamps issued in that year. Eating places are quite pleasant and the solitary philatelic museum has signs leading to it from everywhere. Banks are prominent.

The Liechtensteiners and Liechtensteinerins go about their daily chores quite unaware that they are still being governed as in the days of George III or Maria Theresa.

Apparently it is very difficult to acquire Liechtenstein citizenship and a large proportion of the residents, some of whom were born there, are foreign nationals and will always remain so. After all, it is only a short walk to Austria or Switzerland.

A summary of the 'microstates' of Europe might then read:

Liechtenstein	de facto EU; de facto Schengen; Swiss francs; Austrian trains
Vatican	de facto EU; de facto Schengen; Euros; no trains
San Marino	de facto EU; de facto Schengen; Euros; no trains
Monaco	de facto EU; de facto Schengen; Euros; French trains
Andorra	NOT EU; NOT Schengen; Euros; no trains
Gibraltar	de facto EU; NOT Schengen; pounds; no trains
Guernsey, Jersey, Isle of Man	de facto EU; NOT Schengen; pounds; no trains

53. GRAUBÜNDEN

The most spectacular mountains and scenery in Switzerland are not necessarily those in the resort areas, although what is a resort area to one person may not be to another. To visit the mountains of the canton of Graubünden, the bottom right canton of Switzerland, is quite an adventure.

So we will go to the Rhaetian Railways (RhB) of Graubünden and design a round trip to incorporate the major attributes, and return through Italy for comparison.

Graubünden, Grisons, is one of the largest of all the 23 Swiss cantons and occupies the south-eastern corner of Switzerland, next to Italy and Austria. Without doubt it is one of the most fascinating!

The canton is mostly mountainous and is drained by the Rhine flowing into the North Sea, the Inn flowing through Innsbruck into the Danube then into the Black Sea and the Poschiavo joining the Po then flowing into the Mediterranean. It can claim to be the top of Europe, despite the fact that the Jungfrau region also claims this title.

Its greater fascination comes from the languages. In the north of the canton, the signs are seen in German. In the south, the signs are in Italian. In the Engadine region, in which is the River Inn, Romansch is on the signs and spoken. The average passenger will not notice the language except on the multilingual signs. It does not occur to the folk living in the canton that this is unusual; they go about their business and are as multilingual as their individual circumstances dictate. This means, of course, that those dealing in the tourist trade will also speak fluent English, Italian, German and French. Ability in five languages is thus not uncommon.

This accounts for the plurality of names of the canton and the cities. The capital Chur is also known as Coire and there are another five alternatives.

Announcements on the mainline trains will be in German, in English and then in local *patois,* but may be in others.

Romansch is said to be derived directly from original Latin although it hardly resembles the Latin in which Cicero wrote. In the depths of the Engadine valleys, the language has been left to evolve untouched for 2,000 years. Doubtless the Swiss, having Romansch as an official language, will have ensured that there are TV transmissions in the language. The signs look ghastly with double letters in those words which could not bear them in English, and showing no pretence to imitate the German or Italian of the neighbours.

Every half hour one can take a fast train from Zürich via Sargans to Chur. These are big eight car standard gauge trains with ample space and catering. Proceeding away from Zürich, the train passes a series of glacial lakes which drain into Zürichsee until, a few kilometres short of the Austrian border, it crosses the watershed and into the valley of the Rhine. These valleys can generate wonderful electrical storms, even better than Lake Brienz, and are spectacular from the Panorama cars after sunset. The Rhine here is fast-flowing and of good mountain water; it hardly resembles the Rhine we think of as it passes through Köln in Germany.

Chur, on the Rhine, has been in existence for many centuries and was once, in the time of the Caesars, a Roman garrison town. The architecture is absolutely fascinating, with many buildings dating back further than imaginable. The cathedral and some of the lesser churches are completely unexpected in such a city. One could walk about Chur for days, seeing more every time.

Narrow gauge rail was built in parts of Australia to save money by having smaller bridges, smaller cuttings, smaller sleepers, etc. In Switzerland, the narrow gauge is used in the mountains because of tunnels, tight curves and a multitude of bridges where a standard, horse's backside gauge simply would not fit. So the Rhaetia Bahn, RhB, owned by the canton, runs throughout Graubünden on a gauge of 1,000mm, a little less than the 1067mm gauge of Queensland and Western Australia. The railway has been built up over the years from smaller components and now makes up the biggest narrow gauge system in Switzerland. It consists now of 321km of track at 11kV extending from Chur to Scuol-Tarasp on the Inn, to Dissentis/Muster where it joins the MGB, to Arosa and to St Moritz via the Albula tunnel. The Bernina line runs for 61km at 1,000V DC from St Moritz via Pontresina and the Bernina Pass to Tirano in Italy. Thomas Cook gives a star award for the most scenic routes to the RhB line over both the Albula and Bernina routes, both of which are UNESCO World Heritage listed..

Arosa is a small town with a round-the-year population of under 3,000 and located about an hour above Chur. It's two historical claims to fame are that Sir Arthur Conan Doyle pioneered skiing in Switzerland in this area, and that Erwin Schrödinger developed his theory on quantum mechanics while vacationing in the area. Neither of these is recalled by the ski tourists who flock to the resort each year.

The Arosa-bahn, starting in Chur, is more like a tram than a train. It begins its life in the Bahnhofplatz, where the RhB have cunningly given it a platform, a number and an escalator joining it to the main platform concourse, and then makes its way out of the town via the local streets. Once out of the town it follows the river valley on single track until reaching its destination. Of course it follows the Swiss pattern of leaving Chur slightly after the hour and arriving back immediately before. Trains cross en route at passing loops, hardly stopping, such is the efficiency of the service. Dropping back one train allows over 100 worthwhile minutes to wander around this delightful town.

The main RhB line from Chur follows the banks of the infant Rhine, now coming from the west, to the confluence of the Vorderrhein and the Hinterrhein. The former is fed, still further west, from the glaciers of the Central Alps. Ascending the valley of the latter, the line enters the mountains of the Albula and Engadine regions.

The track slowly climbs into the ranges, up incredible valleys which keep passengers, but not the locals, running from the windows on one side of the train to the other. On its way it crosses a very famous bridge, built from brick, the Landwasser Viaduct, way above the valley, which sends the track into the side of the hill in tunnel. The line passes through the Albula tunnel at about 1,900 metres and then emerges into the Engadine valley, the valley of the Inn running into Austria, drops back to valley level at about 1,500 metres and proceeds to St Moritz. It frequently loops back on itself as it ascends and descends these valleys.

An alternate RhB route leaves the SBB main line at Landquart, passing such ski resorts as Davos and Klosters before reaching St Moritz.

St Moritz is a British resort of the early twentieth century. As in Interlaken, many hotel names are English, like Victoria and Britannia. There would have been a direct train from London Victoria, across the channel to Chur, as well as to Interlaken, in the heyday of St Moritz. St Moritz has a good youth hostel but, if you wish to sleep in a little longer before moving on to Tirano, there is another at Pontresina, one station closer to Bernina, where the door of the hostel faces the railway station. Both have very reasonable prices and are clean and comfortable.

From St Moritz and Pontresina is the Tirano line, crossing the Bernina Pass and continuing to Tirano in Italy. To see all that there is to see on the Tirano line, it is advisable to leave on the first train leaving Pontresina at 0700 heading for the Bernina Pass. The trains on this route are all electric passenger sets, but capable of hauling several freight cars.

The combination of the two voltages once made a train change at Pontresina necessary when proceeding from Chur to Tirano, but a new set of dual voltage trains provides some through working for the *Bernina Express*, the high quality train which uses this line.

The main freight on the Tirano line is timber, in the form of logs. These are brought to Pontresina and shunted in rather interesting movements and attached to the passenger trains.

The climb begins almost at once, rising up the valley occupied by a very fast-flowing stream. The first thing to attract attention in summer is the enormous number of hikers, already out in the early morning, following the Swiss mountain trails. After a few more ski resorts, the train finally reaches Bernina Hospice, the top of the Bernina Pass and 2,253 metres above sea level. As at the top of almost every pass in Switzerland, there is a hostel and a restaurant, this one being part of the railway station. All around the top of the pass are ice-covered mountains and, to the west, is a huge glacier which almost seems to be below eye level. In the valley is *Lago Bianco*, the White Lake, which is dammed at either end. The waters to the north flow into the Engadine, the Inn and the Danube to the Black Sea. To the south they flow down into Italy and eventually into the Adriatic. This is the headwater of a huge hydro-electric project where, although the amount of water is not large, the drop southward is quite significant.

From Bernina, it is possible to walk down to the next station, Alp Grum.

The distance is such that one can remain ahead of the next train, exactly an hour behind. For the whole distance, the glacier looks down on the path and the tiny mortals who dare challenge its land. Tolkien must have been here. From Alp Grum, now at only 2,100 metres, it is possible to see down to the next town of Poschiavo at 1,019 metres, although quite close horizontally. The train almost dives over the edge and begins its zigging and zagging down the mountain; always down. This is the highest mainline train in Europe and the highest with purely adhesion traction. Ultimately the train reaches Poschiavo with as much relief as coming off a roller coaster. In about 30 minutes and 17km the train has come down nearly 1,100 metres.

The remaining journey to Tirano, about 500 metres above sea level, is quite tame by comparison except for the extraordinary view of the mountains behind and the feeling of 'my train came from up there'.

One major attraction is a loop near the bottom at Brusio, where the line turns a complete circle in the open air, using a big viaduct, to lose height quickly. The Swiss do this often inside mountains using tunnels, but this one is in the open air and is an engineering masterpiece. A photo of this loop features on the cover of nearly all Gruabünden tourist brochures. As you may have already guessed from the names, from the summit to the border is an Italian-speaking part of Switzerland. The architecture is no longer the cuckoo clock-style of German Switzerland, but distinctively Italian. The conditions are, however, most definitely Swiss. Finally, after many little towns, including one in which the railway goes down the main street which is hardly wider than the train, the valley crosses into Italy. Suddenly the appearance changes. No longer is there the neat array of Switzerland, there is now an approach to life which belongs definitely to Italy.

Tirano, as an Italian city, does have some really good restaurants which are quite inexpensive. The early morning departure from St Moritz and Pontresina now allows plenty of time for a good Italian lunch. Take care not to confuse this city with Torino (Turin), which is a much larger city further west in Italy.

For some this is the first introduction to the 'bunny-hop' Italian toilet. These make up the facilities at the Tirano Italian station. Perhaps they are sanitary, but they are by no means comfortable to those accustomed to sitting.

An awful way of moving on from Tirano is by the domestic, now standard gauge, Italian train to Milano. While the Italians can run very good train services, they also run really bad ones. The first indication of the standard of the trains is the graffiti on the outside, which is generally continued inside. On a hot sunny day, conditions inside are on the verge of intolerable. The toilets are drop-down, no paper and generally filthy. Still, this is part of the learning process.

The next step on the advertised *Bernina Express* journey is by a once daily bus from Tirano to Lugarno, back to Switzerland, but over many kilometres of Italian roads. Train tickets are valid for this journey but advance reservation is required. On this trip it pays not to watch what is going on. The narrow Italian roads barely take two cars, but the bus drives as if nothing else is on the road. So do all the other cars. Amazingly there are no head-on collisions, not even little scrapes. Ultimately the road reaches the lake shore and now the bus must negotiate the one-lane-wide streets of each little village. Might is right and not many oncoming cars have the temerity to confront a bus. As can be imagined, it sometimes takes quite a while to make a whole line of cars back up to make room for the bus. After the Italian-Swiss border, the difference is immediate. The road now goes around each village or, if this is not possible, tunnels under. The Swiss part of the journey is quite tame by comparison.

From Lugarno the return journey can take the mainline train first to the Swiss town of Bellinzona, the town with the two castles, and then back to Zürich.

From Bellinzona the main line runs back up into the Alps to the St Gotthard Pass. The line winds around the gorges and does many loops of the type discussed earlier, but always inside the mountain. At the top of the north-south pass, after emerging from the St Gotthard tunnel, is the town of Göschenen. Here is a most amazing piece of connecting railway which drops down from Andermatt by following a fast flowing river. Andermatt is on the east-west railway at the top of the pass. This point is effectively the crossroads at the summit of Switzerland. As soon as you arrive in Andermatt, you are aware that there is 'something odd' about this place. And there is. This is the centre of the Swiss defence network. Here is much of the Swiss military and air force, about as unreachable as anywhere in the world. And where is it all? It is under the ground, of course, equally unattainable. Someone pointed out that you do not find military bases with fences in Switzerland. The boundaries of the base are the borders of Switzerland and you are inside the base the whole time.

The new St Gotthard tunnel is being built under this pass and will be around 55km long. It begins not far from Bellinzona and comes out almost on lake level, south of the Lake of Luzern. Life will be different for the Swiss and those others who use the country for transit. More amazing is the fact that there is a station proposed for the middle of the tunnel under Andermatt. Passengers would be able to leave the train there, with skis over their shoulders, and take the lift to Andermatt. What price the spiral staircase?

Not far from Andermatt, at Hospental, is an amazing youth hostel which operates by itself. On arrival you book in by phone with the management, collect your bedding as instructed and stay the night. In the morning the breakfast is all laid out with nobody serving it. It is very difficult to find someone to pay. Dracula comes to mind.

The narrow gauge line from the east, from where we left it in Graubünden, comes down a very steep mountain face, through a series of zig-zags into Andermatt. On this part of the route the management is the *Matterhorn Gotthard Bahn,* MGB, the company we saw at Zermatt. Since the line to the west passes the world renowned Rhône glacier, the luxury train is marketed as the *Glacier Express.* This glacier is the granddaddy of glaciers of Switzerland and feeds from the southern side of the Eiger-Jungfrau massif. Until about 20 years ago the railway line between the towns of Realp and Oberwald, over the Furka Pass, was closed in winter, buried by snow. The Swiss would not tolerate this, so they built a tunnel under the area. The trains now don't pass the Rhône glacier, they go under the mountain. The marketed *Glacier Express* is true in name, but has no view of the glacier.

Railway enthusiasts won't waste anything and the *Dampfbahn Furka Bergstrecke* have grabbed the old line from Realp to Oberwald with glee, brought it to safe operating conditions and found some vintage steam trains to run it. Since a trip on the old line takes over two hours, you can detect that this is a major undertaking. Services operate between June and September. All staff are volunteers. On being asked if he was perhaps a bank manager from Zürich, one conductor explained that he was actually a financier from Köln in northern Germany. This was his rostered rail three weeks and this was his annual holidays. One did not ask what his wife thought of all this. Maybe she was working in the canteen! DFB charge around CHF80 for the two-hour trip.

The carriages are of about 1920-style, as is the locomotive.

For the first hour from Realp, the trip follows the valley below the Rhône glacier and gives some amazing views of the huge expanse of ice. Ultimately it reaches the highest station at Furka (2160 metres), and the train stops for a half hour for coffee and wurst, a lunch in rather pleasant surroundings. The passenger pays, of course, and pays well.

The next stage of the line is inside the 1,874m tunnel. The conductor checks that the windows are all sealed and into the tunnel goes the train. This blackness is now amazing, and up front is the fire of the steam locomotive with two guys working feverishly to keep the pressure up and to avoid their own suffocation. Never today would anyone be allowed to be employed in such a situation; a situation that was considered to be quite normal 75 years ago. After about 10 minutes of this you emerge, perhaps gasping and maybe a little blackened. Today you find that OH&S people have intervened and that a diesel loco is on the front through the tunnel, both to minimise the mess and to give much greater margin of safety. Stopping in the middle of that tunnel with a dragon beside you would be no joke.

The train then quietly works its way back down the valley to Gletsch and then on to Oberwald, where it again meets the main line which would take us back to Brig.

If you choose to take the bus past the glacier, the bus stops at the toe of the glacier and allows time to walk on it. Some entrepreneur has burrowed a hole in the glacier and allows you, at a cost, to walk inside. That is really eerie, because the ice you are standing on can date back to the last ice age, 10,000 years ago. At each opportunity the locals like to demonstrate how far the glacier has retreated in recent years, many kilometres. This is largely a natural phenomonen and it has been observed since well before we began to burn coal. Whether we have accelerated it is another matter.

From Oberwald back to Meiringen, and so to Brienz and Interlaken, is only a short distance by bus which goes over the Grimsel Pass, one of the more spectacular road passes in the Alps. Here one can see where Switzerland generates its electricity.

54. NORTHERN ITALY

In this section, the Italian-speaking part of Switzerland will form the central topic.

Starting once more from Zürich, as we proceed through the Gotthard Pass we enter the Italian speaking canton of Ticino. In this area the cities of Bellinzona, Lugarno, Locarno and Chiasso are relatively prosperous and so the area does not have that Italian down-at-heel appearance, but it is definitely of Italian culture.

You must forgive me if I digress here for a few paragraphs. Above Bellinzona, leading east across the range into Italy, is the Pass of St Jorio. Now my name does not feature very often in literature and it is fascinating to see old St Jorio feature as street names and so on in this area. I have no idea who he was and he is not likely to be connected, as 'Jory' comes from Cornwall.

So there is this pass, the Passio de St Jorio.

A physicist colleague and I determined to brave this pass, simply to say we had done it.

We set off from Bellinzona and spent the night at a mountain hostel, some way up the pass. This gave us an inherent advantage next day, but a complacency which we misplaced.

The climb to the top of the pass was fairly easy, taking us until about noon. During this phase we had to contend with a flock of sheep who clearly believed that they were there by right, we were not, and consequently anything of ours was theirs. We survived. Then we were attacked by a rainstorm, the type which you know comes up mountain passes but you never expect. Fortunately I remembered a small shelter some distance on, from a shorter trip of a few years previously. We made this with nothing to spare. This resembled one of the small shelters on the highway in which dairymen once used to put their cans for collection, and was not as large as a small telephone box. No doubt it was here for the use we made of it. It was only large enough for us both to squeeze into and we found a plastic bag to place in front of us. Then down it came. Had we been caught in this rain, we would have had to retire hurt. After about 30 minutes it stopped as quickly as it started and the sun came out.

Ultimately we reached the top, 2,012 metres, and were in Italy.

Now we discovered three things:

1. It was a lot further down to the lake shore than we had recently come up and we were not going to make it down by nightfall.
2. There was another rainstorm coming up.
3. There was an Italian border patrol vehicle about to drive down the trail.

Naturally we raced over and hailed the guy and he was happy enough to put us in the back with his tools and junk, but nowhere to sit. The trip down took more than an hour, confirming that we would still have otherwise been on the mountain at nightfall. We did not see a soul on the way down. We reached the bottom at Dongo on Lake Como, were duly tipped out by our host, and were able to reach the daily ferry to Colico on the other side whence we were back in the railway network heading for Tirano.

Had we come to Lake Como from the opposite direction, as if coming from Tirano by train, we would have taken the boat at Colico for a lengthy ride across and along the lake to the city of Como. Lake Como and Lake Maggiore are some of the most delightful locations in Italy. This can be judged by the standard of the houses that can be seen scattered around the shores. The trip down the lake is as pleasant as it is picturesque.

Como is a pleasant town and remarkable because it celebrates its favourite son, Alessandro Volta, a pioneer in electricity, after whom the Volt was named. From Como there is a regular train service south to Milan or north into Switzerland.

Another line from Bellinzona goes to Locarno, at the north of Lake Maggiore, from where boats operate through to Arona on the Simplon line.

This again is a worthwhile, but long, journey.

From Locarno, however, a narrow gauge tramway runs for 53km to Domodossala, the Centovalli railway. Centovalli, of course, means 100 valleys, and this line lives up to its name. The line runs up and down valleys, past waterfalls, through tunnels, across gorges and everything else you might imagine. At times it passes over flat farmland terrain or through vineyards. For the locals it is simply the method of getting to market, or perhaps to town on business. For the traveller it is a treat, and a very convenient way of reaching the Simplon line from the Gotthard line.

Milano

Milano is a big commercial and industrial centre, the powerhouse of northern Italy. It is a complement to Roma in almost every way.

There are at least three railway stations at which you could arrive in Milano, all connected by the Metro and within a long walk from each other. Most trains come to Milano Central.

The platforms at Milano Central Station are once more reminiscent of a British terminus, but not so the main concourse hall. This is presented with carvings in marble of both mythological and historical subjects. The cleaning has recently been completed, with all the junk removed and then... The place has been filled with advertising banners so that it resembles a fairground. Perhaps that is only transient. I certainly hope so.

Outside the station is where you don't want to be. The authorities must have somehow excluded these people from inside the station, because all of the homeless and desperate are outside on the grass. This is certainly not a nice place to be at night.

Take the underground downtown and the world is different. Take the Metro to Duomo and come out in the cathedral square, the Piazza del Duomo, to see the biggest (depends on your definition) Gothic cathedral in the world. Some rate it as ugly, but it cannot be disputed that it is an awe-inspiring building.

Across the square is the Galleria Vittorio Emanuele II. It is hard to describe this structure but, as a gallery, it runs for of the order of 100 metres and contains shops and markets of every variety. Its quality is the architecture.

As you emerge at the other end in the Piazza della Scala, there is the Opera House of La Scala, perhaps the greatest in the world, depending again on definition. Leonardo da Vinci stands high in the middle of the square.

Those and other locations in Milano could take you a morning and more to digest.

But you are only likely to be in Milano to change trains.

55. SWITZERLAND, CENTRAL

Starting from Basle once more, the twice-per-hour IC train to Brig or Interlaken Ost takes us via Olten, and then over Switzerland's first stretch of high speed line toward Bern. This line came high on the development agenda because the time between Zürich and Bern was needed to be under the sacred one hour, and a traditional line was not good enough. As well, the line is used by DB ICEs which can make good use of the fast track.

Bern

Every Swiss city is unique and it is tempting to say that Bern is more unique than others, which it cannot be. Bern, however, has a charm about it that is all its own.

Legend has it that one of the dukes of the Middle Ages shot a bear near here and thus set up a town which he called *Bären*, meaning bears, which became Bern. The badge of the city is thus a bear, similar to that of Berlin whose name has a bear origin.

The area around the Hauptbahnhof is as busy as any city but, once you move away onto the peninsula of the River Aare, the most pronounced thing is the series of arcades. The street is lined with colonnades of arcades, which give the pedestrian an opportunity to wander through the areas of the shop fronts without caring for the traffic outside.

In the centre is Bern's famous clocktower, with dials to tell everything and a performance of figurines every hour. More frightening are the fountains, seen as statues in the street, which carry images from bygone days. The most horrifying is the ogre which is devouring babies. This is not thought to have any dark significance, but purely to remind small children of their potential fate if they do not behave.

An unusual element is 'Einstein's House', which is where the great man lived from 1903 to 1905. One becomes weary of the houses once belonging to Mozart, Bach and other classical figures, so the house of a scientist is a welcome relief. It was in Bern that Einstein worked in the patent office and where he wrote the three famous papers of 1905 which revolutionised the understanding of physics. Note that the papers did not revolutionise physics; that stayed the same. They simply changed the way we understood it.

At the far end of the main street is the bear pit, where a small community of bears has learnt the value of performing for an audience, thereby each becoming a professional 'mooch'. Actually they are extremely well cared for. Their notoriety makes sure of this.

Of course, the visit must include a passing reference to the Cathedral and to the Parliament. That could be followed by a nice meal, which Bern can provide.

The Lakes

Having seen Bern, our task then is to look at the area around the central lakes of Switzerland.

South from Bern the line skirts Lake Thun, through the towns of Thun and Spiez. If we are travelling further south, the train will take us through the new 35km Lötschberg tunnel between Spiez and Visp, then to Brig.

The Swiss do not, for ecological reasons, like road traffic going over mountain passes and have done all they can to discourage it. They probably regret initially having built through motorways over the top. The Lötschberg route is one of the few routes from Germany to Italy, and pressure was applied by the EU to have the Swiss allow more through traffic. Their answer was to go under, hence the new tunnel. Once again this is a high speed line and at that speed you hardly notice the extraordinary length of the tunnel.

This part of the line is owned and operated by the BLS, *Bern Lötschberg Simplon*, who also operate the lake ferries. Perhaps a major shareholder in the BLS is the SBB.

It is still possible to go over the pass, through Kandersteg and the old high level tunnel, to emerge above Visp and to negotiate a long descent into the Rhône Valley at Brig. This line draws a star from Thomas Cook in the list of scenic railways.

From Kandersteg a cable car can be taken up to the northern end of the

Gemmi Pass. This leads to a four-hour walk through alpine meadows, past lakes and glaciers to the town of Leukerbad on the southern side. A bus runs down to Leuk on the main Rhône Valley line.

Lakes Brienz and Thun are part of a huge glacial valley coming down from the Grimsel Pass and through today's Meiringen.

The city of Thun is the northern end of the ferry route on Lake Thun, and a ferry can be found within 50 metres of the station. The same does not apply to the next stop, Spiez, where the ferry dock is a considerable hike from the station and down a long hill. The ferries and the train converge at Interlaken West.

DB ICEs, which enter via Basle and continue to Bern each two hours, continue still further to Interlaken West and Interlaken Ost. These are supplemented by two traditional Swiss IC trains plus a connecting service to the Brig train, each two hours, to give a 30 minute service from Bern (and Basle) departing soon after xx00 and xx30 from Basle, Bern and Interlaken West. As well as these, the *Golden Pass Panoramic* service (originating in Montreux) from Zweisimmen to Spiez continues to Interlaken Ost.

Interlaken

At the eastern end of Lake Thun is the town of Interlaken, 'between the lakes', built on the delta of the River Lütschine coming down from the Jungfrau area. The drop from Lake Brienz to Lake Thun is very small, only a few metres, but in true Swiss style there is a hydro-electric power station using the flow.

The view of the Jungfrau, as described below, was sufficient to attract the moneyed gentry of Britain of the late 1800s to make the journey to Interlaken, and undoubtedly to enable the traveller *to be seen*.

The city abounds with hotels with toffy-sounding British names, interspersed with the fancy foreign ones, like the *Bellevue*. A direct train service from London Victoria, including a ferry crossing, would have existed and the top class people (by their definition) would bring a retinue of servants plus huge amounts of baggage with them.

Of course, this way of life no longer exists but the town carries the feeling with it. Today the equivalent personnage flies into Zürich with British Airways and has a chauffeur-driven car to take the family to Interlaken. Interlaken now exists for the ordinary person; but the ordinary person with money. The hotels are posh and expensive. The area caters for skiers in the winter. Hang-gliding starts and finishes in the centre of town. Small buses are waiting to take participants up into the mountains. Restaurants can serve any food you want, but are expensive.

Overlay this once more with the day trippers who are in Interlaken because the train finished here, and are content with a kebab and chips before they move on.

The economy of Interlaken benefits from Japanese tourists. During any morning in Interlaken, one can be forgiven for wondering why Tokyo is not a deserted city. Around 2,000 Japanese tourists, elderly ladies, elderly gentlemen on buses and a few independent teenagers, pass through Interlaken each morning in the high season. This totals about a quarter of a million Japanese per year! If you were a merchant in Interlaken, would you not cater for Japanese tastes? If these tourists are contributing to the upkeep of the local attractions, then who is complaining? But they also will pay inflated prices which reflects on the integrity of the local merchants.

So Interlaken is a many-faced town, liked by all and not a bad place to visit. Exceptionally good in fact.

Jungfrau Region

Standing in front of the Grand Hotel Jungfrau Victoria, Interlaken, on a clear day, looking up the valley of the Lütschine, one can see the triple peaks of The Eiger, The Mönch and The Jungfrau; the devil, the monk and the maiden. This massif is between 3,900 and 4,000 metres above sea level in the middle of Switzerland, more than 3,500 metres above Interlaken. There is one peak nearby which is a tad higher and some peaks on the Italian border likewise, but the Swiss like to describe these three as the 'top of Europe'. It was to see this view that the trains brought the rich, together with entourage, directly from London Victoria Station to Interlaken West.

The local entrepreneurs built narrow gauge railways up into these mountains, the *Jungfraubahn*, so that the rich could see them at closer hand.

From Interlaken Ost the first coupled pair of trains heads mountainwards, divides in Wilderswil and terminates in Grindelwald and Lauterbrunnen respectively. Grindelwald is the focal point of the ski activities in the winter.

A second train, different gauge, then takes passengers from Grindelwald further up to Kleinescheidegg, virtually at the foot of the massif at about

2,200 metres above sea level. Meantime, another train brings passengers from Lauterbrunnen via Wengen. A third train takes viewers from Kleinescheidegg past Eigergletscher, through a tunnel ascending 1,400 metres, to about 3,600 metres at Jungfraujoch, way up on the saddle of the mountain. Here there is the inevitable restaurant, an ice cave and views out over the ranges which are unsurpassable.

The train fare is over CHF 160 return and certainly not value for money. For the Japanese it must be included in a total package, paid for before leaving home, because they fill the trains. Thomas Cook awards this route the star for scenic journeys while UNESCO has declared it a World Heritage site.

It is interesting to note how the height of 2,200 metres keeps recurring. In this climate 2,200 metres is as high as one would want to go without climbing assistance and as high as most of the walking trails extend. Usually above this height the mountains become precipitous. We have already encountered the Bernina Pass, Furka and Passio St Jorio at precisely this height. This just happens to be the height of Mt Kosciuszko, the highest mountain in Australia.

It is often better to see something from afar than to stand close to it, or on it. This is always the case with a mountain peak and, while it is all very nice to take the train to the Jungfraujoch and the view is spectacular, you don't see the mountain.

Adjacent to, but not connected to, the massif is the peak known as the Schilthorn. This has an unsurpassed view of the three mountains, and is the place to visit on a clear day. In the other direction one can see Lake Thun and, further away, Bern. Lauterbrunnen, on the second route, is well inside a subsidiary glacial valley, of vertical sides of about 500 metres and about one kilometre apart. From Lauterbrunnen a funicular railway, on cable and cogs, takes you to the top of the ridge to Grütschalp where yet another train runs you along the ridge to the town of Mürren. Mürren is a delight. For a start there are no cars, only those for essential services which had to be brought up on the funicular. It has the traditional winding village street and standard cuckoo clock houses. From Mürren you can see across to the top of the cliff on the far side, where the Trummelbach Falls have gouged their way inside the mountain down to the valley floor. At the far end of the village is the cable car to the Schilthorn, sitting above at 10,000 feet, obviously set out in these units for advertising purposes; to the Swiss it is given as 3,200 metres. At the top the proprietors have set up a large restaurant plus entertainment complex with plenty of viewing space, both inside and outside. It was from here that James Bond skied down the slope ahead of the avalanche after the restaurant had been blown up in *On Her Majesty's Secret Service*, so you have seen pictures of it, but in some scenes, only of a model. Only by selling the movie rights was the proprietor able to find enough funds to complete it. Unfortunately the proprietor charges over CHF60 return to reach the top. This, in contrast to the Jungfrau, is worth the expense.

In the foyer of Interlaken Ost Station is a video screen which shows live views from the various points in the mountains where a train can take you. Quite often the view from many of them is a blank, seeming more black than white. The accompanying temperature can read negative with two digits on any day in the summer, even when it is perfectly clear. You can thus see what the Schilthorn is like at that moment. Whether it will bear any resemblance to this after the two hours it takes you to go up, is another matter. Never miss a trip to the Schilthorn, but pick your day so that it is clear, and probably very cold as well.

It was my habit to take a party of students each year on a tramp within the Lütschine Valley. These walks gradually became longer by the year as my adventuring spirit became greater but my capacity dwindled. The longest one we ever did was from Kleinescheidegg and Eigergletscher down through the Trummelbach Falls to the bottom of the valley, and thence the bus to Lauterbrunnen. This took of the order of eight hours and resulted in some very sore and weary people, but it was worth it. The last section past the falls is down a cliff face, where the inevitable zig-zag is only made passable by a steel cable pinned alongside the track. The Trummelbach Falls is a series of 12 or so waterfalls, draining the river from the top of the cliffs down to the valley floor, *inside* the mountain.

Brienz

You will have to forgive me for writing in great depth on Brienz, as it is here that I have spent part or all of my summers for the last 20 or so years. Through here have come quite a few Australian students, who have all agreed that I have found *the* place to be.

Lake Brienz is the upstream lake of the pair, running roughly east to west. The River Aare, coming down the glacial valley, enters the lake at the eastern end and flows out at Interlaken Ost at the western end before becoming part of Lake Thun at Interlaken West. On the southern side of Lake Brienz the mountains go up to about 1800 metres, the lake is at 560 metres above sea level, and the bottom is 300 metres further down, straight down. On the northern side the shore is more shelving and can be used for habitation and transport. The lake is about 15km long, 3km wide and one third of a kilometre deep. It is far too deep ever to freeze over. The water a few metres down would be at 4 Celsius all of the time. You may dive down once, but you will never attempt it again. The river in and out is relatively small and provides no current of note. There are, of course, numerous streams or bächen, pronounced becken, singular bach, flowing into the lake all around. The wind determines both the way the water moves and the surface temperature, which is around 18 Celsius by the end of July.

Brienz, a town of 2,000 people, a village by Swiss standards, is on an almost unnoticed promontory on the northern side of the lake, very close to the eastern or top end. The older part of the town, the dorf, is at the Interlaken end and contains the old marketplace and the church. The village is noted in records in 1187 AD. There are parts of the church dating from the 1200s, but the church dates from the 1400s. Where were we in the 1400s? There were not many of us in Australia at the time and it was in 1485 that Richard III was racing around shouting for his horse, only to be done in by Henry Tudor, the father of Henry VIII. Henry VIII became King of England in 1509. Henry's wife was Catherine of Aragon, the daughter of Ferdinand and Isabella who sent Columbus from Spain to America in 1492.

The church is about to run out of graveyard space and they have adopted a fancy solution. From the oldest section of the graveyard they have removed the gravestones and set them up neatly nearby, doubtless on unusable land with a rocky base. They have then overlaid the old area with soil of a metre or so thickness and planted grass. They can now go down the traditional distance (and the legal one) and still not disturb the original inhabitants, thereby using the whole area again. Only the Swiss could dream up something like that.

The road through the village is winding, and in many places vehicles have to be warned of overhanging eaves. Shops and businesses sit along either side of this main street, with the Co-op and Migros supermarkets at either end. Before these arrived, only about 30 years ago, the village was made up of small produce stores to where the local mommas walked each day to buy their requirements.

Now the old dears come once a week in their BMWs to the supermarket, buy for the week and take it home to their freezers. The little produce shops have nearly all gone, with the exception of a couple of excellent bakeries, and their place taken by the glitz of tourist shoppes selling some good stuff but mainly junk for the bewildered tourists. Perhaps the most novel is the Japanese Swiss chocolate factory. The Golden Arches and the Colonel have not reached Brienz, and probably never will. One has to go to Interlaken for a Big Mac. In the centre is Jobin, the wood-carving store which partly gives Brienz its woodcarving reputation or lives off it, depending on your point of view. This is a huge store containing everything that you could not possibly want: cuckoo clocks, music boxes, carvings, Swiss Army knives, souvenir plates and dishes, etc. Granny might like a music box, but you have not enough room in your baggage. Each day there is a parade of tourist buses, filled with elderly Japanese, which pulls up outside Jobin and debouches their load into the store. Here the Japanese-speaking assistants do their best to offload these souvenirs of Brienz, before stuffing everyone back on the bus without them knowing where they have been. The bus takes them to the dock for a ferry ride back to Interlaken and a trip in the train to Grindelwald and to the Jungfraujoch, before returning them to Zürich.

By walking further up the lake for about 12 minutes, one reaches the Jugendherberge, the youth hostel. I have been staying in this hostel for over 20 years and have become part of the furniture of the place. I have my own room (about 3m x 2.5m) and it is there for me when I want it. Of course it is not my room if I am not there, I'm away more than 60% of the time, when I don't pay anything. Everything then goes into a box and is stowed under the roof. The box stays there throughout the Swiss winter, obviating the need to take a large bag back to Australia and return it. In September there are a score or so of cows, bells all ringing, passing regularly along the road under my window.

In front of the hostel is the lake, with possibilities for swimming or purely sitting in the sun doing nothing. Need I describe more?

Brienz is renowned and publicised as *Steamin' Brienz*. Note the language in which this is stated. There are five original steam events in Brienz, on show most of the summer:

1. The *Rothornbahn* from Brienz to the Rothorn.
2. The lady of the lake, the paddlesteamer *Lötschberg*.
3. The local museum steam train, which runs weekends and holidays on the main line. The Swiss Railways have no problem integrating this with regular passenger services.
4. Two launches, each with capacity of about six persons, which take passengers from one end of the village to the other on selected weekends and are purely steam-driven.
5. The steam train of about 30cm gauge, which runs from the dock and along the promenade in the direction of the middle of the village. The train carries anybody for a couple of francs.

It was possible to stand in one place and see all five steam types operating, but this was a matter of luck rather than timetabling.

The dockside railway was a hobby of two retired old men. One of them drove the train, sitting astride the tender, while the other sold tickets and talked to the customers. Both of them wore their engine driver's jacket and engine driver's hat. The steam locomotive was beautifully engineered and undoubtedly an exact replica of a loco of their younger days. It could have been their life's work. They also had an electric locomotive, again a good replica, powered by batteries in the first car. When not in use the locos and coaches were stored in a roundhouse, fully equipped with turntable, at the remote end of the line from the dock, near the bach.

After the Brienz floods a few years ago, their roundhouse was completely buried under tonnes of rock which came down the valley. This appeared to be the end of the service, but it is pleasing to see the track back in place for the 2011 summer.

Ferries

Lake Brienz is home to a fleet of passenger ferries, now down to four unfortunately, which ply the lake between Brienz and Interlaken Ost during the summer months. Once they would have been the sole means of transport between the two ends of the lake and all settlements along the sides. The first railways would have been outwards from the end of the lake, as the sides are, as you recall, rather steep and don't lend themselves to easy construction of roads and railways. Since the railway company, BLS, owns the boats, the Eurail pass covers the boats as well. What nicer way is there to spend a day than to include a three-hour cruise from Brienz to Interlaken and back? If you want more, the boats on adjoining Lake Thun have a five-hour cycle and the two can be coupled for an eight-hour day. The biggest of the Lake Brienz fleet is the *Lötschberg*. The *Lötschberg* is a genuine paddle-steamer with side paddles and a steam engine, which is kept in immaculate condition. It was originally built in 1909 when there were still others of her kind about, and she is licensed to carry 1,000 passengers. During the summer she does two trips a day between Interlaken Ost and Brienz, six hours of round trip, when the number of passengers will warrant. The vessel is maintained on a day-to-day basis by the BLS, but the long-term maintenance is paid for by 'the friends of the *Lötschberg*' who recently subscribed over CHF1 million for a refit. To earn that sort of money would otherwise require a lot of passengers. There is a similar steamer in the fleet on Lake Thun, the *Blümisalp*.

Rothorn

Above Brienz is the ridge which makes up the northern side of the glacial valley. The highest point on the ridge is the *Rothorn*, the red peak, at 1,800 metres above lake level immediately above Brienz. There is, naturally for Switzerland, a train to the peak, the *Rothornbahn*. This non-electrified line, 800mm gauge, from Brienz to Rothorn, is powered by a most ancient but well-kept set of steam locomotives, each belching out vast quantities of vile-coloured, foul-smelling smoke. Perhaps the Swiss like to use this to show how bad others can be. The whole trip is on rack and pinion, which means that there is a huge cog-wheel under the middle of the loco which engages in teeth along the centre of the track. The locos, which push the train up and hold it on the way down, are coal burning, steam driven and have larger wheels on the downhill end, the rear of the loco, than on the front. This means that the fire will always fall into the hearth and not back onto the crew. The whole contraption could not operate on a level track, of which there is none.

The *Rothornbahn* station is across the street from the Brienz mainline station and trains go up every hour in the summer. The fare is about CHF40 up and CHF20 back down. For about an hour this little train steams up the small gorges in the side of the valley, initially in the trees but latterly in the open, and finally comes out at one of the lowest points on the ridge. It continues its journey along the ridge until it comes close to the highest point. At the top station at Rothorn Kulm, 2,244 metres, is the inevitable, for Switzerland, restaurant and lodging house, and a few hundred metres further along is the peak. This is all well above the tree line and on a sunny day it can be very hot up there, with a high potential for sunburn. Not only are you at 2,300 metres, but there is not a tree to be found and the non-natural structures are fairly sparse. The view across the lake is indescribable; that is the only expression to use. The only subsequent comment can be, 'Come see for yourself!'

One of the difficult points for an Australian to appreciate is that there is an 'other side'. Australians are used to the idea that a barrier such as this has more of the same beyond. Not so in Switzerland. Beyond is the next canton with a cable car coming up and with villages and houses visible in the distance. Returning down the other side would result in a long trip home, so the options are to pay to go down, to walk down or to walk along the ridge and down for about four hours to the top of the Brünig Pass at 1,000 metres, and take the train home. Either of the latter makes an interesting day.

Meiringen

Apart from being the kick-off point for the Hasliburg ski fields, Meiringen, the station beyond Brienz, boasts the Reichenbach Falls. It is from a point way up on the path through these falls that Sherlock Holmes struggled with Moriarty and where Moriarty, and for a while it was suspected Holmes also, fell to his death. The falls are quite spectacular and one can ride most of the way up on a funicular railway. A white cross on the face of the cliff marks the location of the fight. The town has made its name from this. Every second hotel has a name including the words Sherlock Holmes. There is a Baker Street and several other location names linked with Holmes also occur. In the middle of the town park is a bronze statue of the great man, sitting smoking his pipe. There are Holmes festivals of all kinds held here in Meiringen. Strangely, the greatest supporters are Norwegian. One can easily spend a full day in Meiringen, visiting the falls, viewing Holmes in other ways and trying some of the restaurants, which are more varied than the much more limited selection in Brienz and not as expensive as those in Interlaken. Alternatively, it is easy to build a quick trip from Interlaken or Brienz to Meiringen into any day's programme, with two trains per hour available throughout the day. It is alleged by some that the *meringue* was created in Meiringen several centuries ago.

From Meiringen there is a tramway continuing further up the valley, to Innertkirchen. One writer described Innertkirchen as a large power station with a small town attached. On its journey the little tram passes the Aareschlucht, a feature several kilometres long where the River Aare has cut tens of metres down into the substrate, but with a width of only a few metres. This is probably in terrain which was a massive landslide which once closed off the glacial valley. The concessionaire will charge you a few francs to walk through on catwalks and through adjacent tunnels, but assuredly you will never have seen anything like this before.

Onward

The train from Interlaken Ost, now narrow gauge, continues beyond Brienz to Meiringen, over the Brünig Pass at 1,000 meters and down to the western end of the Lake of Luzern at Alpnachstad and then on to Luzern. It is easy to see that this line was built many years ago, purely to link Brienz with Alpnachstad. Onward journeys in either direction would have been by steamer. Until a few years ago the tracks on the docks at Brienz and Alpnachstad were still in place.

The Interlaken Ost to Luzern train, of which there are five sets, is old and tired but still up to normal Swiss standards, other than not being air-conditioned and with drop-down toilets. Two of the sets are part of the *Golden Pass Panoramic* service and include a Swiss Panorama car with floor-to-ceiling windows. The locos are each equipped with a driving cog which engages with the track on the rack sections.

From Interlaken Ost to Meiringen the trip is straightforward, as it is along the lakeshore via Brienz. In Meiringen the loco is replaced by another for the ascent.

Shortly after leaving Meiringen the train begins its climb out of the glacial valley and immediately engages the rack. Along this slow climb to Brünig are some of the most spectacular views of the valley you can find. In the winter the trees are bare, covered with ice and the view is unobstructed. In summer the trees are covered in leaves and the view comes in small snatches. The authorities have provided quite a few life-sized carvings of the various animals to be found in the area, and this provides an interesting diversion for those for whom the train is not the feature. The top of the pass is reached, concurrently with the train in the reverse direction, at xx00, or close to, as the system would decree.

Now we go down. The rack is engaged immediately and, after some views of a beautiful green valley with a collection of lakes, the train leaves the rack for the last time at Giswil. At Alpnachstad the line reaches the Lake of Luzern and follows the lake to Luzern Hauptbahnhof. This total journey features in the list of scenic routes by Thomas Cook, but no longer carries the coveted star.

On summer weekends the local preservation society operates a steam train from Interlaken Ost, over the pass to Lungern. This operates with open carriages and is a great family entertainment.

Engelberg

At the eastern end of the Lake of Luzern is the railway to Engelberg in the adjoining canton. The line is also rack and pinion, but made up of narrow gauge electric stock with a similar driving wheel under the cars. Engelberg is a small village at 1,000 metres above sea level and boasts a huge monastery. The town must have a large affinity with the Jewish population, because there are always large numbers of families coming and going, with papa dressed in very orthodox garb including black frock coat and hat. From Engelberg one can take the cable car almost to the top of Mt Titlis, a peak not far short of 4,000 metres. At the top is always an abundant supply of snow and ice and, although it is of little use to the skiers in the summer, it is a source of huge amusement to those on toboggans or to those who are prepared to try to slide on their bottoms. The cable car is a very long haul, as can be guessed by the vertical height and by the expense of over CHF80 return. The trip is a very worthwhile one and, as long as you start early, you can be back to Brienz or Interlaken in time for dinner.

Also from Engelberg is a high level pass, the Surenen Pass, across to the southern point of the Lake of Luzern, which I crossed with another physicist colleague in our younger and sillier days. The walk took about eight hours, went over the pass at 2,291 metres and through a lot of summer snowdrifts. I left my glasses in the hut at the top, so I sent a note to be left with them in the hut by the only other people we saw that day. From Altdorf at the bottom we took a night train to Germany. Two days later I returned to Engelberg and there were my glasses waiting for me in the railway ticket office. This is Switzerland.

Luzern

If it wasn't that I like Brienz so much, I would say that Luzern was the most delightful place in Switzerland.

It has two mountains to climb by train, Rigi (1800 metres) by train from Vitznau on the lake, Rigi by train from Arth-Goldau, Pilatus (2130 metres) by train from Alpnachstad, and Pilatus by cablecar.. Both mountains are worth a visit.

On the huge lake, *Vierwaldstättersee* or the Lake of Luzern, ferries run to all corners including to Brünnen and Fluelen at the far south, which is a return journey of over six hours.

The ancient wall around the city is not fully intact but can be easily traced.

There are rows of small specialist shops which would be a shopping addict's delight. Here one sees the precision of Swiss craftsmanship on display. Granny would like something from here.

Luzern is host to one of the greatest transport museums, certainly in Europe. Like most locations in Luzern, this can also be best accessed from the lake ferries. The museum is not limited to rail transport, although there is sufficient in the museum to justify the whole museum on that. There are further sections, equally as large, on air travel, on road transport and on whatever else you can think of.

Then there is The Lion!

This is an amazing monument, carved in sandstone and mounted on a rockface, of a lion with a spear in his side, obviously dying. It is a memorial to Swiss soldiers who died in the French Revolution. Words cannot describe this lion. There is nothing quite like it anywhere. Perhaps it was from here that C. S. Lewis gained his idea of the dying Aslan in the *Chronicles of Narnia*.

Spend time in Luzern. You'll like it.

From Luzern you can use the Swiss clockface timetable to return to Interlaken, to Basle, to Bern, to Zürich, or perhaps to Brienz.

***

But then maybe this is the end of your journey. A train from Interlaken, connecting directly from anywhere in Switzerland, runs each two hours to Frankfurt, connecting to Frankfurt Airport, from where you can return home.

56. EPILOGUE

Now you, the reader, have come to the end of this little jaunt around Europe, you may either want to do it yourself, or think I am mad. Most likely it will be the latter.

For me the journey will go on, as long as my legs, and the bits above which make them go, will carry me.

Everything is changing, ever-changing, and the difficulty is to recognise that the changes must keep going beyond the end of one's days. There was a time when I believed that anything beyond the year 2000 was out of my life's reach, now I am inviting people to my 85th birthday party in 2023.

All of the things you have read here are my observations and, therefore, subjective. You are invited to check them out for yourself. It is infinitely more fun to do it by train than on a computer monitor.

Some of the things that will happen in the next few years are:

- ICE trains will run from Köln and Frankfurt to London St Pancras.
- The high speed line from Nürnberg to Leipzig will be completed.
- The high speed lines from Frankfurt via Stuttgart to Munich and from Frankfurt to Basle will be completed.
- The Gotthard tunnel will be completed and the times between Zürich and Milano will be slashed.
- The first of the new DB ICEs will enter service
- Britain will do nothing!
- The high speed line between Barcelona and France will be completed and high speed through trains will run from Barcelona to Montpelier and Paris.
- Leipzig and Dresden station undergrounds will be completed.

- Zürich station underground will be completed and more through services will operate.
- Estonia, Latvia and Lithuania might co-ordinate their timetables to allow through travel.
- TGV Est will be extended to Strasbourg and the time from Paris to Basle and to Frankfurt will be cut still further.
- There will be even fewer overnight trains across Europe.
- The U5 in Berlin and the M4 in Budapest will be completed.
- The Hauptbahnhof and Westbahn in Austria will be completed and the time between Vienna and Salzburg cut still further.
- The Brenner base tunnel will be completed.
- Bulgaria, Romania and Cyprus will implement the Schengen Treaty.
- Croatia will be admitted to the EU and to the Schengen Treaty.
- Iceland will be admitted to the EU.
- Poland, Czech Republic, Hungary, Latvia and Lithuania will join the Euro (perhaps by 2014 or 2015).
- Serbia, Montenegro and Poland might accept the global Eurail pass.
- Slovakia and Macedonia might join the Eurail organisation.
- Smoking will be banned on trains in Croatia and perhaps in other non-EU countries.
- Smoking will be banned on railway stations throughout the EU.
- Work on all the projects in Greece will remain in suspense.

Since I first wrote this list, many items have been crossed off as completed and others have taken their place. As these fall off, others will be added. Many of these things will have occurred by the time you have read this.

Even without these changes, there is plenty more to see.

Have a good trip!

ABOUT THE AUTHOR

Rodney Jory spent his working career as a physicist in Australia. His first contact with trains was when he was constrained to ride to high school each day behind a black and sooty steam loco. It was not the physics, engineering or efficiency of the engine, but the efficiency of the operation, which exercised his mind.

After completing his graduate degree in Canberra he took a post at Florida State University where there are no trains but an appreciation of the way other parts of the universe work. His next post was in Liverpool, UK, where there are loads of trains of all shapes and sizes, before returning to his longstanding appointment in Canberra. As part of his duties in his later working years he accompanied groups of students to conferences in various locations around the world, often in Europe. He was also for 11 years the leader of the Australian team to the International Physics Olympiad, which took him annually to locations as diverse as Havana and Beijing. By now he had travel, and in particular European train systems, in his blood.

On his retirement in 2005 he packed his bags and relocated to Europe returns to Australia only for Christmas each year. He maintains that he puts "retired" on all official forms, but on others he simply writes "vagrant".